WALLACE
LEGEND OF BRAVEHEART
BOOK 4

PEACEKEEPERS

SEORAS WALLACE

GW00566774

Ist EDITION

Published in 2020 by Wolf and Wildcat Publishing

Copyright © Seoras Wallace 2020

Seoras Wallace has asserted his right to be identified as the author of this
Work in accordance with the Copyright, Designs
and Patents Act 1988

ISBN Paperback: 978-1-9999170-6-7
Ebook: 978-1-9999170-7-4

All rights reserved. No part of this publication may be reproduced,
stored in a retrieval system, or transmitted in any form or by any means,
electronic, mechanical, photocopying, recording or otherwise, without the
prior permission of the copyright owner.

All characters and events in this publication, other than those clearly
in the public domain, are fictitious and any resemblance to real persons,
living or dead, is purely coincidental.

A CIP catalogue copy of this book can be found
in the British Library.

Published with the help of Indie Authors World
www.indieauthorsworld.com

www.facebook.com/InDiScotland

Wolf & Wildcat publishing
Associate: Jade Macfarlane
+44(0)7766 584 360
www.wolfandwildcat.com
www.facebook.com/Wallace.Legend
Clan Wallace PO Box 1305 Glasgow G51 4UB Scotland

Dedicate to the memory of a great clansman…
RIP
Paul (Pauly) Byrne

Acknowledgements

Big thank you for the writing support from
my hard working family and friends

About the Author: Seoras Wallace

After a career in the film industry spanning over thirty years, in such films as Highlander, Gladiator, Rob Roy, Braveheart, Saving Private Ryan and many more. In 1997 following a serious horse riding accident, Seoras turned his valuable experience to becoming an author, and parallel to his professional life, Seoras has also served as acting chief executive of the Wallace Clan Trust for Scotland.

"An experience like no other," said Seoras, "One of the constants in my vocation has been the revelation of private or secretive documents and accounts from many unusual sources that gave me a wholly different perspective of William Wallace, that shaped him as a man who became a nations Iconic patriot and world hero in the eyes and hearts of many. At first I used to think that the information I witnessed was too incredible to be true, but when certain parts of that narrative repeated from different sources, another story from the academic norm began to emerge. Growing up in a remote west coast village, that was extremely patriotic and nationalist, I was taught from the clan elders at an early age the family legend of Wallace, but that too did not match the publicly available narrative. On my many travels around the world, especially after the release and success of the film Braveheart, people would often say upon hearing my account, "You should write a book about the Wallace." "I have always replied that no one would ever believe it, but following my accident, I decided to leave the family legacy as a fact based fictional narrative for my family and future generations, almost as a historical bloodline diary. The epic account I have written about the Life and Legend of William Wallace has been an inspiration and brought to me a newfound love for the man, the people and the country he fought for. Many who have been test reading the epic series as it developed, have a constant response that stands out more than any other comment, "Seoras, I've researched what you've written, and it's true…" My reply has always been… "Naw… it's just fiction!"

Moray and Brannah

Dawn breaks as William lounges contentedly poking and prodding at the smouldering peat fire making pointless designs in the fine ash. He hadn't slept, thinking of his tryst with Marion; especially the delights of her unexpected nocturnal visit. He laughs thinking that wee Graham was right about sitting up all night considering things you want to say and what you would like to do. Suddenly his happy lazy daze is interrupted when a familiar voice calls to him from outside his obhainn, "Wallace... are yie awake in there?" William replies, "Aye, come on in." The door flaps are thrown open, introducing a blistering flash of bright sunlight, briefly illuminating the dark interior of the obhainn and blinding William momentarily. Stephen and Dáibh come inside to greet him, Dáibh exclaims, "Would yie look at this place..." Stephen laughs, "And look at you Wallace, you're no' dressed yet and half the day is gone already." A confused William enquires, "Is it late in the day already?" Stephen replies. "Aye it sure is Wallace, me foin frisky fella, it's time yie were up."

William sits up yawns, stretches his arms, then he looks around at the scattered clothing all over the floor. He says "Feck, I've lost all track o' time." Stephen grins, "Love will surely do that to a fella. C'mon now Wallace, you need to be getting up and out o' yer pit, all the guests are getting ready to leave for their journey homeward." William, still naked, raises himself from his crib and searches for his léine. He lazily enquires, "Have yiez seen Marion anywhere this morn any o' yiez?" Dáibh replies, "Aye, ah saw her and Brannah no' long ago getting wee Graham to carry all their baggage to their bow-wagon." Stephen picks up a léine, then he throws it at William as he walks over to a water bucket, there he cups his hands and throws cold water over his hair and into his face, washing the morning thoughts away. He quickly throws his léine on, roughly ties it together, picks up his Anam Crios and a leather stud belt with his fathers Royal dirk hanging in the frog and straps it proudly round his waist. Dáibh gazes in amazement at the interior of the obhainn, with its hanging rugs, brats and fleeces, thick soft-cured skins with reed-mats and piles of woollen rugs on the floor, then he notices a pot hanging on the cooking irons, simmering at the side of the fire. "Ach Wallace, can I be tasting some o' the mutton stovies you have going on there, for it sure looks fine and tasty?" William replies, "Help yourselves if yiez want, it's got some real good broken mutton in it. Dáibh, do you know the where-abouts o' Marion now?" Dáibh replies, "Aye she's up at the big house with Mharaidh, Brannah and Daun, ha, and all of them are talking about you I reckon." Stephen says, "Well then?"

"Well then what?" enquires William, grinning as he hops about the floor trying to pull on his boots. Stephen laughs, picks up a fleece and flings it into William's face, "When is it that you two will to be tying the knot then me boy?" William throws the fleece back at Stephen as he replies; "Marion wants to be wedded in saint Kentigerns church in Lanark before the next Fionn's eve. Though we were thinking maybe the next time we hear the bells of the Bahn Rígh Sídhe (Fairy Queen) riding out on the white horse and feelin' the heat o' the Shinin' fire." Dáibh laughs, "Beltane?" Stephen sighs, "Aye that would make sense for you two." William laughs, "Ah don't know what yie mean." Dáibh enquires, "Are yiez not going to be doin' the hand-fastin'?" William replies, "I sure hope so. Though Marion say's she wants to be married the Christian way too." Stephen enquires, "Surely yiez will be having wee Maw commit yiez to the piss-pot at the very least?" William laughs at the very thought, "Marion is very refined yie know." Stephen grins as he scoops out a large ladlefull of mutton stovies, he mutters, "She can't be that bleedin' refined if she loves you."

"Feck off..." laughs William. At that moment, a large number of horses can be heard cantering close to the obhainn. William exclaims, "I hope that's no' Marion leaving now?" He picks up a brat and rushes out the door in a panic. Dáibh and Stephen follow him outside. Dáibh exclaims, "If it is her that's leaving, then she must have a hundred horses pulling her bow-wagon." The three friends see a large squadron of mounted knights riding past, followed by a large retinue of men-at-arms, all flying a variety of heraldic designs of House and Clan. The gliding caparison on the horses wave effortlessly and the long flowing pennant banners flutter behind on their lances, filling the glen of Afton in a sea of bright colours. William notices the lead rider is sir Cospatrick de Dunbar, from nearby Comunnach Castle; a fortified stronghold situated only a few miles away overlooking the confluence of the river Nith and Afton waters, for the protection of the northern gateway to Glen Afton. Watching the seemingly endless line of cavalry, William then points at the sky, "I thought you said it was late in the day Stephen? That there is an early morning sun, and the roosters are only just starting to crow ya feckr?" Stephen replies, "Oh aye, right enough, sorry about that." Dáibh mumbles while still munching on his stovies, "Jaezuz, did you see the size of the big black beard on the fella that just passed us?" William laughs at Dáibh's description. "That's Lord Cospatrick or Blackbeard as everyone hereabouts calls him… because o' the obvious." Stephen exclaims, "Fuck… sure now, isn't that the grandest beard I've ever been and seen." William continues, "Aye he's a queer fella that one. He's the warden o' the border marches and one of the claimants for the Crown of Scotland, but he often resides up here at Comunnach Castle. Ma uncle Malcolm was telling me Blackbeard's making a formal claim for the throne by the rights of his great-grandmother Aida, countess of Dunbar, she was the illegitimate daughter of William the lion, but even with that line o' breedin' Malcolm doesn't trust him much at all." Dáibh quips, "Aye, he's a righteous lookin' big bastard that one." then he enquires, "Wasn't Blackbeard one of the Brix' pact we met down on the plains o' Saint John's a few years ago?" William replies, "Aye that he was…" A petite female calls out as she rides past on a large white stallion, her long black hair tied back similar to the Wolf and wildcat huntsmen, "Co'nas William…"

"Lady Marjorie…" Exclaims William as he waves to her. Stephen says, "Ha, that's a sign for yie right there Wallace. That wee wumman there is yer Bahn Rígh Sídhe o' the white horse." A curious Dáibh enquires, "Who is she?" William replies, "That's Lady Marjorie Comyn de Dunbar from Comunnach castle, Blackbeard's wife. We hunt the Wolf and wildcat forests on the high moors above Comunnach Castle for her. I'll tell you this Dáibh, she's one fine Lady." Dáibh and Stephen look at William with knowing smiles, "Naw ya feckrs…" Growls William, "She really is a fine woman. Marjorie and Mharaidh are good friends, and though Marjorie may look refined, she's a fit and able lass that one. She often comes out on a local hunt with us. I'm thinking she must have been a Gallóbhan Aicé in her younger day's,

10

for nothing I've seen turns away her hawk-like focus on the hunt. I've seen her ride that white stallion full gallop through bracken, burn and over briar patches chasin' a mad wild bull boar, then loose three arrows into its skull before I've loosed ma second flight." Dáibh smiles, "Are you sure she didn't loose four flights?" Stephen grins, "Did she no' spear a spawning salmon at the same time, feed her horse, make the cribs and evening vittals before you loosed your last flight?" Stephen and Dáibh nudge each other waiting for William's reply. William growls, "Fuck off you two." suddenly auld Tam comes rushing over in a fluster. "Stephen…" He stops in front of Stephen, puffing and out of breath. "What's all the fuss about Tam?" enquires Stephen. A breathless Tam replies, "Stephen, I've just come from the doocots, there's a message from your mother…"

Seeing the concern on Tams face, Stephen enquires with a sense of urgency, "What's to do then Tam, what's a message from me maw bein' all about?" Tam gasps,"It's your father… he's passed away, and yer maw, she's needing yie to go home as quick as yie can." Stephen exclaims, "What? Ah mean how could you be knowing all o' this Tam?" Auld Tam replies, "I was checking the doocots a wee while ago when ah saw the message on two o' your fathers birds that had just flown in. I reckon about a day an' a half and no' much more to fly that distance, your Maw must have sent the message from Ireland two nights late past since." Stephen goes grey in the face. After a moment he says, "Wallace, I'd better be goin' up and see Katriona and tell her this sad news. If I've to be getting to Ireland with great haste, it'll take at least four full day's ride on a Fleetfoot and I can't be taking Katriona or wee Stephen wit me." Auld Tam says, "We'll look after Katriona, don't you worry, she'll be fine." Stephen says, "Tam, will yie send a message back to me auld dear to let her know I'll be leaving here right away?" Auld Tam replies, "Aye, that ah will son." William lays his hand on his friends shoulder, "I'm sorry to be hearing this news about yer auld Dá Stephen, do you want me to come with yie?" Stephen replies, "Naw Wallace, but I thank yie just the same. I'll make this journey faster if ah'v only me'self to be thinkin' about." Stephen continues, "I'd better get goin'... I should leave for Invergarvane as soon as I'm packed."

William says, "You get goin' then Stephen, me and Dáibh here will ready two fleet Connemara's and bring them up to the big house for yie." Thanking William and Dáibh, Stephen turns and runs at speed towards Wallace Keep to see Katriona, quickly followed by auld Tam. "Fuck Dáibh," exclaims William, "I really liked auld Stephen. I hope everything will be all right with Stephen's Maw when he gets back to Connaught." On their way towards the stables, a mounted knight veers away from the large column and pulls up behind William and Dáibh. He calls out to them, "Haw, Wallace... Dáibh..." William and Dáibh look round to see who is calling them, much to their surprise they see young Andrew de Moray of Avoch, astride an extremely handsome black stallion. "Moray..." exclaims a surprised Dáibh

"What are you doing here? I've only just passed your message to Wallace here last eve." William enquires, "Aye Moray, what brings you to Glen Afton?" Andrew dismounts and replies, "My father's coming too, both he and his retinue are no' far behind me. He's here to be meetin' with yer Dá and Malcolm before joining sir Ranald Crauford, Cospatrick de Dunbar and Sir Richard Lundie on the caravan to Norham. When he told me he was coming here before his journey south, I thought fuck it, I'd come down and see yie." William ponders, "My father's going too? But Malcolm's no' going to sign the Ragemanus, he say's he doesn't trust the English, so I cannae see why ma Dá would be going?" Andrew enquires, "What's no' to trust about the English?" William sighs and shrugs his shoulders "I've had a few bad run-ins with the English, they no' long since falsely accused me o' bein' an outlaw and they've wanted to kill me on more than one occasion." Andrew is curious, "How so?" William replies, "Ach, a few years ago ah had a fight with them at Invergarvane, then a wee while later, some more English soldiers were going to cut my feckn hands off just for fishing on my uncles land near the town of Ayr."

"What happened?" enquires Andrew, "For I see you've still have all your dinkies?" William looks at his fingers, "It was a madness Moray, I ended up in a fight for my life over some feckn fish, and as it happened, a few o' them there English soldiers got killed, but I didn't have any choice, fuck, I was really lucky to get out of that one, ach but that was then and everything is quiet now, for ah was pardoned." Andrew sighs, "Close call there then for yie Wallace, but there's as many fucked up Scots up here as there are English in this world." Dáibh laughs, "Then that's a bad news for us then, for the English are about ten times more bred out than us Scots." William continues, "My Dá and Malcolm say they don't trust Longshanks, though ah had heard them sayin' that maybe one brother should sign and one doesn't… yie know the old story, just in case." Andrew replies "Aye, that's what most o' the Garda Rígh and council o' Baron's up north are doing, one brother signs, one doesn't, then if everything goes to shit, we won't lose our lands and homesteads through confiscation…" William nods in agreement. "Anyways Moray, come with us just now, we're going away up to the stables to get two horses tacked for my friend Stephen. His auld fella has just passed away to a better place and he's got to get back to Ireland as quick as possible for the wake. Fetch yer horse too Moray, yie can brush him down, feed him and stable the big fella up at the Darroch corrals with ours?" Andrew replies, "Aye, that would be just grand."

Making their way towards the stables, William couldn't help noticing the atmosphere and spirited character coming from the horse Moray has been riding. He's impressed in particular with the proud gait, stride and exceptional long and shining hair of forelock, mane and feathers, he runs his hand down its neck and front legs, then says, "That's a fine horse yie have here Moray." Andrew smiles, "Warrior is what I call him, for he fears fuck all. He's a fine hot blood breed stallion Wallace, big heart with good lengthy and powerful legs." Andrew is obviously proud of his stallion, he continues "Grip those strong second thighs and feel the muscle-back, he's well set and trained to bite yer face and kick forwards... and back." Dáibh laughs, "Sounds like Marion's description o' you Wallace." William smiles as he replies, "Sounds more like Moray is trying to sell him?" Andrew laughs, "I might be..." William strokes Warrior's neck, "Would you sell him?" thinking that a proud thoroughbred stallion is not a bad bolster for his burgeoning ego. Andrew laughs as he playfully pushes William aside, "Would I fuck... Anyway Wallace, how is wee bright eyes, do yie ever see her since Saint Johns o' Dalry?" William exclaims, "Shhhhhhh, for fucks sake Moray." Andrew enquires, "What's wrong?" Dáibh laughs, "Woman trouble."

Andrew grins, "Speaking of women trouble, on our way down here I had the good fortune of visitin' a house of great repute in old Saint John's toun o' Perth. I spent the night with a bonnie wee Egyptian that said she knew you very well indeed." Looking curiously at Moray, a puzzled William enquires. "An Egyptian? Ah don't know any Egyptians." Andrew replies, "Well she looks like one, though she said her name was, eh, what was it… aye, she said her name is Josephine Lamont." William says, "I don't know any lass called Josephine Lamont?" William is curious, "And she said she knows me?" Andrew says, "That was no' her real name… she just uses Josie as her working name at the inn, she told me her real name was eh, aye, her real name is Affric ua Bruan, she's a bonnie wee Ceàrdannan."

"AFFRIC…" Exclaims William, "Awe feck, Affric… ma bonnie wee woodland princess. And she's up in Perth now yie say? How is she doing Moray? How fares her fortune?" A grinning Andrew enquires, "Do you want ALL the intimate details Wallace?" William sighs, "NAW, I mean, how is she, is she fine and healthy, is she still the light o' the night up in the Sin inn? Tell me Moray, is she still a happiest o' happy wee souls?" Andrew replies, "She's a tough wee critter Wallace, as yie very well know, apparently… But she seems just fine and o' a very sanguine disposition, but not so much on a humour when she's talking about you." William appears puzzled, "Bad things?" Andrew replies, "Naw, no' really, but I think behind her bile she really misses you." Andrew looks closely into William's face. William enquires, "What are you looking at?"

Grinning, Andrew replies, "Ahm lookin at you Wallace, I see your big busted nose has healed up a bit since I last saw you. And if you love this maid Marion like yie say yie do, then if I were you, I wouldn't be sticking ma big nose any further into the life and business of that bonnie wee lass Affric." William laughs, "Feck off Moray, that was a long time past… anyways, come on with us and I'll tell you all about the bonnie maid Marion, for she's the one I have my heart set upon." The three friends chat and soon arrive at the stables, still talking about Marion and many things since they last saw each other on the plains of Monadh-abh and Saint John's of Dalry. Meanwhile, up at Wallace Keep, Alain, Mharaidh and Daun greet Lord

Andrew Moray, sir Stephen Lundie, Lady Marjorie and Lord Cospatrick. "Marjorie," exclaims Mharaidh. Marjorie replies with affection, "Mharaidh, it's wonderful to be seeing you, and Daun… you're here too? I didn't know you were down here from the lands of Badenoch?"

The three women embrace then Daun replies, "I came down to meet with wee Maw Wallace at Ach na Feàrna a few days ago, she said she was heading down here to see the family for a few days then she said she's going on up to Perth directly afterwards to be seeing her kinfolk in Kilspindie. While all the men are busy with the interregnum, Malcolm asked Dáibh and I to chaperone her." Marjorie enquires, "So wee Maw's here too?" Daun replies with a knowing smile, "She is." Marjorie laughs, "Do you not think that it's wee Maw who really should be doing the chaperoning for Dáibh and his retinue?" Daun laughs, "Don't be telling the men that or you'll shatter their fragile opinion of themselves."

Mharaidh and Daun put their arms around Marjorie's waist. Mharaidh says, "Let's go to the kitchens Marjorie, the men can talk politics while we talk about things of much greater importance." Marjorie enquires, "What's more important than the state of the realm?" Mharaidh replies, "William and the maid of Lammington, they've just got betrothed." Marjorie exclaims, "Really, oh that's wonderful news, for Marion is a beautiful soul in appearance and nature… and a fine match for William. Come Mharaidh, you must be telling me more about the tryst…?" Sir Andrew Moray meets with Alain as he enters the Keep, "Alain Wallace ma old friend, I've no' seen you for years, is it not about time that you built yourself a fine castle out of stone? Everyone's doing it nowadays, these old wooden ones catch fire far too easily?" Alain laughs, "Ha Moray ya auld crony yie, they don't say wood-warm or stone-cold for nuthin'." The two old friends laugh as Alain welcomes Moray. "Come on inside Moray, come and get a heat in my old home and enjoy the warmth, it should make a welcome change from you shivering in your old cold stone cave yie call a castle up in Avoch." Alain and Lord Moray are met at the door by sir Hugh. Alain makes introduction, "Moray, this is sir Hugh Braidfuite, the laird of Lammington." Lord Moray smiles, "Co'nas Braidfuite?" Sir Hugh replies, "Fine tá. And you?" Lord Moray is about to reply when he feels a nudge by his side. "Would yiez be liking a wee nip of quality Craitur after your long journey good surs?" Lord Moray turns quickly; his great horse-Brat swings behind him to reveal wee Graham standing nearby completely unfazed. Alain enquires, "Wee Graham, where on earth did you come from? With a thoughtful expression Wee Graham replies, "I don't really know sur, the priests said I was a found as an orphan beside the Monastery cludgies, then they fostered me to an auld inn-keeper and his wifey near a Paisley midden, then I moved to..."

"Naw," growls Alain "I mean, ach... it doesn't matter, and aye Graham, fetch our best craitur and fine wines for our guests." Wee Graham winks at Moray, who is trying not to laugh, then lord Moray says, "Good to see you're still master of the craitur then Graham." Wee Graham replies, "Ach aye Moray sur, would you be expecting me to be changing me ways at my age?" lord Moray replies, "Naw Graham, I don't suppose I would be thinking that at all." Nodding his head in approval, Wee Graham sets off on his mission of liquid mercy. Auld Tam, who has walked through the kitchen doors and overheard the conversation, enquires, "Do yie want me to be getting the fare Alain? For I reckon that's the last we will see o' wee Graham till he sobers up." Alain replies, "Aye Tam, I'll be thanking yie if yie would do that for us." Auld Tam turns and follows wee Graham's route to the door when

Alain calls out, "Tam, tell me… what's with wee Graham's demeanour? He seems to be awfy vigorous and alert this day on the refreshment duties, and he's got a strange looking glow about him… and an odd glint in his eyes?" Auld Tam smiles, "I think auld Jean granted him his annual nuptials after the Trystin between William and Marion." Alain and lord Moray look at each other for a moment, then they laugh out loud. Lord Moray says with a wry smile, "Aye well, ah suppose somebody has to love him…"

The council of the west cost magnates and lords join Alain and Moray, then they retire to the great hall to discuss the forthcoming gathering at Norham as *Guests* of the English King. William, Dáibh and Andrew are standing outside the stables when auld Jean sees them from the kitchen doors. She calls out to them "You fella's, get up here, your morning vittals are getting cold." William says, "C'mon with us Moray and get some fine mornin' scran, we're taking Stephen's horses up to save him some time." They make their way up to the big house where William tethers Stephen's horses to the stiles. As the three friends pass through the main entrance and into the Keep, they see the doors to the great hall are ajar; they hear raised voices… "Malcolm, I insist that you listen to me," says an unfamiliar voice to the ears of William. The three friends stop outside the partly open door and surreptitiously peer inside. William whispers, "Moray, do you know who that is talking with my Dá and Malcolm?" Andrew whispers, "That's sir Richard Lundie, he was the Durward to the late King Alexander." The three friends go silent as they listen to an ongoing and very heated exchange between Malcolm and Lundie. Malcolm sounds angry… "How can I swear fealty to a feckn war-monger who say's he's descended from the giants of Syria for fucks sake? Look you to what he has done to the Welsh, the Jews and the Irish. Do you think

Longshanks will change his demeanour towards us because we are Scots?" Lundie replies, "Edward is a great king; I know him well Malcolm. He has been a source of enlightenment for England with his reforms of the law, the Barons council and Parliament." Malcolm scowls, "Only because de Montfort and the rest o' the English Barons forced his hand Lundie. I will tell yie this though; Longshanks cannot be trusted. Why do we not keep our own council? There must be a way we can sort out the troubled throne of Scotland without a civil war or giving up our sovereignty to the King of England?"

"Longshanks is a man of honour," states Lundie as he thumps his fist down on the table, "He gives us his Royal oath that he'll relinquish the sovereignty of our realm back to the new regent of Scotland, no later than three months after the coronation." Malcolm snarls, "And you actually believe that shit? Do all of you noblemen and magnates actually believe that?" Lord Moray speaks, "Malcolm, we have to believe it, what choices do we have?" Malcolm exclaims "Imprison those who would wage a civil war, those like de Brix and his pact, execute them if needs be, for it is sheer madness to sign away our realm into slavery." Alain agrees, "Aye Malcolm, you're right, but nobody will do that will they, not with those noble cliques lining up to be kissin' Edwards arse... Why will no-one outside the Céile Aicé or Garda bahn Rígh listen?" Cospatrick says, "I was a member of the Brix pact Malcolm, would you have it that I lose my head for what I believe too?" Malcolm glares at Cospatrick, "If it were to save Scotland and you were the seed of the discourse, aye, ah would." Cospatrick simply shrugs his shoulders and sups more wine. Lundie pleads with Malcolm, "You must sign the Ragemanus with us Malcolm, or you may be cast aside from all the benefits that could be gained." In frustration, Malcolm throws his flagon into the empty fireplace, "Can you not see my position Lundie? I was council and confidante to King Alexander and commander of the Garda Ban Rígh. I cannot now give my allegiance to a foreign King. My bond and oath can only be given to the legitimate regent of Scotland, and Baliol is the rightful heir after his mother and Margret. It's singularly the duplicity of the Brix pact that has brought us to this precipice of war." Lundie exclaims, "Malcolm you are wrong."

"What the fuck do you mean I'm wrong?" snaps Malcolm, "Baliol is closer to the throne through his mother Devorguilla than his main rival de Brus." Lundie retorts, "NO, I mean, you are wrong in your assumption of the character of King Edward. You must understand Malcolm, you may appear treasonous to many if you and others like you do not attend Norham to sign fealty to good king Edward." Malcolm exclaims, "GOOD KING FUCKIN' EDWARD?" Alain slams his flagon on the table and angrily points a finger into Lundie's face, "Hold your tongue Lundie, you dare use the word treasonous to my brother in my very household, by the Aicé I will have your guts…"

"My lords, please…" appeals Lord Moray, "This fealty is simply but a legal necessity. Malcolm, it's fact sworn on oath by Longshanks that he will return all rights of our regency. He has given his word upon the holy gospels. When the chosen claimant is inaugurated accordingly on the mound of the Liadh Fail, (the stone of destiny) Longshanks will relinquish all of these rights back within three months, he has given his word before God." Malcolm replies despairingly, "And you actually believe Longshanks Moray, and you too Cospatrick? Longshanks intends to place all of Scotland's assets under English authority and tax us heavily in order to aid us… Jaezuz fuck, and we're meant to be grateful and kiss his fuckin arse for that privilege?"

Malcolm laughs sarcastically, "And now we're ordered to give over the keys to all our towns and castles to his army commanders, for the English to protect us? Protect us from whom? What the fuck is it you nobles are thinking, you should be protecting us from our own noble cabal more like?" Cospatrick replies, "What choices do we have left for Scotland Malcolm if we don't swear fealty to Longshanks, for a civil war appears to be our only other option. I reckon that if we do swear fealty, then it's a risk worth taking." Lord Moray says, "Though some of us here may have disagreed when the Pact rose Malcolm, all had Scotland's best interests at heart, and there are many claimants outside Scotland who would bring their armies here to settle this dispute by the sword, do not think it is just nobles inside Scotland who rankle over this dilemma." Malcolm replies, "There are legal and hereditary option's to be found in the laws and statutes of Scotland Cospatrick, had the Pact stayed its hand, we would have settled this internally, now all hope is gone."

"I cannot understand?" says Alain, "Why is it that all the native Scot's wish to follow the order of tenure, yet the Scot's of Norman blood squabble and fight amongst themselves, threatening the very being our Kingdom. If everyone follows our natural hereditary laws, then we would have a Queen on the throne by now and that would have been Yolande, Devorguilla or the maid Margret." Lord Moray sighs, "If only it were that simple." Malcolm rages, "It is that fuckin' simple." Alain says, "It would be that simple if the Norman Scots nobles respected our ancient laws according to the rules of cognatic primogeniture, but it seems as though you fuckin' Normans will always stick together when in dispute with the original people of the lands you nest in like cuckoo's." Lord Moray reacts sternly, "You should be minding your words Wallace."

Malcolm glances at Lord Moray, "I meant no offence directly at you my friend." Lord Moray smiles and accepts Malcolm's apology. After a moment's consideration, Malcolm speaks with a calmer voice, "Moray, you're married to Euphemia Comyn, sister of Lord John Comyn the Lord of Badenoch. Cospatrick, you're the husband of Marjorie Comyn who dines with Mharaidh next door, both of you with the Balliols could bring three great houses to the fore with an army that could stand by the shoulders of the Garda Ban Rígh and quash any thought of a civil war." Alain agrees, "There are also the Douglas, the Grahams, Stewarts and many more great Clans and families, fuck, there's even Lord Stewart's borderers and the Gallóbhet of Galloway who would stand with us to fight against Longshanks and protect our sovereignty."

"This is exactly what we don't want," says Lord Moray, "Another raising of an army would certainly set Scot against Scot, this time there would be no stopping it until Scotland is drowned in its own sea of blood." Lundie says, "It's impossible Malcolm, there are too many divisions amongst us. If it were possible, don't you think we would have set everything in play by now to achieve this? Longshanks arbitration is the only way Scotland may avoid shedding the blood of generations." Malcolm, obviously frustrated in the feeling that not one nobleman or cleric appears to hear his lone voice of concern says, "Then all of you, mark my words, for if we resign our realm and castles over to Longshanks, I cannot see that the English King will ever give any of it back. We are handing to him our realm on a pauper's plate. Most nobles who go to sign this Ragemanus, do so only to protect their vested interests in England and France, they should be made to follow the law of Scotland's interests first, or suffer the penalties therein." Lord Moray says, "Wallace, I will ignore your second attack on my Norman blood, but no more of these unwarranted slights." Cospatrick says "And I." Lord Moray continues, "Many of us from mixed blood feel as you do Malcolm, but it would appear your enflamed discourse cannot be settled this day. I see that is so, but believe me; I love this realm and covet our sovereignty as you do my friend. I also respect your reserve, but we must see this poisoned chalice through, its too late now to do otherwise, too much is set in motion to stop what appears to be our destiny." Lundie speaks, "Moray is right Malcolm. My friend, I must tell you, the signing of the Ragemanus to settle Scotland's ill's is the only way to avoid further bloodshed, and we must do it with the Garda ban Rígh, or we will do it without you, there is no alternative."

Malcolm sits at the table appearing exhausted, "My lords Moray, Cospatrick, Lundie, I sincerely apologise for impressing that your birthright was of lesser importance to our sovereignty than my own, for that indiscretion I humbly apologise. Moray, you've been a lifelong friend to me, as have you Cospatrick and so too you my lord Lundie. But I tell you this truth, I will not sign the Ragemanus, and there shall be one force standing alone, armed and prepared if it becomes a reality the Liadh Fail, Great Seal or any Honours of Scotland be touched by anyone other than a true Regent of Scotland. If that should come to pass, there will come a day of reckoning with the Garda cinniúint na laochra dubh." Lundie laughs cynically, "The Black Warrior guard of Destiny? Malcolm, you go too far with this churlish retort. I grant you, this romantic old-fashioned notion of ancient warriors returning to save our beloved realm sounds very heroic, but these feeble threats are but futile gestures from a time long since past that merely falls upon deaf ears my friend. Perhaps old men of the Garda Ban Rígh waste their time by telling such stories to frighten little children, but now is the moment we join the civilised world. Your petulance does risk Scotland's rightful place and her true destiny under the leadership of Longshanks." Malcolm exclaims in a fury, "The Garda Ban Rígh… old men and wasters?" he throws his hands in the air and looks to the roof, "Fuck you Lundie, there will be a reckoning we will all pay for some day if we disregard the Garda ban Rígh and their protections. Do we not have civilisation of our own making already established in this realm? Lord Moray, I beseech you, are your people not known as the Freemen of Moray? Are we not all free to worship in private whatever deity serves our prayers, purpose and needs best? We own beasts, but we do not own men, is this not civilisation?" Cospatrick interjects, "Malcolm, I believe our friend Lundie is correct, in that, Longshanks is much respected and a visionary, who encourages common men of merit to rise into acclaimed positions within English society. He shows his intentions openly towards enlightened meritocracy, as did the late king Alexander show to all within our realm. I believe King Edward's great stewardship will lead us out of this darkness." Malcolm sneers, "Longshanks and meritocracy in the same breath? Meretricious feudalism would be the words you seek Cospatrick, or simply put, slavery, a much more accurate word for the courtly sycophants of Longshanks. Unlike you and Lundie, I will not whore myself or lick-arse a foreign king for my own court privileges."

Lundie flies into a rage, "You infer a slight upon those who would sign the Ragemanus in good faith Wallace, that we do prostitute and whore ourselves. Would you accuse your brother here of this same salacious behaviour for his own avaricious ends?" Malcolm glares at Lundie; "Are you certain in your own beating heart Lundie, that you're not being fooled by Longshanks vulgar attractions of wealth, simply to obtain your signature on oath and seal of nobility, all in exchange for your self-serving avarice and servile obedience? Naw Lundie, I'm convinced Longshanks ambiguous offer of arbitration is nothing but a pretence and cunning deception. These baubles he offers brings forth the true characteristics of meretricious men who would whore themselves for silver, gold and personal gain?" Lundie is incensed, "I swear to you Wallace, you push me to the limits of my restraint. If you do not understand what profound inspirational leadership Longshanks will bring to our realm, then you and other jester fools like you, are a greater threat to Scotland's peace than the Brix Pact could ever have been. Perhaps we should apply your own judgment of imprisonment or the headsman's sword for you and your likes." Suddenly there is an uproar in the hall, Lord Moray swiftly brings order, "Good sirs please, we must have order, I beg of you. Order…" Lord Moray looks at Sir Richard, "Lundie, you must surely define your inference regarding the leadership of Longshanks? Must I remind you that we are not being led by Longshanks, he merely arbitrates at our request and by his own magnanimity."

Drinking from a wine goblet, Lundie looks at his peers, "My Lords, friends… my words were uttered in the heat of passion and ill chosen, as I believe was Malcolm's words when he too became enflamed. I merely meant King Edward's great example of politic, judgment and affairs of state, are the leadership qualities we should aspire too." Alain says, "We already have these qualities Lundie, and more. We here are free men of Scotland, we hold no slaves by any other name, our church is independent, we are independent, and as important, if not more so, we are a proud and independent sovereign realm, and as far as I know, we were nigh on joining the European Union of the Hanseatic Varjag. What course does Longshanks offer to take Scotland that would inspire or benefit us further to better this? Do we submit and obey this English King and then must do what he bids or commands of us to do under the guise of some false union of equals, or do we choose freely our own destiny to do with what we will with the rest of the world. We already have great trade links with the rest of the known world, and without having to be taxed by the English crown for a privilege we already own. In fact, if we remain independent, we would no longer have to pay extortionate taxation by being forced to use English ports instead of our own shipping channels as he proposes under the Ragemanus declaration on the rolls at Norham." Malcolm sneers, "More like a Ragman's roll if you ask me." Malcolm continues, "And aye Lundie, a moment ago you talked about Longshanks, his affairs of state and his leadership qualities? Yet everyone here knows that Longshanks has near bankrupted England with his constant warring and territorial disputes. Yet we declare war on none and prosper greatly under the legacy of Alexander. I agree with Alain, why be tied to a bankrupt realm that requires Scotland simply for our resources, why would we even think of giving up these merits? It is total control of our people and resources the English King truly seeks, mark my words."

Pausing for a moment, Malcolm looks around the table; he sees exhausted faces, but he continues, "Longshanks' repressive taxation on his people for the sake of his own aggrandizement has been the near ruination of England. Wasn't that really what the English Baron's rebellion was all about? Naw Lundie, I don't trust this treaty of Norham, I'll not attend it nor will I support it. I believe Longshanks seeks to acquire Scotland as a mere province simply to be bleeding us dry of all our wealth, trade and resources forever and a day. Mark me well, he will subject all our young men to fight and die in England's Imperial and expansionist wars, why on earth would we want to do that? That my friends is what my gut tells to me." Lord Moray says, "I do admit, you have a credible assessment of the situation Malcolm that is not lost to me, I've also heard many court rumours myself, that Longshanks does aspire to sit himself upon the Liadh Fail whilst wearing Llewellyn's crown, then saying to all that will listen, that his inalienable right to rule over all of us comes from some distant or fabled King called Arthur of the Britons. Though I do believe that Longshanks is an extremely intelligent man, but I also believe he is a dangerous fantasist, he has brutally colonised Ireland and Wales, now it would certainly appear that he requires Scotland to become prostate to the throne of England, calling it, his *Great Cause.*"

"Bah…" Sneers Lundie, "You all do make up outrageous and scandalous stories simply based on old wives tales and court gossip. Longshanks has enough concerns to be dealing with governing England, his provinces and estates in France, Ireland and Wales. He only lends to us Scot's his valuable time to enable us, nothing more." Cospatrick agrees, "When the new Regent is greeted by the Olambh Rígh, (royal poet) upon the Liadh Fail and addresses the new Monarch's genealogy and honours the regal personage *Beannachd dèRígh Alba*, (God Bless the regent of Scotland) It will be but three short months from that day till Longshanks will forever relinquish up all proxy titles he holds on behalf of Scotland to the rightful heir." Malcolm's frustration is wearing thin, "I cannot understand why such an ominous premonition that makes sense to me and other imminent Garda Rígh commanders, is being ignored by the magnates and nobles." Malcolm speaks again, but this time he carries tiredness in his voice, "I also do not understand your single minded adoration of this foreign English King Lundie, nor do I understand those who wish to acknowledge him as our overlord and Magnus supreme, why, for what purpose? What do we do if Longshanks wishes to hold on to these newfound titles of Scotland, especially with his army entrenched and ours disbanded? Have any of you seriously considered what may happen then?" Alain says, "I may appear to be a corn-fed country hunter, but I have read much in my day, and one thing that strikes me when reading the tactical histories of great king past, is that when they set their desires upon another realm, many times, in fact, in all times of note, it is the targeted realm where the noble classes are bought off cheaply for a small pot of gold, and their task, to simply put down the concerns of those that cannot be bought..." Lundie looks at Alain curiously, as does Cospatrick... Lundie says, "I do hope that you were reflecting on history Wallace, and not making another slight upon those of us with Norman blood, for if that is so..."

"My friends," says Sir Hugh, who has been listening quietly, "Alain has many concerns that I also share. So please my lords, if I may, do reply to me thus Lundie, or you Cospatrick if you have the answer... Longshanks has many demands that we must accept before he will commit to arbitration. We're supposed to give up all our Castles, Keeps and port's over to his soldiers and commanders. Our realms administrative officers from the court of Canmore are to resign and be replaced by his own officers. Our sheriff's constables, bankers and district judges are to be replaced by his own Governors implanted from England, and all of Scotland is to be placed under martial law by four of his constables, so tell to me if you can... who shall pay for this, who funds these English expenses, including all monies to pay Longshanks for his time?" Lundie enquires, "How should I know...?" Cospatrick simply shrugs his shoulders, both bereft of any reply.

Malcolm shakes his head, exasperated, "This entire scheme of arbitration is an utter madness, the lords are giving away our realm as though we'd fought and lost a war, then we're expected to pay compensation to Longshanks for this privilege?" Ranald speaks, "Assuming sir Hugh is right, our armies disbanded, Edward's bankers and taxmen controlling all our fiscal institutions, an English army hoarding our trade goods to guarantee Edward's demands for compensation through taxation, what is our plan if we cannot pay this foreign arbitrator, what do we do with a foreign army sitting in all our castles under the control of his administrators? What do we do when in receipt of demands we don't agree with or cannot afford to pay, what then is our recourse my lords Lundie… Cospatrick?" Again there is no reply from Lundie or Cospatrick. Ranald continues, "If our nobles, magnates and Bishops sup like hogs at Edwards table, my main concern is, should he wish to actually keep control of Scotland, who is going to stop the him crushing our very freedom? Who then becomes the independent voice for the good community of Scotland?"

"This is a bloodless coupe by any other name," states Malcolm, "The first sign is this imposition of martial law to put down any common sedition, as they did previously in Galloway and Carrick. That will be the English King's excuse to brutalise any voice of dissent throughout the entirety of our realm. I ask you again my lords, how cheaply bought is our realm without a leader?" There is a long silence in the hall as everyone considers the question. Alain speaks, "Scotland is being bought cheaply by this foreign English King. We'll be paying for our own bloody extinction under the guise of arbitration and filling the purses of our avaricious noble cabal for many generations to come. I fear this is your answer Ranald." Malcolm drops his head, "Then what hope is there for Scotland my lords?" Alain says, "Your concerns are well understood by me brother, and for many of us they're shared.

Unfortunately our great nobles and Bishops are irresponsive and merely brush our deepest concerns aside." Malcolm says, "My friends, I beg of you, heed my words, should Longshanks arbitration as Overlord Supreme threaten our very existence as a realm, I will compel the Garda Rígh to take up an armed resistance." Lundie sneers, "Don't be so foolish Malcolm…" Ranald interrupts "No Lundie, Malcolm is right, many have met a bloody end at the hands of Longshanks under the pretext of his guise of giving aid or succour to a struggling sovereign realm. I'm beginning to believe this Ragemanus treaty may be just a Trojan horse for military intervention and a complete takeover by the English."

Lord Moray appears concerned too, he says, "We must proceed consistently in favour of our realms singular interests to achieve our goals. We must not to be led by or dictated to by Longshanks. Scotland is respected and highly regarded abroad, as can be seen by our many foreign trade treaties, we also have the Flemish, Hansa and Genoese missions establishing embassies in Scotland as we speak. But they'll only remain here if we stay strong, stand firm and remain independent. We cannot be subservient or be a mere province to the English crown… or we shall lose it all." Ranald agrees, "It cannot be a surprise that Longshanks does covet our trade, tax and resources, we should not be letting our wealth be stolen by our so-called fuckin' nobles by giving away our inalienable rights to sovereignty. Alexander kept a firm iron grip on our sovereignty, yet many of our Norman nobles now act against his legacy and seek to give it away as though it's their God given right." Alain speaks "Has the thought ever occurred to any of you that Alexander's death may not have been by the hand of God, but by man's duplicitous intervention?" Lundie laughs out loud, "Alain, now you go too far with your fantastic machinations.

Tell us, where is your proof? Where is your witness or evidence to support such idiotic and preposterous notions? None I would wager." Cospatrick laughs too, "Now you make a farce of these deliberations Alain, regicide…? This is too much." Outside the door, William, Dáibh and Moray listen intently to the heated debate. William whispers, "It's a good thing lady Marjorie is no' listenin', for she has no love o' Lundie." Andrew says, "Lady Marjorie… Dunbar? She's a cousin to my step-mother Euphemia Comyn, sister o' the black Comyn." William says, "She's in the kitchens wie Mharaidh and Daun if you want to meet her?" Andrew hears a noise behind him; he quickly spins around to see what he could only describe as a vision of nature's beauty. He nudges William, "Wallace…" William says, "What is it Moray?" Andrew enquires with a tone of delight in his voice. "Wallace, who is she?" William turns to see Brannah and Marion watching them. Marion tiptoes across the hall with Brannah to kneel beside William. Marion giggles then she whispers, "What are you all doing here sitting beside this door like little frightened mice?"

"Eh… nothing." replies William, "We were just coming in to see if Stephen is ready to leave for Ireland and then to get some vittals from Jean." Marion holds William by the hand. "Then come with me, Stephen is already preparing to leave at the front of the Keep." Brannah smiles coyly then she nudges Marion, "William," says Marion, "Where are your manner's?" William replies, "Oh, ahm Sorry," He says, "Marion, this is Andrew de Moray of Avoch and Petty. Moray, this is my beloved Marion. And this beautiful maid by her side, this is her wee sister Brannah." Andrew clasps Marion by the hand and bows his head in respect. He gazes at Brannah, clasps her by the hand and bows courteously. He raises his head and their eyes meet. William, Marion and Dáibh smile.

Dáibh sighs, "Right, that's it, ah'v had enough, I'm away to find Daun, for all this young love reminds me of what I am missing when Daun's no' by my side." Marion sighs, "Awe my, is that not the sweetest thing a husband could ever say about his dearest wife in the company of others." William smiles, "Aye, that's what I like about Dáibh, he and Daun are loved by all who know them by their good grace and countenance towards each other. A lot of men could learn how good a man can be when truly loved by a beautiful woman such as Daun." Clasping William by the hand, Marion says, "Come on with me now William, we must go to see Stephen before it's too late and he departs this place for Ireland." William walks away hand in hand with Marion, they see that Andrew and Brannah are stood still gazing at each other, as though all wit and good sense had vacated their thoughts, left with nothing evident in mind but inane smiles. William enquires, "Do we look like that?" Marion laughs, "I hope so." William says, "Naw, I can't believe Moray and Brannah are romancing each other already, they've only just met?" Marion holds both William's hands and pulls him close...

"We did Wallace." then she smiles, folds her arms and gives him a minor but a very effective look. "Naw..." laughs William, "Have you and wee Maw been talking?" Marion enquires, "WHY?" William doesn't know if he should be smiling, or obeying. He replies, "Ach, it's just that I recognise the folded arms and the kinda *look* you're giving me darlin'." Marion enquires, "Wallace, do you not believe in love at first sight?" William looks at Marion then laughs to himself getting his first chastisement, and a young version of the Look. He thinks of how beautiful Marion appears, even when in this temperament. She enquires, "And what are you grinning at Wallace?" William smiles, "You Marion. I just think that you are so beautiful. I'm also thinking of

32

how lucky I am to be in love with you." Marion smiles coyly, "Why, thank you William. At least Moray has the advantage of not smelling like chicken shit or wee Grahams whisky sick when he and Brannah met." William exclaims, "What?" Marion gazes at him with a passion; then she grips his little goatee beard and pulls him close enough to kiss. "I really do love you William Wallace..." Marion kisses him on the lips; then she tells him to hurry up and get a move on or he will miss Stephen, soon to be leaving. William calls out, "Moray, Brannah, will you two chaperone me and the maid Marion this morn, if it pleases you?" When Marion and William exit the Keep, they see Stephen is already mounted and leaning over on his saddle kissing Katriona fondly, then he reaches over to wee Stephen held in the arms of Katriona and kisses his son on the forehead. Gathered to bid him farewell on his journey, are Dáibh, Daun, Auld Tam, wee Graham, Jean, Mharaidh, Marjorie, Margret and wee Maw.

William calls out "Stephen..." He runs over and grips the horn of Stephen's saddle. He enquires, "Stephen ma friend, are you sure that you don't want me to come to Ireland with yie? Do yie no' remember the red Earl and how we left him? We might have rattled his teeth sure enough; and even though he still might have not much to say yet, I'm sure we didn't dislodge his feckn memory." Stephen sighs, "Now then don't be frettin', I'll be all right there foin enough Wallace, there's no' a sionnach (Fox) in auld Erinn more evasive nor wily than me'self now. I'll be sendin' a message back to the doocots here as soon as I get to Monaghan, and ah'll be letting yiez know what's all happening. If I think I might stay awhile longer, I'll send for Katriona and wee Stephen to come over to Ireland to be joinin' me." Wee Graham steps up, "Would yie like a wee nip o' craitur afore yie go son? Ah'v a couple of flagons and a couple o' leather bladders o' ma finest craitur blend stashed away on your pack-horse too, and mind and save some for your dear auld fathers wake…" Everyone smiles at wee Graham's care and kind thoughts regarding Stephen's sustenance on his forthcoming journey. William also notices the deep concern evident in wee Graham's voice. Ever since Stephen had married Katriona, he has become like an only son to wee Graham. The growing affection between them as a loving tight-knit family is there to be seen, and warmly felt by everyone. "I'll have one to be sending me on me way then fadder-in-law." Stephen takes the drinking horn from wee Graham and downs his craitur gift in one, leans over from his horse and kisses Katriona once more, long and passionately; then he looks towards wee Graham… "Mind and you take care o' the wee one for me." He winks at wee Graham then says curiously, "And mind the other wee one too." Wee Graham takes a step back from the horse and replies, "Ah will do that son; they'll be safe and sound enough here. Now you mind and take good care of yourself, and mind to let us know how things are when you get there."

Wee Graham and auld Jean both put their arms around a tearful Katriona, to comfort her in seeing her loving husband depart. With a wicked smile, Stephen winks at Katriona, then he spurs his horse, tugs on his packhorse and begins to canter along the North road to then turn westward towards the lands of Carrick, and finally, onwards to the shores of Invergarvane, there he will catch a Birlinn for Ireland. Everyone cheers and waves goodbye to a much-loved son and friend, wishing him well on his journey. Wee Graham whispers… "May the Aicé speed yie till wee meet again son…"

An Eala Bhàn

While Glen Afton basks in a glorious setting sun, wee Maw sits quietly alone on the edge of the Keep promontory, gazing towards the long empty road that Stephen had taken earlier on his heartbreaking journey back to Ireland. William is watching her intently, there is something different about her demeanour, but he can't fathom out what it is or what it could be. It's as though wee Maw is watching for someone to return from some long journey. There's also an air about her that makes him feel uncomfortable, he's distracted when Marion walks towards him while everyone else makes their way back into Wallace Keep. He notices wee Graham and auld Tam close-by enjoying the contents poured from a large jug of craitur, both laughing and talking about the old giant salmon that they never did catch… yet. Marion approaches William and stands beside him. They link arms, sharing for a moment the wonder of the Glen Afton vista…

"So beautiful," says Marion, she laughs then points, "Look at that William, down beside the Craig n' Darroch stables." William looks to where Marion is pointing and laughs too when seeing their chaperones Brannah and Andrew sitting together on a small haystack, completely oblivious to everything else, chatting as though they are the only two people in the world. Marion notices something else and pulls on William's léine sleeve... "William, Katriona's so upset about Stephen's departure, I think I'll go over and comfort her awhile." William feels a pang of emotion while observing Katriona's distress. She had remained stoic for Stephen, but now seeing her with tear-filled eyes, moves him. He knows how wonderful the love between Stephen and Katriona is. The two of them have become inseparable with the combined strength of old twin-oaks when together, yet almost incapable of life without the presence of the other in separation. William pulls Marion close and whispers, "Aye bonnie darlin', her hurtin' needs all the soothing your care may bring her. I'll go and sit with wee Maw, for she's not looking her usual self sitting over there."

The two lovers gaze lovingly into each other's eyes, Marion studies William, this man so handsome and thoughtful of others, a man who shows her naught but infinite understanding and a gentle caring heart, a man who offers offence to none and is committed to her in a way that makes her heart and soul feel eternally entwined with his. William makes her laugh, with his innocent almost naive observations that are true to him as he sees life, giving her an amusing view of the world through his eyes, a view she welcomes as her own, and of course, his smile. She thinks 'You just melt my heart.' "William Wallace..." says Marion. William replies, "Aye darlin' what have I done now?" Marion giggles, "I love you." Smiling, he pulls Marion close. His beautiful loving sweetheart meekly complies with a twinkle in her eye. "Bonnie Marion, I love you so much that I think I'm the luckiest man on this whole flat world." Marion giggles at William's version of romance, she taps him on the end of his nose, "Wallace, you're so funny." He's bemused, "What dyie mean?" Marion smiles while holding him close, she kisses him gently on the neck, cat-nipping his skin, sending thrilling sensations throughout his body. He closes his eyes, exhilarated by the feeling of holding her in his arms, her sweet scents fill him with a longing… suddenly he thinks to himself in a panic… "Awe naw…" Marion immediately stops moving, they both stand absolutely still with her lips still pressed against his neck, her warm breath caressing his skin.

They remain motionless as though frozen in time. Marion begins to feel his hot passion rising as her own lust wells up inside. She whispers, "Wallace?" a nervous William replies, "Aye ma dear?" Marion whispers, "I hope that's your dirk pressing against my stomach?" William grins as Marion says in a rebuke, "I said, your Dirk Wallace…" William laughs then he stammers, "Eh ah… I hope so too." Marion pulls back and gazes into his eyes, she smiles approvingly at this unfortunate and very embarrassing moment for him. She laughs, then with a cheeky glint in her eyes, she says, "Away you go and see wee Maw, I'll go and tend to Katriona, and hmmm, perhaps Wallace, eh, perhaps we may continue this discussion later…?"

Grinning inanely as Marion walks away, William studies her tall slender body, her long black hair flows gently behind her like a heavenly moon-kissed waterfall. His eyes follow down the curve of her back as she sways her hips ever so slightly, as women do. Marion's svelte figure makes him feel the need to follow as her feminine movements mesmerize him. *'By the Aicé, she is so feckn beautiful, and I love her so much with all my heart… and she loves me? How lucky am I? Feck… and she wants to continue this discussion later?'* Elated and almost dizzy with loving thoughts flying around his head… William's attention is brought back to wee Maw who is still sitting quietly on her own, unnoticed by everyone other than himself. There still seems to be something different about her demeanour that is concerning him.

He walks over and sits down beside his wee Maw, then he puts his arm gently around her shoulders and pulls up her shawl, tucking it in about her neck and shoulders to keep her warm in the typically Scottish brisk early summer's eve. He enquires, "Granny, are yie feelin' all right?" Wee Maw is startled by his voice and his presence. She stammers, "Oh, is that you Billy?"

"Billy?" Exclaims William, "Naw Granny, it's me, William." Wee Maw mumbles, "Oh aye William, is that you son?" William enquires, "Are you feeling all right Granny?" But there is no reply. He looks at wee Maw as she continues watching the drove road intensely. "What's wrong with yie Granny?" Then he notices wee Maw has tears in her eyes. She replies, "Ach there's nuthin' wrong son." Wee Maw catches her breath with a little sob then she pulls at the sleeve of William's léine and blows her nose, "Sorry about that son." William looks forlorn at his sleeve, sticky with wee Maw's deposit; he sighs, smiles and carefully tucks his sleeve up and away, "It's fine granny, that's what grandsons are for..." Wee Maw looks at him and raises a wrinkly smile; then she says in a surprised voice, "Oh, it is you William. I thought you were me darlin' Billy there for a moment. Do yie know son, did I ever tell you that my Billy has been coming to me in my dreams of a late?" Wee Maw looks into William's eyes with a childlike innocence... "Aye, almost every night he comes to me, but when I wake I'm sorely saddened to find that my Billy has returned to Tír na nÓg without me, and him leaving me here all on me own so very much alone..."

William listens intently to her words, though they un-nerve him slightly as she continues, "Son, it makes me so very sad to wake from my dreams where your grandfa-ther and I will meet in a world of peace with such a loving care for each other, ach, so much so we are still in love and young again in that place. And there too are all my friends now gone from this life… then, when I wake, he's not there… they're not there." Wiping tears from her eyes, she pulls at his sleeve again, blows her nose and tucks his léine sleeve back underneath his arm. "Oh William, its just that I've lived such a long life and seen so much. Sometimes it's been so very rich and full of all the joys that life can bring, yet there is other times when the sadness and loneliness can be so heartbreaking. It makes me wonder if it's at all worth it to be carrying on so… Son, I'll tell yie, the older yie get, the more yie realise time is relentless and ruthless. One moment you are a wain running about the place without a care in the world, the next moment you're old and feeble like me, yet you don't really feel any different inside in all that time, just a wee bit weary of it all."

Looking into the bright steely blue eyes of wee Maw, William exclaims, "Whoa there granny, you're no' old, and you're definitely no' feeble." Wee Maw smiles "Well this day I am feeling my age William, and seeing young Stephen leaving to be by his dear mothers side, when it's likely to be the last time… William, my heart feels that raw pain so much, it's a heart breaking raw pain to think I will never again see my old and dearest friend Stephen H'Alpine in this lifetime. Oh William, my old heart is so very tired of it all, sometimes I wish could just go back to the land o' dreams, to a place where my Billy waits for me and there I may stay forever in peace with those I love and never to be waking here again." Tears begin to run down wee Maw's face. William is shocked, he pulls wee Maw close and begins to feel very emotional as tears begin to well up inside of him too, sensing wee Maw's pain and seeing her so very vulnerable… he's never seen this side of her before, but he knows he needs to be strong for her, then he begins to sob gently himself as his own emotional strength deserts him caused by her distress. He never could have thought to imagine or even consider a life without his precious wee Maw, but now he feels that cold reality touching his heart. They sit quietly together when wee Graham and auld Tam come walking over, for they too have noticed wee Maw's distress, they are ominously curious, sensing that something is greatly amiss. They say nothing as they sit beside wee Maw and William, they just know. Auld Tam sits beside wee Maw and puts his arm around her waist as wee Graham kneels in front of her and lovingly holds both of her hands. William looks away; he doesn't want them to see his emotions, he can't understand this moment of love, care and confusion. Wee Graham speaks in a sombre caring voice as he gently strokes the back of her hands…

"There there Bheitris, we miss big Billy too." Auld Tam says, "We understand Bheitris, ah miss ma bonnie wife Aoife and there's no' se' many o' us left now, so we must be looking after one another. Would you be wanting me to go and heat up a wee hot honey toddy for yie bonnie darlin?" Wee Maw begins weeping and buries her face into the shoulder of Auld Tam. She sobs, "I miss him so much Tam, so much…" Auld Tam replies, "We know yie do Bheitris, we all do." Lifting her head up and wiping away her tears with Tams léine sleeve, she says, "I wish sometimes that the angels would come for us and let us have peace and love again." wee Maw sobs, "Sometimes I'm so very lonely Tam, even when the family are around me it can be the loneliest time of all, it's then that I miss Billy the most." William sees the tears well up in wee Graham and auld Tam too, this moment is breaking his heart, he's never experienced these emotions before, and being beside two men renowned for their skills in war and in the killing of men by ruthless endeavour, men free from emotion in the art of the dispatch, now showing such tender loving care to a fragile little old lady they both love so dearly, she is clearly their special Aicé. Wee Maw smiles feebly, then she grabs at William and auld Tams léine sleeves to wipe her eyes and blow her nose again. She laughs at the same time as she weeps, causing everyone to laugh, and so very much relieved that she now appears free from melancholy. "Jaezuz Granny," says William, "Yie fair had me worried there." Auld Tam sighs, "Jings, me too, ah think ah need a wee nip after that." Wee Maw says, "Aye, ahm awfy thirsty too boys…" Wee Graham grins, "Would yie like a nip o' ma really special honeydew craitur now Bheitris?"

"Aye, go on then yie fly auld rascal," replies wee Maw, "Yie still know the way to a girls heart, don't yie me auld friend. Aye, I'll be having a big nip of your finest toddy if yie please." With little skip and a jig, wee Graham retorts, "Then it will be my pleasure me bonnie lady o' the Morríaghan Sídhe." He glances at William and winks, "I'll be making sure it's the finest o' the finest o' toddies Bheitris… and ah'll be making sure there's no' any spillage on me way back." Auld Tam and wee Graham stand up; then they share a concerned glance with William. Suddenly wee Maw calls out. "Wee Graham, Tam…" Her old friends turn to find out why she has called out to them. She says with a warm smile. "Ta'padh leat… Thank you." With cheery waves, Auld Tam and wee Graham go on about their medicinal errand while William and wee Maw sit together once more, peacefully viewing the resplendent vista of Glen Afton. Curiously, William and wee Maw hear strange noises nearby, like two giant blacksmith bellows getting closer… and much louder. William exclaims, "Look granny". He points towards the skyline just above the Afton flow. A jubilant wee Maw cries out, "Awe Liam, an Eala Bhàn (The white swan) Didn't I tell yie William, and there's two of them, look see, they're flying westward too." William and wee

Maw watch intently as a pair of magnificent and regal white swans fly serenely overhead, with a grace and dignity reserved only for these angelic creatures borne of such elegant poise. "Oh William," exclaims an excited wee Maw, "That's my Billy, ah told yie didn't ah, he's come for me… and he's brought the spirit wings to carry me away with him too." William looks at wee Maw and sees the delight in her eyes as the swans fly low overhead, making the unmistakable *whump-whump* sound as their wings beat the air in wondrous flight. Wee Maw and William watch the white swans that uncannily appear to respond to the passionate and emotional senses emanating from a joyful wee Maw.

The tow swans slowly complete a circle over the great glen of Afton to fly low overhead once more, close enough for William and wee Maw to see into the blacks of their eyes and feel their presence looking back. William senses a magical connection in this spiritual moment, then he notices wee Maw reaching up, as though she is running her fingers gently along the soft underbelly of both the swans as they pass overhead to fly onwards and along the crescent ridges of Glen Afton. Wee Maw happily rests her head on William's shoulder, coorying in to keep warm as they continue watching the majestic birds flying across the glen of Afton one more time, then they make a final turn to continue their journey westward, towards the sea. "Oh I'm so happy now William," says wee Maw "Now I want to go home this day to Ach na Feàrna and wait for my Billy." William enquires, "Are you feeling a wee bit better now Granny?" Wee Maw regains her composure, "Aye son, ah do. Sometimes things can just get a wee bit overwhelming and very emotional at my auld age." Comforting his precious grandmother, William says, "You were talking earlier of grandpa Billy granny, I wish I'd met him." Wee Maw smiles "Aye son, and I've said this to yie often, that of all the family you are the most like him in looks and the way you carry yourself. And when I saw you and the maid Marion together, it reminded me so much o' when I met your grandfather and we romanced." William smiles at the thought as they sit a few moments in silence, then he enquires, "Granny, there's a curiosity I've had for such a long time, I've always wanted to ask you this question, and now with me and Marion betrothed and hopefully the patter of wee tiny feet soon to be in the offing, I need you to sort something out in my head about grandpa."

"What is it about that you need to know son?" enquires Wee maw. William says, "Well granny, there's uncle Malcolm, now his father and mother are Adam Wallace and Christina Kilbane is that right?" Wee Maw replies, "Aye son, that's right." William continues, "And aunt Margret's father, that's uncle Ranald the sheriff of Ayr, and her mother, wasn't she Cecelia Campbell of Auchenames o' Loudon?" Wee Maw replies, "Aye that's right too William, so what's your question?" William explains, "Well, if uncle Richard of Riccartoun is Malcolm's brother, why is it that my father Alain is not mentioned as a brother in Paisley Abbey records, nor is grandpa Billy?" Wee Maw sighs, "Ah… it's a wee bit complicated that one son, but ah'll tell yie anyway. The confusion about the brothers comes from a time not long after the Normans started arriving in Scotland many years ago. The story goes as far back as your great-great-great grandfather, which really relates you to the high steward of Scotland and Beatrix Douglas, the countess of Angus, that's the name that I carry forward."

"So, we Wallace's are related to the Douglas?" William exclaims. Wee Maw replies, "We are, and also to the great Scott, Moray and Comyn clan's too." William is surprised, "Ah never knew about that granny, but what about Dá and grandpa Billy?" Wee Maw smiles, "Grandpa Billy was born from the loins of an old Gallovidian Dál Riatan chief called Ualaicé, the son o' Giric MacRath, foster brother o' Feargus mòr, son of Eochaidh and Aedan macGabrin, then so to the blood o' Cinaed MacAlpin an Ferbasach (The Conqueror) William exclaims, "Kenneth MacAlpine, the first king of Scotland? Is that why we have a close relationship with the ua h'Alpine family?"

"It is son, the wheel turns full circle for both our families, with wee John and Rosinn getting wed." William is curious "But why is there two sources of our name?" Wee Maw replies, "Right William, when the Normans first came here they wanted to be identified with the native folks of this land, so they adopted local names. One o' those Norman fella's was a big knob called Elmerus Gramus Galerius, he's supposedly the main prodigenator as they call it of what was commonly known as the Riccartoun Wallysch family. Have you got that son?" William nods in the positive as wee Maw continues. "Lazy Norman scribes used more what a name sounded like than to be bothered following a set of hereditary rules." William replies, "Aye granny, but ah thought that Elmerus fella was the name of some old Roman César?"

Wee Maw smiles, "Aye son, that too, those Normans had a great sense o' humour when they gave names to their wains." William laughs as she continues, "Then there's the native Wallace family o' this land, entirely different from Norman humours, for our native origins go back into Cruathnie Dál Riatans and Cymrans o' Strathclyde history, they folks were Wall-Aicé from the Aicé lineage's if you remember ma stories correctly?" William grins, "Aye Granny, I know the legends o' the Aicé, how could ah forget." Wee Maw says "Right son, now we have two established families of distinctly different names and separate origins, but they sound alike, the Strathclyde Wallaicéo' yr Hen Ogledd alt Cluid and the Norman

Wallysch o' Riccartoun, have yie got that?" William smiles, "Aye granny, ah'v got it." Wee Maw says, "Good. Now, your father Alain's mother, the poor wee soul, she died giving him birth, now his dear mother's name was Murraghd nic' Lunna, (Raven, Daughter of the moon) your father was called a foundling, and as such he became a ward of the Cluniac priests of Paisley Abbey. Adam Wallych's family took him in as their own in fosterage, that's why your uncles Richard is o' Riccartoun and Malcolm is o' Ach na Feàrna and Auchenbothie… and why they're titled so." William now understands something that has puzzled him all his life, but he hadn't realised how important wee Maw's answers are till now. He enquires, "So how did me Dá, now a Wallace, end up here in Glen Afton?"

"Well son," replies wee Maw "In him being a foundling, he couldn't assume a hereditary title, because he's no' a blood son of Adam, but he rose through personal grit and merit to be King Alexander's personal huntsman in the Wolf and Wildcat forests, and in time, your father became a Knight and master tenant o' the Kings hunting lodges o' Kyle and Carrick down here in the bonnie lands Glen o' Afton." Still curious, William enquires, "I thought Dá was already a knight?" Wee Maw replies, "When a foundling grows to manhood within a titled family, he can either gain his knighthood through acquired possessions or sometimes he can even purchase a title. In your fathers case, he earned it because of valuable services rendered to our late King, but you know yer father William, he never liked the title anyway, as the royal court knobs always thought of him as what they call a *Lowly knight*. Mmmm… A bit like a rich mans bastard son so to speak."

Laughing at the description of his father, William enquires, "And what about ma uncle Malcolm then?" Wee Maw replies, "When Malcolm and your father Alain received their knighthood's, they decided to take on your grandfather

Billy's spelling o' the name, they were the first to spell Wallace this way." William exclaims, "Ah granny, now I understand why some folk say the Wallace are from France or Wales and some say we're from Strathclyde… it's a merging of two families who now use the same name." Wee Maw smiles, "That's it me boy." William enquires, "But granny, you haven't explained about big Billy and yourself, you haven't said about that part of the family?" Wee Maw sighs, "Ach son, many years ago me and your grandfather had many children, aye, me and Billy had nine wains all told…." William exclaims "Nine?"

Wee Maw replies nonplussed, "Aye nine, we would have had more, but six of them died in childbirth. My first born was a wee girl, her name is Dorinn; she survived and later she married sir Tam Halliday of Corriechd near Moffadh." William enquires, "So what happened to Dorinn granny? I remember her when ah was young but she left and ah'v never seen her since." Wee Maw smiles, "Aye, that Halliday was so wild and fond o' a braw fight, so he went on the Crusades, but he didn't like it much at all, he said it was too hot. I remember once that he told us he had more of a liking for Saracens than his own folk anyway, so he went away to Flanders as a soldier of fortune and Dorinn went with him, but I have heard they're to be coming home very soon." William enquires, "What about your other children?" Wee Maw replies, "After Dorinn, I lost a six more wains, by the time I was eighteen summers, I had twin daughters, Aoibheann and Brìghde bless them. After that it was no' possible for me to be birthin' again, the goddess o' Magda mòr must o' reckoned I had done my fair share o' earth birthin'. Anyway, bonnie Brìghde, your mother, she was your father Alain's first wife,"

William sees that wee Maw is getting very emotional thinking of her late daughters, she looks at William and smiles, "My bonnie lassies used to be annoyed by two big stupid looking gangly half-brothers who hooted, whooped and jumped about our wee Balloch for years like a pair o' deranged half-wits. Oh William, my they were awful creatures, doing the most annoying and stupid o' things to gain the attention of my bonnie wee girls, till it came the day that those two young fella's became fine young men and asked for the hand of my daughters in marriage."

Engrossed by the story, William looks at wee Maw, "My father and uncle Malcolm? Wee Maw laughs, "Aye, the very two, the biggest rogues in all o' Strathclyde they were, and they were inseparable, just like you and wee John... like you and Stephen ua H'Alpine are now if the truth were to be known." William enquires, "So ma mother really was your blood daughter?" Wee Maw replies, "Aye, Malcolm's first wife Aoibheann was her sister. Malcolm had two daughters by Aoibheann, Uliann and then Aunia, sadly, our bonnie Aoibheann passed away. But Malcolm soon enough found love again and married Margret Crauford, his second wife. As yie know, they had three sons, Malcolm, then William, your namesake who died in childbirth, and then they had gentle Andrew." William says, "I never knew any of this before granny."

"Your father Alain and Brìghde had you and wee John, but it was terrible times for us all when Brìghde died giving birth to wee John. When Alain married Mharaidh Scott, they begat bonnie wee Caoilfhinn." William says, "So Granny, your daughters married two bonded but no' blood brothers?" Wee Maw replies, "Aye son, that's how it was. When your grandfather Billy died at the battle of Largs, my two lassies o' Malcolm and Alain died soon after, I stayed on at Ach na Feàrna to help both your father and Malcolm with you and all o' the wains, and I've been there ever since." Sighing, William sits back and gazes across the flowing landscape of Glen Afton, "Now I understand Granny, It's puzzled me for years. I tried to find out by following the female line in the parish records, but they don't record daughters and mothers in the records of the church for some feckin reason." William immediately puts his hand to his mouth "Ahm sorry granny I didn't mean to curse." Wee Maw laughs aloud, "Ach son its fine," she laughs, "Though that Christian God works in many mysterious ways they say, and honouring a wife and mother as equal to any man appears to be not one o' them. Though it does say in their Greek scriptures that any man who turns away from the female face of God sure won't get intae their heaven." William laughs, "Then that's his loss then granny, I will tell yie this granny, am so glad ah'v been brought up Céile Aicé." Wee Maw chuckles as she glances across the glen, "Me too son."

Still curious, William enquires, "So what is ma real Bloodline Granny?" Norman, Welsh, Dál Riatan or Cruathnie?" Wee Maw smiles again, "You're Cruathnie Dál Riatan Cymran true-blood Wallace through your grandfather Billy, your mother Brìghde and through my blood all the way back to the bonnie Aicé Morríaghan. And then from bonnie Murraghd Lunna and your father..." Pausing a moment, wee Maw looks into the inquisitive eyes of William. "And do yie know that Leckie mòr Lunn is the brother of your fathers mother?" William exclaims, "Auld Leckie... he's ma grand uncle?" Wee Maw smiles, "Don't yie know?" William sighs, "Feck... I do now, I can understand a lot more about the special attention he used to mete out to me and wee John. Oh, another thing Granny... You mentioned a couple of names in our family there, Murraghd, which sounds a wee bit like Moray, and another you also mentioned the Douglas? I met three really fine young knights at Monadh-abh a few years ago, a fella called Andrew de Moray who's here today with his father Lord Moray, and a knight called Hardy Douglas. There's another fella called Graham, they said they're Céile Aicé and showed to me their earliest family coat-of-arms, each of them has different coloured Dragon. Are we related to them too?" Wee Maw replies "Aye son, those fine families are of the Céile Aicé faith too. They have Norman Flemish and Cruathnie bloodline in their families, but mind this son, Normans are not all bad, like many Scots are not all good, though ah wish ah hadn't said that." William laughs, "Granny, do yie see that young knight away down there by the riverside, walking along with Brannah?"

Wee maw screws up her eyes "I think so..." William continues, "That's young Andrew Moray of Avoch, he's Céile Aicé." wee Maw replies, "Aye that's right, their auld ancestor Friskin married the grand Aicé Graunia, o' the Avoch Cruathnie, it was from her family your father Alain's dear mother hails from. Now take Marion and Brannah over there," ponders wee Maw, "They too were ward foundlings, just like your father, awe, but it was so sad for them after the killing of their good folks away down in Rosbroch, and for no reason. But it was a great day for us all when sir Hugh and lady Johanna took them in." William nods, "Aye granny, ah remember yie told me." Wee Maw says, "You look after Marion son, for you're a Wallace, a Céile Aicé and a man after the heart of your old grandfather Billy." Wee Maw pauses, then she says, "Ah love you dearly William, but now... I'm feeling a wee bit tired for I am no as young as I used to be."

William enquires, "One last question Granny... where was I born, Glen Afton, Riccartoun or ach na Feàrna?" Wee Maw laughs, "Do yie really want to know where yie were born son?" William replies with excitement in his voice "Aye granny, of course..." Wee Maw sighs "Then I will tell yie son... you were born on a Sídhe Chailleann (She-hallion - Fairy hill) in the middle o' Catterhaugh..." William laughs, "Ha, agallamh na seanórach. (Tales of the elders) Granny, ah know the colloquy of the ancients. But seriously, where was I born?" Wee Maw is about to reply, when suddenly, she begins choking and coughing up blood, she quickly goes grey in the face and begins to fall over in a faint... "GRANNY..." shouts William as he catches her from falling over completely. Deeply concerned, he helps her to sit back up. "Here William..." calls out auld Tam as he and wee Graham come rushing over from the kitchen doors and gather round wee Maw. Auld Tam holds a small horn cup filled with hot honey blended whisky to wet her lips, he says, "William, quickly, go and fetch Mharaidh and your father." Coming round from her faint, wee Maw Growls, "I'm fine, I'm fine, just be leaving me alone..."

Mharaidh, Daun and Marjorie come rushing over to help, they immediately take wee Maw by the hand and lead her towards the kitchens. Mharaidh says, "William, go and get Malcolm and your father." Wee Maw calls out, "Billy..." she calls out once more and holds out her hand in search of someone, "Billy... where are yie?" William reaches out and holds her hand. Wee Maw enquires, "Is that you Billy?" William replies, "Naw Granny it's me, William." She whispers, "William son, I want you to get my wagon ready, for we're going away home to ach na Feàrna, we're going to follow the white swans west and you must be taking me home right the now." Mharaidh and William look at each other, then wee Maw says, "Don't you lot be fussing about me... just get ma wagon ready. It's still early enough in the day and I need to be going home right now, and William is taking me. There will be no stoppin' me if yiez know what's good for yiez. William, Tam, wee Graham, uze help get ma wagon ready and I will be saying farewell to my family here in Glen Afton."

William and Mharaidh look at each other with a knowing that something in wee Maw's voice make any thoughts or arguments about her staying in Glen Afton, moot. Later that afternoon, wee Maws bow-wagons are ready for the trip north and west. Alain and his retinue are also preparing to travel in caravan with Lord Moray, sir Richard Lundie, sir Hugh and Cospatrick de Dunbar for their journey to Upsettlingham on the northern side of the Tweed, the Scots camp marking the border between Scotland and England. William has his pack ready and sits on the banks of the river Afton, throwing pebbles into the soft flowing Spey when Marion comes down from the Keep to join him.

"Oh ma bonnie darlin." says William, "Ahm going to miss you." Marion, with a hint of sadness in her voice says, "I will miss you more." William laughs then says, "I'll miss you moreover than that…" They both laugh as Marion sits down on the Afton riverbank beside him, resting her head on his shoulder. Marion enquires, "Did you know about the condition of Katriona?" William is baffled by her question, "What about Katriona?" An excited Marion replies, "She's with child…" William exclaims, "Ah ha… So that's why Stephen said to wee Graham to watch the wee one twice, I wondered what he meant by that. So how is she?" Marion reaches over and holds William's hand, "She's upset and so very sad that Stephen had to go, that's why I went over and stayed with her awhile, at a time like this it would be very easy to lose the child." Laying back in the grass William smiles at Marion, "I'm really glad you have a good knowledge o' motherhood bonnie Marion, for we must keep trying for a family on a regular basis soon, as often as possible in fact… in ma humble opinion." Marion states tersely "Wallace…" then she relents, "When do we start?" They both laugh as she strokes his face with a grass stalk. Marion lies back down beside him and puts her arm across his chest. "How many children would you like William?" With a broad smile, William replies, "At least one... a year." Marion giggles then she leans over and kisses him softly on the lips. It's not very long before they are kissing passionately. They pause, with Marion laying her head on William's chest. He enquires, "When do you leave for Rosbroch?" Marion replies, "This eve I think, then we go to Edinburgh, after that we go to Berwick where father is to meet with Flemish and Hansa traders. My father sends all his wool to Flanders, he has a great friendship with a Flemish knight sir Guy de Dampierre and he's also meeting with some of his other Flemish business partners. Brannah and I are buying things for a house my father built beside the bruin house in Lanark town."

They both lay back content to watch the clouds float past, William enquires, "Marion... I've often wondered, why do they call the house you manage the Bruin house?" Marion looks at him curiously "I thought you would know the answer to that Wallace?" He shakes his head, "Naw, tell me?" Marion holds his hand, "Apparently the name comes from the example of the woodland bear that stores food for winter hibernation, that's also why we store food, for the poor and the needy. It's where we give them food, seed, cheeses, salts, fiongeur and wort to ward off the winter hunger. We supply weaves to keep them warm too, that's why they call it the Bruin hoose...the bru, the bears house?" William says, "It's sure a good thing you do at the Bru hoose Marion." She smiles "Thank you William. It's an important position to be responsible for the poor and the needy, if I were to make any mistakes at all, if just one poor soul suffers needlessly because of our lack of care, I could never forgive myself."

"Well darlin." William grins, "If we are going to spend most of our time trying to make many wains, it might be that I may have to go to the Bru hoose for assistance myself. If I cannot hunt through a malady caused by spending my time giving you my all for the sake o' a family... I might be in need of your understanding and charity." William expects a playful slap for his bawdy humour, but nothing came his way, he looks at Marion, she smiles at him and says, "I do love you Wallace, I was wondering if you..."

A familiar voice calls out, "WHERE ARE YIE BOY?" William exclaims, "Awe feck, Awe naw, no' now, please..." Auld Tam and Wee Graham approach the two young lovers. Tam says, "Marion, your father wants to see you now. He's ready to depart for Lammington." Wee Graham says, "Aye Wallace, c'mon son, for yer wee Maw is near enough ready to travel too, Malcolm has her bedded down in the back of the leadin' wagon, Daun is looking to her needs and everyone is waiting for you to get up there so they may leave." William and Marion stand up and brush the grass from their cloths. Marion sorts her hair then they make their way up to Wallace Keep arm in arm, chatting and laughing together.

"When shall I see you next Wallace?" enquires Marion, William replies, "I don't know darlin' I had hoped to see you when you got back from Edinburgh in three of four weeks, but I'll have to see how wee Maw is when we get back to ach na Feàrna." William pauses, "You still want to get married on the Beltane don't yie?" Marion replies, "Of course, but what shall we do about arranging the wedding William? I had hoped we could have made those arrangements while we were here, but I understand that you must leave now with wee Maw, and it appears we will be leaving very soon too, what shall we do?" William replies, "Why don't we wait till both our fathers are back from the Norham Gathering and you're back from Edinburgh? And as soon as wee Maw is feeling a lot better, I'll come down to Lammington and we can make our the arrangements then?" Marion exclaims, "Oh William, this is so exciting." William pulls her close, he says, "Ah know," he continues, "I have got such a feeling racing round my body, I can't hardly wait ma bonnie darlin." Marion exclaims, "Oh Wallace, je t'adore." William smiles as he holds Marion in his arms, "Je t'aime, mon amour." The two lovers passionately kiss, then make their way to the foot of the Black Craig where the bow-wagons and everyone waits to leave for ach na Feàrna.

They soon arrive at the lower corral where three bow-wagons with riding horses tied behind them are waiting. Malcolm and Margret are sitting in the lead wagon, with wee Maw tucked up inside, Dáibh and Daun are now in the second wagon. The last wagon is full of wild summer hunt provisions tethered for William to drive. "William," says Alain, "Wee Maw needs you to be close to her just now, and when she's fit and feeling better up in Ach na Feàrna, I want you to take your wagon on up to Perth Saint John's for wine, ale and important vittals. On the way back down, stop at the Ceanncardine flats for salt and fill the spaces in wagon with as many salt sacks or barrels as yie can fit in. We need stocked up for our autumn hunt and salt ready for our winter provisions when yie get back."

Alain pauses, then he says, "And mind and leave some space in your wagon for some barrels o' that fine Perth ale son." William replies, "Aye Dá" then he enquires, "Oh Dá… when will you be back from Norham?" Alain replies, "We leave tonight. I reckon we'll be back in about three weeks, maybe four at most. There'll be a lot of debatin' fat chewin' and lots o' shit talkin' amongst the nobles. I reckon three weeks to a month before we get this mess sorted out." William throws his kit bags into the back of his bow-wagon as Mharaidh comes over to him. "You look after wee Maw William, she needs you now. And look after yourself too." Mharaidh gives William a long embrace then he sees Marion walking arm-in-arm with sir Hugh coming towards the wagon. "You take care… son," says sir Hugh. He laughs then he continues, "And mind this too, I'll have plenty for you to do when you come down to see us in Lammington." William replies with a grin, "Aye sir Hugh, noted…" Malcolm calls out, "Come on boy," as he cracks the whip on his lead Oxen. The front wagon slowly pulls away, followed by Dáibh and Daun waving good-bye to everyone. Marion comes round the blind side of William's wagon alone, where the two passionately kiss and embrace for a few moments longer. "Marion?" enquires William, "Why should we be waiting till Beltane to be wed? Let's just get married when our fathers come home? I love you and I need you… and I just plain hate leaving you, why should we wait any longer?" Marion gazes enthusiastically into William's eyes, "I'll speak with father when we leave here for Rosbroch. I'm sure he'll give us his blessing."

William feels a warm glow inside his breast as he studies Marion's beautiful face. He reaches out and gathers up a piece of soft silken mane of jet-black hair falling across her face. His fingers gently brush her cheek. Marion shudders as butterflies beat their wings in her heart and thoughts of sensual pleasures warm her very soul. Gazing into his eyes, absorbing the meaning of his expression, Marion lovingly smiles at him as she reaches out and strokes his face, he puts his arms around her waist and pulls her close, irresistibly, they begin to move their hands over each other, slowly, passionately, as if both are trying to touch the other's inner soul by this gentle and sensual embrace. As they gain closer, their lips never touch till their resistance completely melts, their lips brush so briefly, so tenderly, then they passionately kiss… Suddenly, William exclaims, "Oh feck

Marion, ahm so sorry about this…" Marion giggles, "Not again Wallace." William goes red in the face "Ahm afraid so ma darlin." They laugh together, then they kiss once more, but this kiss is different as both become extremely hot and passionate, feeling the edge of wild abandon take over their instincts, the air fills with a brilliance of energy and a lustful passion emanates from their love for each other, then a voice nearby says, "Excuse me," The two young lovers look to see Mharaidh and Marjorie grinning while they point cautiously towards sir Hugh, who is waiting impatiently. William and Marion both appear very flushed. Mharaidh and Marjorie look at each other and laugh.

Giving each other a knowing look, they turn away from the young lovers, smiling and waiting… William whispers, "Marion, I've never felt anything like this in my life." Marion giggles and holds him close, "Wallace, neither have I." William exclaims, "Feck Marion, if I don't go now, I don't know what I'll do." Marion laughs then says, "Go Wallace… Or we will both do something that we may not regret, but everyone else might." They both laugh then kiss long and passionately once more, eventually he turns and jumps up and into the driving bench of the bow-wagon, cracks a whip and waves goodbye to every-one, all the while, both young lovers never taking their eyes from each other as his wagon rumbles forward.

'They all look so happy,' thinks William, then he sees Marion blowing him a loving kiss, he catches it and blows a kiss back to her, suddenly wee Graham jumps up and catches it and holds the kiss close to his heart, much to the mirth of everyone. Respectfully he passes the magical kiss to Marion in cupped hands. William and Marion glance at each other as he follows on behind the other bow-wagons. As the train nears the northern gateway of Glen Afton, William pulls his wagon to a halt and looks back to see a rider galloping at full speed after them. He locks up his wagon wheel and waits. After a few more moments, the horseman eventually arrives. "Moray…" exclaims William "What are you doing here?" A breathless Andrew dismounts and replies, "I said I'd came down to see you didn't I? I am no' going to waste my time with a lot of bloated nobles down at Norham when I could be throwing salt sacks up in Ceanncardine with you."

Tying his horse to the back of the bow-wagon, Moray jumps onto the driving bench beside William who enquires, "What about you and Brannah then lusty boy?" Moray grins, "Now there's a woman that we must talk a lot more about Wallace, the legend of this land with so many honest men and bonnie lassies is awfy true indeed." William replies, "That's for sure." A jubilant Andrew enquires, "Are yie ready for the road then Wallace?" William replies, "That I am Moray, are yie ready too?" Andrew enquires, "How fast can this wagon go?" William stands up in the foot-well then he raises his whip and replies with gusto, "Lets find out Moray… you get ready and hang on to the bench-bar for dear life." Moray grips the bench-bar tightly, "I'm holding on tight Wallace." William calls out, "Then lets do it." "Do it." Shouts Moray. William reaches high in the air and cracks the whip with great gusto. With a sudden lurch forward, the old bow-wagon creaks into a crawl, Moray is speechless, both friends look at each other… then both burst into laughter as they trundle north towards the Loudon Hill, then on to Ach na Feàrna.

ΠΟRᏅΑΠ

Alain Wallace rides beside Lord Andrew de Moray towards the Scots camp beside Upsettlingham as part of another contingent of Scots nobles and magnates, summoned by the English King, Edward Plantagenet, to attend the treaty of the Ragemanus conference being held across the River Tweed near the English exclave of Norham. When Alain's deputation finally arrive at the gates of the Scottish camp, they pause awhile and gaze across the border river towards England, there they see many hundreds of great and colourful pavilions hosting a vast sea of regal flags and banners, all fluttering and flying brightly in the early morning sun upon the Norham Castle precincts on the English side of the border marches, representing all Scots and English Magnates, Bishops and nobles of note. This unusual gathering is intended for all landowning nobles of Scotland to witness then affix their seals on an interregnum agreement between the two realms, confirming King Edward as Magnus Rex, Feudal Superior, Overlord and Lord Paramount Supreme of all England, Wales, Ireland and upon the Ragemanus ratification… Scotland.

Alain says, "I don't like this Moray, I don't like it at all. I reckon this English King Edward fella will soon be exploiting this situation to his vantage. Our fool nobles should never have brought us to this bloody debacle; how is it so?"

Moray nods his head; "Most of the nobles initially rejected his offer in the first instance Alain, for fear this submission would give Longshanks much more than just a symbolic authority over Scotland." Alain enquires, "How did we end up in this feckn situation?"

Moray replies, "Longshanks made a series of demands in order to avoid a civil war in Scotland between our warring nobles, for they still bicker over their individual claims to the throne. The first demand was that we relinquish our realms sovereignty; the second demand was to acknowledge him as our Magnus Supreme. The third was for us to surrender all of our Castles and Ports; then he would send in an army of peacekeepers into our realm, that's why we first declined him as arbitrator. Wishart stated to his face there was neither historical evidence nor precedence for these fantastic conditions. Wishart also told him that since there was no King or Queen of Scotland, the Guardians Council was not in any position to surrender Scottish sovereignty over to the English King, since only a rightful Scottish King or Queen could do so. But it would appear that Longshanks' plans were not halted by this, for he and others who are expert in legal matters exploited an ancient Scots coronation statute, whereby Edward could adjudicate if three or more claimants applied for him to do so, allowing him in law to judge and make such a decision, apparently he now has the legal authority for such a ploy."

Alain ponders, "Who in their right mind would appeal to a foreign King to make a decision in their own sovereign realm, this is feckn surreal Moray, like a bad dream. I fear that what we do here will bode us no good for the future. How did Longshanks find any claimants in Scotland to lodge this appeal, who would do such a thing?" Moray replies, "Somehow Longshanks found nine willing claimants, with

Robert de Brix leading the charge to pay homage to the English King as his feudal superior, other claimants in seeing their opportunity for kingship slipping away, had no choice but to recognise Longshanks, that's how we find ourselves in this situation." Alain shakes his head as they ride on.

At the centre of Norham's magnificent tented city is situated the grand pavilion of the King of England, unmistakable by its size and royal insignia of magnificent vexila and gonfalons flying in sequence on sidewall poles, demonstrating the power of the royal English household. Longshanks' personal coat of arms from the house Plantagenet, a quartered flag, two squares red with three Golden leopards on each, two squares blue with the golden fleurs-de-lis of France attached, stands proud and centre, flying highest overall. Longshanks stands In the middle of this fabulous Pavilion warming himself at a brazier while studying in detail, large maps of Britain, Ireland, Western Europe, the Holy Land and all of known Asia. As King-in-Council, Edward is hosting a Privy Council meeting. In attendance are the co-architects of his plan to dominate all of Western Christendom. In this particular Curia Regis, Robert Burnell, Edward's Lord Chancellor, is first to speak...

"Sire, for the Scotch to relinquish possession of all their major castles, ports, towns and then put them under the authority of our Constables and Taxation Collectors, then to stand down their various armies and fleets to nominate you as arbitrator that you may apply your judgement on the succession of their realm, and even more astonishing, they must pay you handsome recompense for such privileges... this is beyond my understanding of their wit." Edward walks away from the great maps and sits in his sumptuous throne beside a glowing central brazier. He too is incredulous that he's about to gain complete control of Scotland, an independent, proud and civilised realm, a realm now reduced to a status no greater than a provincial colony or shire to his English throne, for a mere fraction of the cost of his recent Welsh and Irish campaigns and without raising a martial finger. Edward is almost ecstatic that Bishop Anthony Bek of Durham, with his Chancellor Robert Burnell, has successfully negotiated the terms of the treaty with most of the Scots nobles. Burnell exclaims in a joyous fluster, "I have never known the likes my lord, that a realm should deliver up the determination of its sovereignty and crown estates to the court of another, without war or conflict? Sire, this is undoubtedly a gift from God demonstrating his approval of your wit and zeal. It's extraordinary that any Kingdom should simply give away their sovereign rights and liberties with no resistance and at little cost to a foreign King."

"That may be so." says Edward, "One can always rely on the avarice and cupidity of men to influence their loyalty, or betray their own." Burnell says, "The Scotch nobles have gifted to us a cheaply bought estate sire. The avarice of the Scotch nobility has been bought with little financial incentives, the small amount we've given over to their perfidious nobles to sweeten their insecurities, is but a fraction of the costs of our Welsh and Irish campaigns combined. I've distributed a mere twenty thousand Pounds and inferred personal Per Dium allowance return from their English holdings of five Pounds Silver in the taxable hundred."

Displaying little emotion, Edward replies, "Such cheaply bought possessions Burnell, if only it were so elsewhere." He pauses and looks at the faces of his council. "If I were a Scotch simple, I would find it unforgivable that my emissaries would allow a foreign army to govern my Kingdom," Edward laughs, "And then levy upon them a debt of repayment they can never hope to repay, this is sheer madness my lords."

Burnell laughs too; then he says, "We also hold their gold and silver reserves sire and all of their international trader charters and trade contracts as a surety." Edwards shakes his head, "This would be ridiculous to even consider had it not been for the duplicity of the Scotch nobles. After the Scotch sign and seal the Ragemanus, we will immediately impose a levy of taxation upon them at breakpoint by employing both austerity and martial law. The Scotch will be sucking at our teats barefoot and in servitude for a thousand years or more, they'll even be indebted to our children's children for their folly this day." Burnell laughs "The children of the Scotch will also pay in base servitude for this privilege for that same thousand years."

The elation in the pavilion is palpable. Burnell shakes his head too, almost in disbelief. "Absolute genius sire, this absurdity of requiring the Scotch nobility to stand down their army then paying their highest ranking officials a pittance to exile or imprison their own seditioners under the pretext of martial law rather than they lose your patronage, this must be the most ridiculous yet most satisfying removal of a sovereign crown from any kingdom in world history, I warrant you this." Laughing to himself, Edward says, "Tacticians and political theorists will be in awe of this strategic victory for a millennium... what say you Burnell, how profitable a business is this removal of Scotch sovereignty now?" Burnell replies, "Sire, my gauge is that Scotland will be able to return to us two hundred and fifty thousand silver Pounds per annum in land, port, town and country taxes. That's my estimate of their annual returns on their home and international trade, even before we tax them for our armies costs within their realm." Looking to another of his trusted councillors, Edward enquires "And where are these Scotch sheep grazing now my Lord Brabazon?"

"Sire…" replies Brabazon "The Scotch feast and drown their sorrows on cheap French and Tuscany wine for nigh three weeks now, whilst still bickering amongst themselves across the river Tweed in their dreary camp at Upsettlington." Bek gloats, "It would appear that they are a tad confused with all of the proceedings being conducted in archaic Norman and then the records of these proceedings notarised by our scribes in both elaborate Sermō Vulgāris and the langues d'oïl text sire."

Allowing himself a rare smile, Edward say's "I'm quite amazed that the Scots could be so foolish as to deliver Scotland to me thus." He queries Burnell, "My lord Robert, review to me the Scotch conditions that I may understand their frivolous concerns." Burnell replies, "Sire, Lord Brabazon and I urged the Scotch to recognize you as their overlord supreme, that without their co-operation enabling you to engage proceedings as sole arbitrator in law, without actual nominal possession of Scotland, you could not legally confer upon the realm a chosen monarch. Their agreement upon the successful conclusion is to be known as The Award of Norham. Brabazon and I instructed the claimants who present their individual claims to you under oath, must therefore accept your judgment as their overlord supreme as legal and binding. In that, they agree to submit and swear fealty to you as their sovereign lord to sanctify your judgment."

Brabazon continues, "Sire, most of the Scotch have accepted all of our terms, as they currently dwell in a realm with no King and no proper leadership. Other than the Guardians, the Scotch nobles are still divided between those claimants with estates in England and your territories in France who wish to sign sire, and those who only have estate in the realm of Scotland who do not wish to sign. We impressed upon the non-signatory's they would forfeit their estates and be personally liable for all the expenses and interest incurred by the Treaty if they reject your generous offer of arbitration. And with our northern army standing at the border waiting to take over martial responsibility in that realm, those Scotch nobles who are so busy looking after their own purse strings are blind-sided to the reality." Edward enquires "And they truly do consider signing their realm into my royal estate?"

"They do sire." replies Brabazon "We also explained that for the duration of the interregnum and protections of Scotland, all royal castles, Keeps and fortifications of the Scotch realm must be given over to our governance immediately, under the jurisdiction of our good prince Bishop of Durham here, Anthony Bek, as your Lord lieutenant in Scotland, and they fully accept sir Brian Fitz-Alan of Beedale as sole Guardian of that realm. They also agree to Bek overseeing all English interests in Scotland. The Scotch are also informed upon their sworn agreement, that a standing army of English yeomen, men at arms, knights, constables, sheriffs and governors wait at the border, all prepared to proceed with their given authority into Scotland as Peacekeepers for the protection of that realm."

Edward ponders awhile, then he enquires, "And the justification accepted by the Scotch for our the naval blockade of Berwick, Leith and Saint Johns port?" Burnell replies, "The Scotch have been notified the English fleet does provide a secure blockade from Durham to Inverness in order to protect Scotland from any out-borne invaders during their time of flux." Brabazon says, "As a sign on good faith in you as acting Lord Paramount of Scotland, we have required it so that every Scottish official of merit must also resign their office immediately. They shall be replaced by your impartial official representatives, this is also before you agree to arbitrate and make any decisions sire." Finding it difficult to contain his elation, Edward laughs, almost predicting the answer to his next question, "My lord Brabazon, have the Scotch yet handed over the keys to their castles and fortified towns?"

"I am pleased to say they have already done so sire." Replies Brabazon, "On arrival at Upsettlingham, in order to take part in proceedings, the Scotch are required to hand over all keys and charters of submission relevant to this requirement." Edward laughs, "This is a foolishness by the Scotch beyond comprehension my Lords." Burnell continues, "Upon receipt of each Burgh and fortification keys sire, We in turn are sending squadrons and detachments of soldiers, Constables and sheriff's into that realm, all carrying with them the proper legal writ warrants and documentation, authorising them to take control of each assigned jurisdiction. Some of our men do travel as we speak sire, moving through the east coast to Berwick, Rosbroch, Edinburgh, Perth, Dundee, Saint John's port, Aberdeen Inverness and Moray. Our entire western army of peacekeepers await your orders to cross the border into the west coast of Scotland and take over there too sire." Edward enquires, "Commanded by John De Warren the early of Surrey?" Bek replies "Yes my Lord."

Savouring all of this good news, Edward smiles, "If this treaty was not given by God's blessed hand, I would believe I am dreaming in some enchanted forest by the gift of ease to which the Scotch do deliver to me their kingdom. The Scotch submit to us like famishing mice being fed old stale cheese." Brabazon says, "Sire, we have also confirmed with the Scotch, that should any claimant, their supporters and families reject these conditions, fiscal remuneration for your own personal expenses, legal liabilities and satisfactory recompenses shall be placed upon their individual personage for dissenting. However, should they agree to your request, then favourable compensation and taxable leniency would be theirs to vantage at a later date." Edward enquires, "Are there any dissenters?" Bek replies, "Robert Wishart, the Bishop of Glasgow sire, Will the Abbot of Sautre, Subtilis the Franciscan Doctor and John Dunn's Scotus. They are the sole dissenting clerical voices we are aware off. It was not till we satisfied them Scotland and their temple customs would remain independent and not be subservient to the Church of England did they accept and submit. I gave my word as a prince bishop, sworn by oath upon the holy cross and relics of Durham."

Burnell says, "Some of the lower Scotch Knights showed dissent in acknowledging you as their sovereign overlord sire. It is those nobles that have proved particularly difficult to deal with, for they still refuse to accept you as Magnate Supreme, this is what has compounded the lengthy adjournment. We gave them until noon this day to sign the instruments of fealty and complete the Ragemanus with their arms seal of matriculation affixed, or face the fiscal penalties mentioned prior. We have assured them proceedings will resume based on their acceptance of this final condition… when a monarch is chosen, you will faithfully restore the realm of Scotland and sovereignty in its entirety to the successful claimant."

Edward appears concerned as Burnell continues, "Sire, I think that when the Scotch previously invited you to send a peace keeping army to the Galloway marcher lands until the fighting between de Brix and Baliol ceased, and then they bade you remove our soldiers, to which you removed every single English soldier and his buttons, this did please the Scotch greatly. And when you forgave them all assaults placed upon our loyal soldiers by declaring an amnesty upon all transgressors sire, it didst lull them so meekly."

Bek sighs, "So cheaply bought are the Scotch Sire. They give no thought nor consideration that by us trading a few worthless soldiers lives would be a fair exchange for their realm." Brabazon agrees, "Its true sire. By you forgiving all previous slights with no punitive reaction, this impressed the Scotch that you took no vantage when they were at their most vulnerable."

"Ah," utters Bek, "And they hadn't even the wit to notice our clerics removing and replacing their records of antiquity from their universities with our own versions, they were so busy turning their little ploughshares of wrath upon each other that they missed entirely the sword of God at work, but that is the way of it for heathens and non-believers." Edward smiles, "When the Scotch gather this day and I have full and titled possession of the sovereign realm of Scotland, I shall elect a council of eighty-four of our well-paid chosen Scotchmen and twenty-four stout Englishmen to nominate a favoured monarch. Once the thirteen competitors have submitted their seals on the rolls and sworn under oath accepting me as their liege lord, I'll conclude the process of king making." Brabazon says, "Sire, I propose an addendum for your perusal. In that, all lowly Scotch who does own any property or does let property, should also be required to pay homage to you, either in person or at one of the designated locations of your forthcoming visit to Scotland, by the twenty-seventh of July of this year."

Edward's demeanour changes as he carefully chooses his words "Make it so... Now my Lords, we must focus our attention on this day of gift giving from the Scotch. It is imperative that we guide these witless sheep to the fold. We've gathered them in a field nearby, we must now ensure nothing blocks their path as they enter through our stock gates this day, treat them well and we shall close the gates permanently behind them." There is a murmur of approval from the council as Edward continues, "Once I accept their submission I will engage in a reasonable term of legal deliberation. This will gain us valuable time for our Northern armies of De Warren and Fitz Alan to become entrenched in the wicked fastness of the Scotch. Whomever I judge to be their King will soon find out that he inherits a worthless empty throne. To wit my lords, I have had approaches from several Scotch burghs such as Edinburgh, Rosbroch and Jedburgh, they have sent discreet representation wishing to have all their cases of law and dispute settled in English courts from this day hence." Brabazon says, "Sire, this is another unexpected gift from the despicable Scotch, that they would surely reject their own Monarch courts in favour of your justice and wisdom..."

Smiling, Edward shakes his head almost in disbelief, "A lesson for us never to trust a Scotchman my lords." He continues, "In good time Brabazon, we shall hear bleating pleas of the Scotch in our courts, but first we must allow for our Governors such as Lord Cressingham to thoroughly examine the Scotch treasury and fiscal annuities and also to gain us time for Lord Fitz-Alan of Beedale to be well established as my new Governor of the province. I shall require de Warren's army to entrench a strategic force of military superiority. Subsequently, when we require the Scotch to supply us men for the Great Cause, they will be obliged as loyal subjects of the Crown of England to attend me."

"Burnell?" enquires Edward, "You are my lord chancellor; I know that you do covet silver and gold more than David of Judea himself. The Holy Spirit in our campaigns and crusades has forever blessed us with your astute taxation prowess, but you describe these Scotchmen as bog living creatures and outlaws, yet you then expect me to believe that by securing this kingdom, we shall find enough fund resources to host another successful campaign of subjugation or Crusade? You truly believe we shall unearth a hidden horde of wealth in that realm to support my blessed vocation and God-given right to be Magnate Supreme of Christendom?" Burnell replies, "I do sire. It shall appear that we have come to solve all of Scotland's ills and problems, and at their own expense too sire. Once embedded in that realm, we will soon know to what extent their fiscal standing may truly be."

Edward looks across the great table, "Brabazon, what say you my lord, what have you found out from your spies in that realm?" Brabazon replies, "My Lord, Scotland has extremely valuable and necessary forest resources to continue building our expanding towns, castles and navy, we also urgently require their wealth reserves to invest in modernising and re-equipping our army and fleet, Scotch men and boys shall serve as battle fodder in future conflicts to preserve our stout English yeomen for the seeding our new territories." Burnell says, "Sire, The Scotch no longer have any possible means of resistance, the key to this has been the bribery of a select few of their principle nobles. Soon we will have all of their wealth."

"On the subject of wealth," ponders Edward, "We must be resolute in eliminating corruption, from our Governors to the ordinary soldier who mans their castles... Brabazon, you must ensure in law, the punishment for corruption will be to suffer a long and torturous reward, followed by public execution. Corruption will be seen as treason, and as such, penalties will also be visited upon transgressors families and confiscation of their estates." Burnell acknowledges Edward, "Sire, we shall include corruption penalties in our martial law writs for Scotland, including the immediate implementation of emergency taxation to fund your peace-keeping force to compensate our treasury for all and any associated expenses caused by your just arbitration. These laws will be ruthlessly implemented and remuneration forcibly extracted." Sitting at the Kings table, Burnell begins reciting from a large parchment book, "Sire, records show that many of the Jews you previously exiled from England had fled to Scotland, it is there they've helped bring those backwaters to a point of trade that exceeds our own revenues at least two-fold. The pogrom of the Jews was a masterstroke, but their revenues and properties confiscated in England does pale to a fraction should we subdue absolute and bring the kingdom of Scotland to your service. The manpower our nobles will extract freely and by pressing the Scotch into crown service will equal our own standing army twice in size my lord." Bek says, "The resources, taxes and manpower from Ireland and soon Scotland sire, is thrice England's crown estate revenues and will overmatch that of Philip of France." Edward ponders, "And what about the Welsh?" Brabazon replies, "Wales is all but a fully colonized dominion sire. Apart from a few heathen outlaws and tribes in the mountains who will soon be starved into submission and hanging from a gibbet, none shall trade with or give them succour, for the native simples fear your wrath much more than the scourge of famishing outlaws."

Edward nods in approval as Brabazon continues, "The execution of the Welsh Princes of Gwynedd, young Llewellyn and his brother Dafydd, has effectively ended any further attempts at Welsh independence Sire. To wit, the Welsh campaign has now produced some sixteen thousand infantry and ten thousand longbowyers into our army. Your imperious design upon Scotland should exceed nigh on thirty thousand infantry, cavalry and knights." Brabazon bows his head and takes his seat. Edward enquires, "And what then of Ireland?" Burnell replies, "It could be a substantially larger fiscal return than the Welsh and half the potential to that of Scotland sire. Since Pope Adrian's papal Bull confirmed that you are the sole sovereign Lord protector of all Ireland and again ratified by Pope Nicholas, we have established the lands of the Pale, Duhblynn, Ulster and all surrounding precincts of that wretched land as properties owned by the crown estates of England." Bek says, "Sire, the blessed church in Ireland vigorously and enthusiastically supports your endeavours in bringing Christianity and Gods blessing through taxation to those bog-living savages. As the Irish of the fringes continually fight each other, it will not be long before all Irish are meek and in bonded servitude like the Welsh. Once subdued, I cannot foresee the Irish will give England any problems of any worth, now or in the future." Edward laughs, "At least the witless Welsh and bog Irish had the fortitude to put up a fight, these Scotchmen disappoint me in that respect. Perhaps I was wrong to think their passion for war would be an asset. It would seem they have lost the will to stay awake, never mind fight back."

Sitting quietly throughout meeting, Edmund enquires. "My lord, have you reached a decision upon who you shall crown as King of Scotland?" Edward sups some wine then he replies, "I am dismissing Eric of Norway's claim, as his claim is not a principle I favour, whereby ascendants are eligible to inherit Scotland's crown. I will advise Cospatrick de Dunbar, de Vesci, de Ros, Golightly, de Soulis and de Pinkeny to withdraw their petitions too, I have other plans for them." Edward continues, "I would have chosen Lord Brix, but his temperament by his example of waging war in the south of Scotland against my wishes, greatly disturbs me. I do not doubt his loyalty, but I do question his ambition. I also have it on good authority that it was his hand behind the demise of the maid of Norway." Burnell glances at Edward, "We too have heard this account sire, it is well known de Brix had no love of the maid to be ruling over him, he was sorely vexed. His mistaken belief that Alexander wished him to have the throne makes his ambitions much too unpredictable."

"Or too predictable…" remarks Edward. Edmund enquires, "Sire, I thought the maid of Norway died of malady on her journey from Bergen?" Sitting back in his throne, Edward looks curiously at Edmund, then he leans forward, slaps Edmund's shoulder and laughs, "Of course she did brother… of course she did." Everyone laughs, except Edmund. "Sire," says Bek "Our good friend Bishop Narve of Bergen who did accompany the maid, has confirmed to me in person that a malady of consumption was the cause of her death." Edward smiles, "So, my old friend Narve is up to his old tricks again… I trust he was fully compensated for his duties?" Bek replies, "He assures me he will use the compensation wisely sire." Edmund is confused, "What happened to the maid if she did not die of the sickness?"

Ignoring Edmund's enquiry, Edward speaks to his council, "It matters not her demise by whom-ever, even if it was by the hand of de Brix or Narve, conveniently they have aided my cause, not thwarted it. Her timely death simply annuls any claim Eric of Norway may have upon Scotland. I shall now propose the betrothal of my son Edward, the prince of Caernarvon, to Philips daughter the princess Isabella. I then intend to offer my hand to Marguerite Capet of France, Philips sister, these contracts shall guarantee the next generation of French royalty to be that of our Plantagenet Angevin bloodline." There is an audible gasp from the gathered council; then Edmund speaks, "Sire, you truly are a tactical genius. With Scotland secure, Isabella and young Edward producing the next heirs to the French throne, and you married to princess Marguerite Capet… absolute genius sire, I heartily applaud you." Edward smiles, "Why thank you brother Edmund, but to answer your earlier question. It is widely known that although Robert de Brix swears fealty absolute to the English crown, he does imply that this fealty only applies when he is in residence in his English estates, yet he expects full autonomy as a King of Scotland."

Edmund utters, "Ah, whereas, Lord John Baliol has complete fealty to offer to you my Lord. He has been nothing other than a loyal and faithful servant to the crown of England, and I must agree with you, de Brix does have a foul temperament. He has already displayed this trait with his reckless campaign in Scotland where he almost dragged us all into a greater war than he could have ever have imagined... But Lord John Baliol sire, he is loyal beyond question, perhaps he lacks ambition and vision, but that suits our purpose." Edward replies, "I do favour Lord John Baliol for those reasons Edmund and more, old de Brix is a leftover from another age, he even suggests that I visit my judgment in his favour by dividing Scotland into three principalities between the houses of Brix; Floris the count of Holland and sir John de Hastings of Abergavenny. He implies these are the only men who can prove direct descent from the earls of Huntingdon, King David the first of Scotland."

Edward pauses, then he says, "No matter who is King of Scotland, I shall break him, I will deprive him of all power till that realm rejects him as indolent. I want Scotland as a vassal province that we may transfer all assets and properties to my crown, for as you say Burnell, we need their trade revenues, resources, and their manpower for the Great Cause." Edmund smirks, "Sire, the Scotch do refer to your arbitration of their flux as the Great Cause." Edward blusters, "What say you?" Edmund replies, "It is true sire, the Scotch actually believe the Great Cause is your arbitration on their sovereign destiny." Edward laughs aloud, "Surely you jest

Edmund? You say that the Scotch actually believe that they are somewhat of a Great Cause?" Edward shakes his head in disbelief. He continues, "The Scotch are nought but a flea on a fat sows back, but they do make great humour for us with their foolish grandiose and self-importance in the scheme of things. Ha, this trivial paltry realm does greatly amuse me. I am planning a dynasty that will last a thousand years and beyond, reaching from the frozen northern tundras to the basking shores of Asia, and the Scotch believe that their shit-infested realm is the actual pinnacle of my ambition?"

Rubbing his chin thoughtfully, Edward says, "Though their self-induced delusions may suit our purposes my lords, if the Scotch are known to be using this term, the Great Cause, in thinking it does apply to them, it may be prudent if it's a term used by the populace of that realm regarding this paltry matter of Scotch sovereignty, for the true Cause will then be screened by their pathetic self esteem and bleating machinations to the Pontiff." Edward sups some wine then he continues, "This day I shall accept their total submission and fealty, then I shall appoint one hundred and four Auditors to discuss the evidence of the claims, with their conclusions to be presented to me at Berwick castle in late August, after the summer harvest recess."

Everyone sups more wine while digesting Edward's thoughts. He continues, "Burnell, my lords... since my return from France I am keenly aware that England has faired extremely well under your guidance, including the ongoing colonisation of our Irish and Welsh territories." Edward smiles at Burnell; then he continues, "Also Burnell, your administrative assessment of the hundred roll's has been outstanding work, pray do tell us more about your findings?" Burnell addresses the council... "Sire, the hundred rolls assessments are now complete and does present a finite comprehensive and detailed account of every shire in England, including a scrupulous accounting recording of all revenues and manpower available to the crown. All foodstocks, livestock craftwork, farms villages, towns and any possible means of revenue are now recorded in greater in detail than the previous book of Winchester. Taxation practise in England currently realises the recent treasury projections and can be extended de facto throughout your provinces by simple application of your warrants."

Edward glares at Burnell with ice-cold eyes, he says, "Our revenues are stable Burnell, but they only increase at a mere three per cent per annum… this is not good enough." Edward smashes his fist onto the table, "We need substantial increases in taxation good sir…" At that moment, a herald enters the pavilion and calls out, "Sire, my lords… Bernard de Got, the Archbishop of Lyon does beg an audience." A tall handsome man enters the pavilion dressed in the purple and black cloth of Rome. His rich textured black silk robes flow freely as walks towards the council. On his breast hangs a heavy chain of silver, supporting a large silver bejewelled crucifix. The visitor casts an impressive gait as he walks over to Edward, bows and kisses the King's ring of Royal office.

"Welcome my dear archbishop…" says Edward, "Pray take a seat, your attendance is very well timed this day." de Got replies, "Thank you sire," The Archbishop of Lyon takes his seat between Bek and Burnell, Edward compliments de Got on his recent elevation in the Catholic Church. "I am extremely pleased to be addressing you by your new title my dear 'Archbishop.' You have certainly came a long way since you were my young chaplain." De Got replies, "Why thank you my Lord, you are too gracious." Edward enquires, "How best has been are our interests served with His Holiness?" De Got replies, "His imminence and his bishops struggle with the concept of your Royal authority and the whole relationship in general between Kings and subjects. The pontiff constantly debates with his bishops about the enigma of the Northern kings and their growing sense of power between monarchs and the civil life of their realm. His Holiness believes it's becoming inimical to the institution of the Catholic family." Edward enquires, "How so?" De Got replies, "The Holy Father is convinced the northern Kings are forgetting they are nought but princes of Rome, and that their royal powers are increasingly being used independently of Rome by these same ruling monarchs, in that, they do appear to believe those given rights are absolute. And you sire, your personal introduction of elevating ordinary men of the field to the power of jurists by using their own ingenuity, is deemed to be possibly heretical."

"Does the Holy Father mention me by name?" enquires Edward. "Not as such my Lord," replies de Got "Though your parliamentary liberties does cause him great angst, but he is more concerned with King Philip of France, who advances and exceeds your example of meritocracy somewhat. It would appear the false enlightenment of the French monarchy imitates your jurisprudence of the vassal courts. The pontiff shows great concern that these monarchical advances in freeing the thoughts of the common man, are based on a very dangerous principle of political theory, purporting that all societies within a kingdom are now appearing to be the ruling monarch's jurisdiction and not the authority of Rome." Edward ponders a moment; then he says, "Then His holiness must surely realise that to alienate the all the great kingdoms of the north would not be in his best interest?" De Got replies, "Sire, after the eighth Crusade and the vital truce of Gaeta, King Philip causes a great concern with His Holiness by making severe demands for reimbursement and subsidies from Rome, and he is pressing for a speedy settlement sire. If the Pontiff wishes for continued aid from Philip, he must not be seen to hinder Philip's plans to elevate the populace and the monarchy." Edward speaks thoughtfully, "Perhaps then Philip's wisdom and that of his council does demonstrate a sharp countenance that could be of great service to us methinks." De Got replies, "Philip is using the pontiff's vulnerability with the fractious Mediterranean league of Kings to strengthen his position, at the expense of ecclesiastical immunities." Edward appears to be delighted at the news between his adversary Philip and the Pontiff's political disagreements. De Got continues, "Twice Philip has sent the pontiff a formidable list of grievances, stating clearly these complaints are on behalf of the bourgeois universities and commoners of France and not merely a request from Philip alone. By Philip stating these just grievances as part of his realms authority, he boldly declares these grievances come from the whole community of his Kingdom, now Philip makes demands to negotiate a new settlement treaty with Rome that's favourable to France."

Sitting back, Edward laughs aloud, "This French upstart stirs up a hornets nest, but I do have admiration for his lust. I thought him simply as a lamb born amongst wolves, but he is a lamb fattening himself for the Easter feast. Tell me then de Got, does His Holiness favour Philip to my disadvantage?" De Got replies, "No my lord, I believe his Holiness needs you more than ever." Edward enquires, "Explain your observations?" De Got replies, "My Lord, as you so wisely predicted, his Holiness has elevated me to the Archbishopric of Lyon on the very borders of France, he requires me to keep a close watch on Philip, as Lyon being a free and independent sovereign city with the jurisdictions..." Edward concludes impatiently, "Being the sole authority the archbishop himself.

Pray get to the point…" de Got continues, "I have instructed Rudolf of Habsburg to publicly demonstrate a martial interest in rattling the affairs of the Suebian Burgundian Duchy and the nearby Besançon in the Bourgogne-Franche-Comté as you requested sire. Habsburg is at your disposal and readies with a standing army." Edward smiles, "His presence on Philip's eastern borders will rattle my feisty little French lamb."

De Got continues, "Before I left Lyon, my spies informed me that Philip will soon be making claim for the sovereignty of Lyon, and in preparing his claim he is already building up great files of merit." Edward is extremely pleased to hear that Philip is publicly unfolding disputes he himself has pending with His Holiness and the Vatican. He says, "Never has it been so important for France that Philip should be amicable to the Archbishop of Lyon. You are well placed my dear Archbishop." De Got relaxes a little, smiles, then continues, "I agree sire; Philip brings to light the fundamental relationship between the Pontiff, King, Church and State. Philip's advisers are making no secret their aim is to have an independent and sovereign state of all France, governed solely by the Monarch. Nor do they cloak their enthusiasm for the premise which intimates an existence for France entirely free and independent from the yolk of Rome."

"I too have heard it so sire," says Bek, "The French advisors to King Philip openly debate that the Pope no longer has any more jurisdictional rights in temporal and state matters. They do declare that Philip may act within his own realm as Sovereign de facto, individually magnanimous and beholding to none." Burnell speaks, "This indeed is a grave matter for His Holiness. By Philip making these thinly veiled but serious threats against the authority of Rome, and he being the papacy's sole supporter in its struggle with Arogonese brotherhood of Kings and the Caliphate, then the papal state must surely be left with no other choice but to recognise Philip's claims, thus it follows sire that all Kingdoms of the Holy Empire must speedily adopt these same benefits." Edward enquires, "And what has been the reaction from His Holiness?" De Got replies, "Publicly, His Holiness has demonstrated a consensual response to these requests for these jurisdictional freedoms sire. But to prove how impartial his past severities on matters of jurisdiction is with you sire, the Pontiff is sending a special embassy to publicly lecture you on your shortcomings regarding your own disputes with His Holiness." Edward exclaims, "I'm to be chastised by Rome?"

"It should appear so to Philip sire, as His Holiness apparent favouritism for England these last few years on similar matters of jurisdiction must now be curtailed, particularly when you have consistently enforced your will with no unfavourable chastisement by the return from the Pontiff." Edward grins, "I am almost grateful to Philip... In his youthful ignorance, the Great Cause is being served without a Merk or Pound of silver being spent. He would be a useful ally if it not for his dogmatic insistence that he is my Lord superior." De Got says, "Sire, Philip threatens to alienate all of Roman Catholicism and inadvertently, he may bring many on this side of the Pyrenees to the bosom of our Northern brotherhood of Christian Kingdoms, and this moment shall free us to further pursue our own needs in Godly pursuits. Though I do believe that King Philip is of more use to us bickering with Rome than he ever could be as an ally." Edmund enquires, "Sire, how does this aid the Great Cause if Philip is at odds with Rome?" Thinking a moment, Edward replies, "The true reason for the loss of the Holy Land is not the wit and armies of the Saracens, but the Pope's reckless preoccupation with the war against the Kings of Aragon,

Greece and Sicily. It should be the Mamluk Sultan who is the pope's enemy, not His Holiness own allies…" Edward sups some wine then continues, "These bitter little eunuch's of Rome profess to be the sole beneficiaries of Gods all seeing eye, but they are entirely unaware the Arogonese Kings and League of Mediterranean Kings are now acting secretly as the Sultan Qalawun Al-Malik al-Mansur's allies, sworn to recognise whatever conquests God allows the Sultan to take, be it Egypt, Syria and Jerusalem."

Edward continues, "The Arogonese Kings do pledge themselves to inform the Sultan of any plans for a renewal of Crusades made between His Holiness, the eastern Christian princes and also the Mongol hordes should they plan to attack the Sultanate armies. The Arogonese and brother-hood of Balearic and Khazarian Kings have also sworn upon oath, to make war on the Pope's crusaders and give no aid to the Pontiff's Christian forces en route to the Holy Land." De Got says, "In return sire, Qalawun has committed to the Arogonese Kings whatever conquests castles provinces and slaves they might take from France on their side of the Pyrenees." Edward laughs, "Sultan Qalawun is very charitable indeed… almost Christian charity you could say." De Got continues, "Sire, I have heard Qalawun has agreed that all Northern Brotherhoods may also keep existing holdings and have freedoms to build new Christian enclaves in the Holy Land under the Sultan's own laws of ahl al-Dhimma."
(Christians under protection of the Sultan)

"This then will be His Holy Father's future downfall my lords," says Edward, "When our Northern Kings alliance has secured a new Christian Empire in the north and also when the gateway lands of the Balkans is in our possession, we will have a mighty army that will dwarf any imperial Vatican army in it's history." Edward looks at his gathered council, "I hear what you are thinking my lords. But the power and authority of Rome dwindles as the sovereignty of our Northern Christian Kingdom alliances grow. Though I shall offer the visiting embassy from Rome my sword to do God's will, my hand to lead a crusader army and I shall offer once more to personally carry the Holy Cross and pledge my life as God's champion, should the Pope declare another Crusade. Though I believe he may wish to offer that honour to Philip to appease him, which may be a public slight that I must mildly refute. Nonetheless, if a warrant is issued to rally Christian Europe for a new assault on Islam and the holy land, I will publicly give it my wholehearted considerations." Bek says, "If Philip goes to war, then it will probably be against the Arogonese, Sicilians, and Castilians, not their Moorish allies."

"That being so," says Edward, "With our Germanium and Cumin allies, this would be an opportunity to implement our own Crusade in the Balkans and falsely secure France as part of our defensive dominion. Then we may proceed toward our collective goal of securing Constantinople." Edmund enquires, "Who then is left to bring into our Brotherhood to open up the Baltic trade routes to Asia and the Holy Land sire?" Edward replies "Emissaries of Nogai Khan of Isaccea on the lower Danube have promised me his Magyars as allies. If we also treaty with King Uros Milutin and his brother Prince Dragutin of the Serbo-Hungarian alliance, they will also join with us, for they too are most eager and vehemently declare they have no love of the Pontiff. Then my lords, the northern gateway to Constantinople will be under the domination and control of the Northern Brotherhood of Kings." De Got exclaims, "Ah sire, now I understand the name given you by the Bishops of Rome." Edward enquires, "Do tell to us my Lord Archbishop, how is it they do refer to me in the prattling cloisters of Rome?" Once again the silence in the pavilion is like a tangible weight descending upon everyone as they cautiously await de Got's reply... "Well?" enquires Longshanks impatiently. Nervously, de Got replies, "Sire they call you the Justinian of the North." There is a moment's tense silence as everyone holds their breath, then Edward laughs aloud, "Very prophetic de Got... and extremely complimentary I do believe." The relief in the pavilion is felt by everyone, and noted by Edward...

"Our alliance strengthens each day my lords. Once we have secured these Islands, isolated and disposed of Scotland and then Philip, the Northern Brotherhood of Kings shall elect me as Overlord and Magnus Rex Supreme of all known Christendom. The Pontiff may keep his faith with God on the far side of the Pyrenees, for I shall rule from Scotland to Asia and all lands north as the King of a new Christian world." Edmund appears perplexed. "This is all very interesting brother, but I don't understand... what has this to do with Scotland?"

No one speaks for fear of stirring Edward's wrath. After a moment he replies "Edmund, my dear brother... Scotland is the last sovereign realm in these Islands to be quashed and brought to boot, and we must surely conclude it this day. If Philip does calls upon Scotland as an ally, everything is undone. If I cannot be seen to rule these paltry little islands, how then can my brother Kings have any faith and support me in the Great Cause as the undisputed leader of a new Christendom?" Edward glares menacingly at his gathered council, "My Lords, make no mistake upon the course of my wrath if thwarted, for this day, we shall make these Islands of Albain one sovereign kingdom. I want Scotland subservient and begging absolute before I leave this place for France. There can be no sedition or rebellion by the Scotch.

If none be left alive within that realm... so be it, we must turn our swords of God to cleanse the road from Scotland to Constantinople."

"Sire," says Bek "You are absolutely correct, I fear that if we do not eliminate Scotland as a threat right here and now, His Holiness, allied with Philip, will surely have a deadly ally sitting at our back door, The Pope already shows the Scotch favouritism by referring to them his Favourite Daughter. If any conflict does arise between the Northern Brotherhood of Kings and the Pope, he may support the Scotch and the Irish with monies and men-at-arms." Another moment of silence follows then Edward stands and everyone rises from their seats, "My lords, perhaps we might break for good fare then continue this discussion later." A pavilion guard calls out, "My Lord... an emissary has arrived from the Scotch who carries with him the Ragemanus Rolls." Edward laughs, "I almost forgot the Scotch were still here." Everyone laughs as Edward commands, "Bring me the Ragemanus rolls... immediately." The guard brings forward two large chartered rolls of the Ragemanus and lays them on the table. Edward declares... "My Lords, behold, *The Scotticum Ragemanus.* These rolls contain the acts of fealty, seals and signatories applied by all the nobility of Scotland." He opens them up and scrutinises each of them, then he passes the Ragemanus to his council for further examination and scrutiny, everyone looks to Edward.

There is a palpable atmosphere of elation and euphoria within the pavilion. Edward speaks, "We have achieved the impossible my lords. We have successfully stripped a sovereign Kingdom of its throne, power, trade, industry and dignity, by simply applying bribery, collusion and the hunger of men's avarice. The Scotch nobility has given up their sovereignty without a sword raised in defence."

Brabazon speaks, "Sire, there are no words enough to describe this utter folly of the Scotch. You have rested that realm from the nobility of Scotland and delivered what none has ever achieved in an armed conquest of that land, be it the tribes of Germania, Saxon Kings, Norse invaders or even César's great armies of Rome. You have so easily delivered the realm of Scotland into your bosom for a few mere pounds of silver and some worthless estates in England." Looking at his council, Edward sighs, "The Scotch nobility... what a parcel of ignoble rogues in a realm who does betray their own people, all in exchange for a few bags of silver. But now my Lords... We must make haste and move our armies into Scotland immediately. Once there, we must assume complete control and begin the Scotch diaspora. My Lords, you know what to do, the Scotch nobles await my personage, but we shall make them wait awhile longer methinks. Edmund, I want you to go to our commanders and set in motion our plans."

Edmund bows and leaves the pavilion to execute his orders. Edward turns to his council, "My Lords, there cannot have been such an easier crown removed from any kingdom... "Burnell, de Got, Bek..." commands Edward, "You will all remain here awhile, that we may scrutinise and study these Ragemanus and meticulously examine all of these rolls, there shall be no small errors or even a hint of dubiety. I want anyone known to be missing from this unholy list identified and eliminated, regardless of their station." Burnell says, "Sire, we should expect some resistance to be shown to our brave soldiers who go to occupy our new province. There will always be some native fool who will raise his head in defiance." Edward frowns, "Brabazon, do we have lists from our spies in Scotland, that we may eliminate these seditious miscreants at the outset?" Brabazon replies, "Sire we do, other than Alexander's cousin, Duncan the earl of Fife, there are no other dissenters of that rank or station. The lists of lower nobility dissenters has also been completed and delivered."

"Didn't we eliminate MacDuff?" enquires Edward, Burnell replies, "We did sire, de Courtney did a great service, for Duncan MacDuff was also a Guardian of Scotland, making it a very risky business indeed, but de Courtney laid a fine trap for both him and his supporters." Edward enquires, "How so?" Burnell replies, "Many men of his own house and clan were swiftly caught and hung or beheaded for his base murder." Brabazon says, "The Scotch do not suspect anyone else's involvement in the affair sire, it was a task well delivered by de Courtney. He manipulated a falsehood when Yolande gave a stillborn birth, he set a claim abroad that MacDuff in collusion with Yolande, had switched the royal infant of Alexander to spawn a direct heir to their throne, this falsehood made it imperative that Duncan and as many of his supporters were speedily eliminated, and it has been so. Even the brains of his closest family infants were all dashed asunder. Sire, there will be no Canmore or any MacDuff dissention, for the blood of those houses are now ended."

"Indeed." says Edward, "Pray then, do tell me Bek, when Brix and Baliol raged about southern Scotland in a petulant dispute, who was responsible in containing their zeal from spreading throughout the realm... and what force of arms did they use? To have the strength of arms to contain such men as Baliol and de Brix, it must have taken minds of great wit and fibre." Bek replies, "Sire, the main pacifier was Bishop Wishart of Glasgow." Edward sighs, "Ah Wishart, I should have known, he is of the Cluniac Brotherhood as am I. Tell me then, what force did he command that defied the warring factions during the interregnum, and obviously strong enough to cause de Brix to falter?" Bek replies, "They are called the Garda Rígh and the Garda Bahn Rígh sire.

The King and Queens bodyguard and former Guardian army of Scotch King." Edward pauses for thought, "Then tell me, who is the commander of this Royal Guard, and is he with us here this day?" Bek replies, "A knight called sir Malcolm Wallace sire. He was the personal confidante and a close friend of the late King." Edward spends a few moments scrutinizing the Ragemanus, "His name does not seem to appear on these rolls? Who is this Knight who does not swear allegiance?" Bek replies, "Sir Malcolm Wallace of ach na Feàrna sire. He is or was the hereditary Guardian to the Queen of Scotland. An engagement of the blood and not by elevation..." Bek pauses. Edward demands, "What is it that leaves your mouth agape Bek?"

"Sire..." exclaims Bek, "Wallace believes Scotland and her people should not be subject to your crown authority, but equal in all measure as a friend and good neighbour. He will not swear oath nor go on bended knee to any other than a bloodline monarch of Scotland." Bek pauses. Edward glares at him, "Why do you falter Bek?" Bek continues, "Sire, this Wallace miscreant has also been heard to say publicly that he refutes your claim as Overlord, declaring to all who will listen to him that it's preposterous that you lay a claim of dynastic authority hailing from the Diocletian kings of Syria, Troy, Giants and other so-called falsehoods. All of these claims he says is in order that you may justify your barbarous conduct towards Scotland. He refuses to submit to you and swears he will never yield sire." Edward rages upon hearing these words, "You see it clearly now my Lords, scratch the skin of this wretched realm and you will find underneath the body of plague vermin. The opportunity for this low born Noble to fall on his knees has passed, we must deliver a message by example that encourages all of his kind to the bosom of Gods chosen warrior, make it so that his timely end is made a legal elimination." Burnell says, "Sire, we may have an opportunity punish the house of Wallace for sedition very soon. His younger brother Alain Wallace of Glen Afton is here. He wishes to represent the family by signing the Ragemanus Rolls and swearing fealty sire, in that he and his may gain your blessed peace." Edward replies, "The Scotch have given over to us the use of their courts and laws, I want you to eliminate Wallace and all other seditious traitors in that family by those same laws."

Burnell acknowledges Edward; then says, "Sire, with the Ragemanus now in our hands, we can legally and immediately apply martial law upon the households of Scotland, as all laws passed in England automatically becomes our God-given right to prosecute in our provinces once an English boot stands firm upon the land." Edward replies, "Martial law yes, but my lords, we were much too forgiving with the Jewry, Welsh and Irish. They did cost us a great expense chasing their dissident population, we shall engage a much harsher regime on the serfs, simples, and traders of Scotland, you may use them as you will, for they are of no account. Those you do not eliminate, I want pressed into servitude in my other provinces or in our armies. I want their youth removed from that realm alive… or dead, it makes no difference to me. We shall employ severest measures upon the Scotch, more than we ever applied to our Jew, Irish and Welsh simples. And as for the house of Wallace… make an example of them as soon as possible." Edward continues, "Are there any lower nobility other than the lick-spittle Scotch gathered here today that could cause dispute?" Burnell replies "There are sire… the remaining barons council of Scotland. These are a hundred lower born knights, mostly of native blood, they refuse to swear fealty, though they have brothers fathers and sons here this day who represent their families or clan's." Edward speaks,

"Heed me well my Lords, I want every one of them dead, I want you to use the law in every case and without exception. None shall escape our justice, for the law exists to be set upon these lowborn creatures heretically describing themselves as noble. Should any Scotch man, woman or child, look directly into a noble Englishman's eyes before bowing first or looking to the feet of our soldiers and emissaries this also may be construed as treasonous. By the law we will have law, are you with me my lords?"

Collectively the jubilant council replies, "We are sire." A satisfied Edward continues, "I want you all to leave now, go with much haste and make it all so. I want our army entrenched in Scotland before ratification is completed by August. Now my Lords, I shall be entertaining our Scotch guests later this eve, gracing them with my presence to satisfy their angst that I'll maintain the tranquillity of that realm and arbitrate in all disputes, and of course, mete out justice with legal impunity." The Privy Council take their leave, allowing Edward the solitude he needs to scrutinise his strategic plan in the peace of his pavilion, but the success of the Scots capitulation distracts him from his thoughts. He looks at the Ragemanus laid out before him then calls out, "GUARD..." A guard rushes through the pavilion entrance; "Sire?" Edward commands, "Fetch me my Lord Cressingham… now."

"At once sire." As the guard speeds off to carry out his command, Edward ponders over this incredulous delivery of a realm into his fold. He sups fine French wine from his own Tuscan vineyards, feeling very satisfied knowing that a long hard campaign of war has been averted. As soon as Scotland is under his brutal martial regime and any dissent crushed, he can turn his focus back to his plans of ridding France of Philip, then he will finally secure Western Europe from

Scotland to Constantinople as his own personal dominion, verily blessed by God. "LORD CRESSINGHAM SIRE," calls out a guard. The doors open and Lord Cressingham comes rushing in to greet Edward. "Sire..." says Cressingham. He struggles to keep his bulky balance on one knee as he holds Edwards hand and kisses the royal signet.

"My Lord Cressingham... do sit with me, for I have duties only your eh, your particular delicacies can fulfill." Cressingham replies, "Sire, what is your will?" Looking at a map of Scotland, Edward says, "You are to leave for Scotland immediately. I require you to take up residence in Stirling Castle as my assessor to the treasury of Scotland, there is no other I trust for this vital task but you. De Warenne and Fitz Allan are moving up the east coast with their armies as we speak, De Percy will move an army into the west of Scotland by mid-morning. I require you to leave immediately after this meeting, but I would ask you a question first." Cressingham replies, "Sire?" Edward enquires, "Other than the Barons and nobility upon the Ragemanus rolls, who in Scotland may discreetly assist you to set an example upon any troublesome Scotch rebels?" Cressingham replies, "There is Sir Richard of Lundie, Cospatrick de Dunbar, Lord Menteith..."

"No you fool..." snaps Edward tersely, "Discreetly I said," Cressingham flusters "There are Templar's sire, the preceptors of Ballentradoch, all Norman English by birth. Walter de Clifton, William Middleton, John de Husflete Roger, de Akiney, Hugh de Conyers, Ranulph Corbet..." Edward frowns, "They would need authority of Jacques de Molay from Paris. Do they have no Scotch Templar's in Scotland?" Cressingham replies, "None sire, other than the those who do service as menials. The only other Scotch templar's reside in English preceptories, Scotch Templar's sire, are very few indeed." Edward sighs, "Hmm... My Lord Henry De

Percy will be leaving shortly to take position as governor of Ayr, Carrick and Galloway, have you heard of his bastard…?" Cressingham replies, "Marmaduke De Percy sire, isn't he sir Henry' de Percy's own bastard?" Edward laughs, "Yes, and England is full of bastards. I believe at times such as this they have their uses." Edward notices Cressingham's discomfort, it amuses him. He thinks a moment; then he says, "Cressingham, I require you to take the young bastard De Percy with you, he will assist you to service this need for me. He's young, ambitious and he needs to quench his spurs. Take heed though my faithful Cressingham, I want you to guiDe Percy in some, how should I put this, ah, more delicate practices in the execution of these particular duties I have in mind. I require your worldly experience in the more delicate skills you have in these matters."

Cressingham relaxes as Edward bestows a form of compliment upon him. Edward continues, "I require you to employ your specific form of punitive and public examples enacted upon the populace in Scotland at your earliest opportunity, ensure by public example and execution that no Scotch would ever wish to be outwith my favour, if you get my meaning. I am aware that the bastard De Percy is young, but he has potential, but both of your particular skills are most suited to the tasks I have in mind. I trust you do understand me Cressingham, and that you shall not fail me?" Cressingham replies, "Yes sire, no sire." Edward glares at Cressingham then he continues, "De Percy awaits an audience with us and ferments his ambitions in a pavilion close by. I have sent for him to join us, but while we await his presence, I will detail exactly what I want you to do." Marmaduke De Percy sits impatiently waiting on his call to audience with the great king Edward. His mind races with thoughts of what it could be, he knows his service with Lord de Courtney has been exemplary and his excursions into Galloway during Scotland's civil war has gained him a fearful reputation amongst his peers. Could this now be the time he will be recognised and be free of his curse of illegitimacy. A guard walks into the pavilion where De Percy waits and calls to him "You are now granted an audience with King…"

Before the guard could finish, De Percy rushes out of the pavilion as fast as he can and runs directly to the pavilions of Edward Longshanks… The Kings pavilion guard calls out, "Sire, Marmaduke de Percy…" De Percy nervously walks through the hallowed entrance and begins to sweat profusely. He feels his throat dry up as he looks around the splendid majesty of this great sanctum; then he sees standing at the far end of the pavilion, King Edward and lord Cressingham. "Ah de Percy…" says Edward. "Come over and join us." De Percy immediately rushes over to Longshanks, bows and kisses his Kings hand. Edward scrutinises de Percy, "I have heard much of your progress from lord de Courtney. And your father sir Henry; he speaks very highly of you too." De Percy utters, "Sire… I… I am honoured." Edward smiles when seeing the terrified expression on de Percy's face.

"May I call you Marmaduke?" enquires Edward, laughing to himself at the nervousness of his young guest. He hands De Percy a goblet of wine, "Sire…" replies de Percy. Cressingham looks on, astonished at the informality of his King; clearly he can see that Edward favours this upstart young squire Marmaduke de Percy. The three talk in depth awhile about the special duties required of them till Edward feels it is time to make his attendance at the pavilion of the Scots and perform his ceremony of acceptance as Overlord and arbitrator. Edward scrutinises De Percy closely, then he says, "There will be great rewards if you please me Marmaduke. The Scotch will be here at least another three or four days, both of you have this time to make speed north and prepare a hot bed for their return. There may even be position and estates in this for you if you continue with such fastidiousness attention to detail as you have previously shown to me... Which I expect will become even more of a skill that I may rely upon. What say you Cressingham, what say you, will Marmaduke serve us well?" Cressingham replies, "Sire, I do believe he may have some honourable traits, somewhere in that skin that holds the fermenting little bastard in his place." Edward grins, "A tad harsh Cressingham, I'm sure he will be a great service to you."

Edward waves his hand, "Leave us now boy." De Percy kneels, kisses Edward's hand and hurriedly leaves the pavilion, eager to fulfill his master's wishes. Turning to Cressingham, Edward speaks, "He is enthusiastic and ambitious Cressingham, make sure there are no mistakes in his eagerness to please though, any errors made that could be embarrassing or cause us concern, you have him to throw to the wolves in your place. Now Cressingham, I have here a list of names here for you. All of those marked red on the list I have no need for, you may eliminate them, and those names marked in black, attend to them as though they were my dearest friends. Should you encounter any native Scotch who are not listed at all, do with them as you please." Cressingham looks at the rolls and list of names, "I will sire execute your commands with due diligence sire." Edward replies curtly, "Good, very good, now leave me and proceed immediately good sir, for I have many perfidious Scotchmen who wish to prostrate themselves and kiss my feet." Cressingham replies, "My Lord..." he then exits the Kings grand pavilion. On his way to gather his soldiers, Cressingham looks around for his men-at-arms, he is perturbed when sees De Percy ordering his manservant to fetch his personal retinue of a hundred men, He hears De Percy call out, "All of you, make sure you are well armed and carry enough provisions for a two-day journey, and make good speed about it you famishing scoundrels." Cressingham thinks… You impudent young fop, you order my men to heel as though they are yours… You little bastard, you would lick the Kings arse to gain his praise, even if it were caked dry in shit. De Percy mounts his horse when he sees Cressingham approach, "Come sir Hugh, we will soon be making merry sport upon the Scotch. We must make haste to carry out the king's wishes." Cressingham mounts his steed to follow De Percy when he notices a particular knight pass by, he recognises the turquoise blue Dragon clutching arrows with diced blue and white surcoat bars… Alain Wallace, of Glen Afton.

Cressingham spurs his horse to a Canter, following De Percy and his men across the border river Tweed into Scotland, on their journey towards Ayr town.

King Edward is being prepared by his wardrobe servants to attend the Ragemanus ratifications when his guard enters and calls out "A *Visiteur* Sire." Edward looks at the guard, "What do you mean, a *Visiteur*? What language is this you dare to use in my presence?" The nervous guard replies, "Sire, he said to inform you that he is a… a *Visiteur*?" Edward, now losing patience with the guard demands an answer, "Did he not give you his name up to you? What does he look like you idiot?" The guard hastily replies, "Sire, he is dressed in the garb of a commander of the Temple." Edward exclaims, "Fool… Go and enquire his name?" The guard quickly exits and soon returns, "Sire, Lord Brian Le Jay, master of Ballentradoch, preceptor of the Knights Order for Scotland." Edward orders his servants to leave immediately as the arrival of this special 'Visiteur' pleases him. Sir Brian le Jay enters the pavilion, a powerful looking warrior dressed in the flowing garb of a stark black surcoat emblazoned with large white cross pattée over all body chainmail.

"Ah Frater Brianus…" expresses a delighted Edward, "Welcome pauperes commilitones Christi Templique Solomonici."(Poor Fellow-Soldier of Christ and of the Temple of Solomon) Sir Brian Le Jay goes down on bended knee and holds the Kings hand. "Sire…" He kisses the royal signet as Edward enquires, "How long has it been my old friend?" Le Jay replies, "Not since the Saracens attempted assassination upon you in Acre sire." Edward says, "Too long Brother, too long." Le Jay releases his heavy mantle from his shoulders, he says, "I have long missed your company Brother." Edward continues, "And I yours Brother. Your work with the elimination of the Scotch King was exemplary, you have done fine work for the house of Plantagenet over these past few years brother Brian." Le Jay replies, "Why thank you Brother Edward, it is by the will of God that we have such continuing successes." Edward enquires, "Have you heard the news from abroad?" Le Jay replies, "The Great Cause sire, I have heard much from Edmund. He apprises me on a regular basis." Edward says, "Good… Then you know that we have much to discuss. But first, I must attend to the Scotch who do wait for my blessing. Will you attend me brother?" Le Jay replies, "It would be my honour brother." Edward says, "I hear you have a reserve army at the ready in Llangybi Tregruk with my old friend de Clare down in Monmouthshire." Le Jay replies, "We do sire. Many of those who have returned from Jerusalem wish only to serve, they await your orders sire."

"Good, good…" says Edward, "Now, I urgently require you to send word and ready them to march north to Berwick." Le Jay enquires, "Do we invade Scotland sire, if this is so, it is against the laws of Templar chivalry and agreed royal principles for those who serve the Temple to invade another sovereign realm… and your Barons…" Edward interrupts, "My Barons will be forced to join this venture Brother, for they are sworn to arms should England be invaded by a foreign power." Le Jay is curious, "I don't understand sire…" Edward smiles, ""Our loyal servant de Brix and his son Robert Brus have been stirring dissent upon the Scotch border lands, I have made sure that de Brix is commander of my border stronghold at Carlisle. And soon I expect the Scotch will react, and when they do, as I predict, they will cross that border seeking vengeance, on this premise the knights of the Temple Order can then assist me in the defence of this Just and Christian realm brother…"

Surprised, Le Jay exclaims, "You shall trick the Scots into invading England my lord…?" Edward replies, "Yes Brother, not yet though, but when they do attack Carlisle Castle, we shall be waiting with our armies on the border near Berwick, with our Northern armies already entrenched in the north and east of that country, we will then destroy that realm in its entirety, but it must be before all saints Easter. It is imperative we have control of Scotland by the twenty eighth of March next year, at least before Easter Sunday, or we may lose everything that we have planned for all these years." Le Jay enquires, "Why is that particular date so important to you my lord?" Edward replies, "The Scotch intend to sign membership with the Varjag and Hanseatic federation on that date, they are a powerful European Union and an unholy alliance of ninety one city states and they grow stronger each day. Even though I may be Overlord of Scotland during the Interregnum, I may yet lose this opportunity to bring them to my fold. If the Scotch do join this European Union, then the damned Scotch will be protected forevermore and potentially they will become the wealthiest realm in all of Christendom, and this I cannot allow. I want, indeed I require their resources and wealth for the purposes England's glory, for without their wealth and resources, I fear that we are undone… the Scotch cannot be allowed to join this pestilent European union of heathens, we must eliminate their notion and threat of independence for all time… we shall enslave them or destroy them, it matters not to me. We have already bought their nobility, and as we speak, I have many paid interferers causing instability in that realm, and now the Scotch are destroying their own realm from within…"

LÜBECK ALE

Wee Maw and the family have long since returned to Ach na Feàrna after their trip to the Glen of Afton. William has remained by her side awhile till he was certain that wee Maw has fully recovered from her malady, then he leaves the Balloch of ach na Feàrna with Andrew Moray, Dáibh and Daun, driving their wagons northeast towards the international river docks and busy markets at the inland seaport in old Saint Johns toun of Perth. After full day's travel, they cross into the old Cruathnie kingdom of Perth then enter Saint John's Toun port on the banks of the river Tay. They have travelled for provisions and valuable salt for the Wolf and wildcat hunters that William is to take back to Glen Afton. Salt being a necessary and vital tool for hunters as a preservative for their summer catch of fish and meat for winter consumption.

Early next day, William and Moray are at the Ceanncardine quarter salt markets loading the provisions on the back of a large bow-wagon. "What a mornin'." sighs William, "It's been relentless rain for near on ten days now." Andrew says, "It's good that those are tight barrels and this is a covered wagon or all that salt would be ruined." William laughs, "For fecks sake Moray, you've been sat there poking your finger in and out of some wee leather bag and sucking on it all mornin' while I've been loading this wagon by ma'self."

Andrew remonstrates, "I don't want to be getting soaked in all this rain Wallace. Anyway, those salt barrels are heavier and bigger than I am… and you need the work, you're gettin' fat anyways, besides, I've been busy all morning on your behalf."

Glaring at Moray humorously, William throws on board the last heavy barrel of salt then proceeds to go round the wagon tying and securing the cover-sheets. He glances into the back of the wagon then enquires, "Well?" Andrew is puzzled, "Well what?" William continues, "Did you manage to find her?" Andrew replies, "I did." William exclaims, "You did… does she want to meet me?" Andrew laughs, "She does, she said she'll meet us at the Sionnach Inn down at the docks, but not before mid-day, she said that she needs her morning sleep as she works long nights." William laughs, "If you're one of her best customers Moray, it's obvious that she works short knights too." Andrew laughs and punches William on the shoulder, "Fuck off Wallace…" William laughs; then Andrew says, "Come on Wallace, let's get this wagon rolling and I'll take you to meet the bonnie Affric."

The two friends ensure the wagon is made completely water tight then Andrew ties his horse to the back of the wagon and jumps on board with William. They drive down through the tight little streets of Saint Johns Toun towards the Sionnach inn and hopefully, the bonnie Affric. William ponders, "Ho Moray…." Andrew enquires, "What is it Wallace?" William replies, "I should be looking to take something back for Marion, for I'm seeing things here I never even knew existed." Andrew replies, "Wallace, yie'll no' believe the kind o' things that gets imported here, there's a whole new world out there we should explore some day." As they trundle onwards, Andrew says, "Old king Alexander sure made Scotland a strong linking partner with Europe in this place. There's so much here that I think both Marion and Brannah would enjoy, things like Iberian and Asian silks, even perfumes from the Saracen and Moorish Caliphates. There's fine wine's here too, really tasty, not like the horse pish you get in that wee village on the river Clyde that you took me too on the Molindenar Burn. What's it called again?" William replies, "Glaschu?" (Glasgow) Andrew replies in humour. "Bless you."

Driving on through the tight streets, William is curious at the myriad of strange objects and sights being sold by the traders in the lanes and market squares of the old town. He enquires, "What do you think Marion would like?" Moray replies, "Whatever items of luxury or comfort you could afford to buy her Wallace, yie can get it here. If she likes cooking and baking there are dried fruits, spices, nutmegs, peppers, ginger, figs, or here, what about getting her fine wine or some perfume? There are so many different varieties of wines here, or there's a great thing called vegetable honey, that would really please her." William looks at Moray curiously, "Vegetable honey, what's that?" Andrew grins with delight, "Awe Wallace, wait till yie get a taste o' this stuff, it's somethin else when you put it on food." William enquires, "What… Yie mean in stew or on stovies or what?" Andrew thinks a moment then shakes his head, "Naw, I don't think so, it's like putting bee honey on apples or pears. Some folk use it in their Ale if they can afford it, though it takes more than its own weight in gold to buy it."

Andrew pauses and pulls out a small leather bag, "I've got some right here, here they call it vegetable honey, but the Iberians call it Sukar, here, try it Wallace, try a wee bit, but wet your finger first." Dipping his finger into in the little leather bag, William pulls out some rough brown-coloured crystallized grains sticking to his fingertip, he sniffs it first then he sucks on it for a moment… Suddenly his eyes light up in pure heavenly bliss… "That's incredible Moray, it is like honey only it's lumpy and crisp too. I reckon wee Caoilfhinn and little Stephen would love this. I'll need to be getting some." Andrew replies, "Aye, it sure is fine stuff all right." Licking his lips, William enquires, "Can I get some more?" Andrew replies, "Aye sure, but only a wee bit mind, for yie can't hardly buy this stuff, it's only meant for princes and the highest o' society." Looking at Moray, William enquires, "How did you manage to get a' hold of it then?" Andrew laughs, "Well, Dáibh happened to find a wagon belonging to that new English constable o' Dundee, and would yie believe it, didn't a couple o' wee barrels just happen to fall out o' the wagon right at his feet." William laughs as he dips his finger back into the little bag, he says, "Aye, Dáibh fair knows how to find a good deal."

Andrew agrees, then he says, "Ho Wallace, do yie remember you're supposed to get some barrel's of fine Perth Ale to take back with you to Glen Afton too?" William replies, "Aye… so what?" Andrew continues, "Don't buy it, its pure shite… wait till you taste this stuff they call Lübeck Ale, it's from some Kingdom called Saxony. They sell it down at the inn we're going to. Ah reckon that yer auld Dá, Tam and especially that wee Graham will surely praise yie to the high heavens if you return to Glen Afton with some of this stuff, It tastes great but it's a feckn killer." William enquires, "Is it that good?" Andrew replies while kissing his fingers, "It is the tastiest Ale that has ever passed ma lips." William says, "Then lead ma lips to this nectar then Moray." William grins and glances at all the stalls, where he sees many new and wonderous things for sale or to trade brought in from ships from Europe and beyond. "This is some place right enough Moray." Andrew replies, "There's nowhere like this over on the west coast. Yie should go down and visit Berwick sometime if you think this place is great, they have things traded down there that hasn't been thought off yet, from places that doesn't exist, that's how good it is. The traders all call Berwick the Alexandria of the North because of its variety and trading wealth. It's the biggest and richest seaport in Scotland, yie should go down some day."

The two friends talk about all the amazing things William could take back from Saint John's Toun when they become aware of the long columns of English soldiers marching through the town, all coming up from the docks. William enquires, "Where are all these English soldiers coming from? I thought that everything would be settled by now down at Norham." Still sucking on his vegetable honey, Andrew replies, "I was down at the inn this mornin' talking with some of those English soldiers. It's strange what's going on, apparently it's our nobles... they've made some sort o' deal with the English King to avert another civil war in Scotland. Longshanks, that king of England, he's going to arbitrate from the appeals and disputes of each claimant, then he'll decide who he thinks should be our next King." The two friends continue to watch large patrols of English soldiers and horse squadrons moving throughout the town. William enquires, "So why are all o' these soldiers here?" Andrew replies, "Apparently to keep the peace." William enquires, "Are they just coming to Perth, or is it the whole of Scotland?" Andrew shakes his head, "An English soldier told me that it's the whole of Scotland. He said they're here to occupy all our major towns, castles and seaports so that no usurper may take them to their vantage during the interregnum."

William and Moray continue observing the endless columns of English soldiers marching past. William laughs, "They should try some vegetable honey to put a feckn smile on their miserable-lookin' faces while they're here then, what a sour-faced looking bunch they are."

While manoeuvring the wagon deftly through the small streets, the two friends discuss the appearance of the English army and what possible affect they could have as peacekeepers. Suddenly Andrew exclaims, "Wait Wallace, hold the oxen a moment, there's some friends o' mine." William pulls his wagon to a halt as Andrew calls out "LORNE, COMYN... SCRYMGEOUR..." Andrew turns to William, "Fuck, they can't hear me with all the noise from the rain and these English soldiers chattering like idle women. Wallace, drag the wheels while I go and get my friends then we can all go down to the inn together. These are wild fella's at a hop Wallace, wait till you meet them." Jumping from the wagon, Andrew runs over to a small group as William drives the wagon slowly down the old street, he notices Andrew pointing to the wagon and watches as the small group make speed through the rainfall and jump aboard, bundling in and roughly crushing in beside him on the drivers bench.

"Wallace..." says Andrew, "These are my friends Duncan o' Lorne, John the Red Comyn, son of the Lord o' Badenoch, and this big skinny fella here is Alexander Scrymgeour, his Dá used to be king Alexander's fancy sword-master along with auld Leckie mòr Lunn. Fella's... this big fella here is William Wallace o' ach na Feàrna." They all make an acquaintance as Andrew directs William towards the inn, where he will meet with his old friend Affric. "Comyn," Says William, "I think we're related down the line somewhere." Comyn enquires, "Is your father Malcolm, the confidante to the late King?"

"Aye, well..." replies William, "That's my uncle Malcolm, he is, or he was commander of the Garda Bahn Rígh. My father is Alain Wallace the Kings hunter from Glen Afton, down in the Wolf and wildcat forest. Lady Marjorie o' Comunnach Castle is a good friend and neighbour and she's your blood isn't she?" Comyn exclaims, "Feck that's where I have seen you before, Marjorie is my stepmother's sister." William enquires, "Do you know Dáibh Donnachaid o' Badenoch?" Comyn replies "Aye ah do, he's a real good friend." William says, "He's a good friend of mine too. Dáibh and Daun have only just left us to go get provisions in the old town markets. So tell me Comyn, why is it that you fella's from Badenoch are known as the red this or the black that?"

Everyone laughs in the bow-wagon, "No disrespect intended Wallace..." replies the red Comyn "Do yie not think it might be because of my red hair?" William sighs, "Awe Fuck... I couldn't tell because you're wearing a feckn hood and yer soakin' wet." Comyn smiles and points, "What about my red beard then, is that maybe a clue?" William laughs, "Aye ah suppose so." They all laugh as they continue on their journey through the town. No one on the wagon notices an English soldier staring intently as he passes by going in the opposite direction. The English soldier stops and looks at them with curiosity, he's sure he recognises the wagon driver, he cant remember from where or when, but he's certain he has seen him somewhere before, but it just eludes him, suddenly his sergeant pushes him sharply in the back. "Move it Fitchett."

William drives the wagon through the streets and out into a large open dock square, when Andrew suddenly stands up and cheers, "That's us nearly there Wallace, that's the Sionnach inn over there on the corner of the square, do you see that row of wee bothies that stretch all the way to the banks of the river Tay beside the docks? Those are the wee houses of great repute in Saint Johns toun. So pull the wagon over there between the inn and the wee cotters croft beside it." William drives the wagon close to the inn doors and hauls on the block brake as everyone jumps off the wagon and runs towards the inn doors. William shouts, "I'll feed the oxen and be there directly, and ahl feed your horse too Moray, as it seems yie have forgot." The torrential rain lashes down as Andrew reaches the sheltered door of the inn. He calls back… "Tá Wallace, I'll get some of that fine Lübeck nectar ready for yie. Yie won't be drinking any other shit Ale again after you've tasted this stuff." Andrew is getting soaked; he quickly pushes through the open door of the inn for shelter. After securing the wagon and feeding the animals, William runs to the doors of the Inn and barges his way through, he stands for a moment, absolutely soaked to the skin. Looking around the dark interior, William sees it's busy with sailors, bargemen and English soldiers enjoying continental ales, beers and the working girls plying their charms and trade.

A voice calls out to him above the noise of the packed crowd. "Here Wallace…" William looks across the crowds and sees Moray and his friends near a large stone inglenook fireplace. The low ceilings and thick Cruk beams of the inn cause him to stoop because of his size, and the bulky brat on his shoulders broadens his frame to nearly twice the width of an ordinary man. It's impossible for him to move through the inn without bumping into people and getting noticed. Eventually he reaches the fireside to join his friends

"Look at the size o' him…" exclaims Comyn, "Fuck, I knew you were a big fella when we jumped onto the wagon Wallace, but feck me, you really are a big feckr." William laughs, "It might be something to do with ma size, is that a clue for yie?" Everyone including Red Comyn laughs then he replies with a grin, "Aye right enough, fair play Wallace, yie got me there." Scrymgeour moves along the bench making space, "Sit down here Wallace or you're going to get a sore neck standing there." Sitting down on the bench beside Scrymgeour, William enquires, "That's an unusual name you have there, where's it from?" Scrymgeour replies, "Its an old

Cruathnie name from hereabouts, my father was given the title by King Alexander. It means the sword-master." William nods "Aye, ah met your father down at the plains o' Dalry a few years back. He was with my father at the face-off with the Brix Pact." Scrymgeour replies "Aye, Ah was there too, that was a close run day that one."

Andrew hands William a large flagon of ale, "Here, try this Wallace, this is that Lübeck Ale I was telling yie about, but watch yourself, it's strong stuff. Your head stays fine but its like someone cuts your inside ropes and everything else that holds you upright, especially when you take too much of it." William replies, "Slainte Moray," he takes a sup of the Ale. Slowly… a look of pleasure spreads across his face. "Feck me, this is great Ale Moray, you're right about that." Andrew says, "Ah told yie. Ho Wallace, this fella here is MacDuff, nephew of the late King, and before you start drinking too much o' that ale and it comes to you later, the answer is Aye, we're all Céile Aicé." William is surprised at what Andrew has just said, and he is getting an instant liking for his raucous newfound friends. He lifts his flagon of the tasty Lübeck Ale and makes a toast, "Mo càirdean, do dheagh Slàinte." (your good health my friends) Andrew stands up and replies "Slainte mòr a h-uile làchi 's nach fhaic." (Great health to you all every day that I see you and every day that I don't) Everyone raises their jugs and flagon's and shouts out as one "A' Céile Aicé…"

After a good few moments of riotous celebrating, they all settle down and chatter away amidst the throng of music and noise of the inn while swallowing plenty more of the tasty Lübeck Ale. William speaks with the innkeeper and agrees to purchase six barrels of Lübeck Ale. He loads them into the back of his bow-wagon then returns to the Inn. William enquires, "How much do I owe you for the barrels innkeeper?" The innkeeper replies, "Come and see me in a wee while when it's not so busy, we can work out a deal that suites us both then... Wallace, is that your name?" William shakes the innkeepers hand, "Aye William Wallace is ma name and I'll be thankin' yie innkeeper, for it's the strongest ale I've ever swallowed, and the best tasting too." The Innkeeper says, "Ach your fine Wallace, away to your friends and we'll talk coin later, ah trust yie." William returns to sit with Andrew and his friends beside the big fire. He enquires, "Moray, where's Affric now do you think?" Andrew smiles and raises his hand in an open welcome as he replies, "Here she is now Wallace." William turns round to see Affric standing behind him, looking just as he remembers her, the very essence of a beautiful wee elfin woodland princess.

"AFFRIC..." exclaims William. He immediately stands up and crashes his head into the ceiling, breaking all the dung-plaster. Disregarding the chaos and laughter from his friends, William picks up little Affric and embraces her, spinning her round joyously while knocking drinks off tables and barrels, much to the dismay and chagrin of the surrounding drinkers. He exclaims, "Affric ma wee darlin, feck, I have missed yie so." She throws her arms around his neck and hugs him dearly. For many moments they hold on to each other, then she pulls back and looks longingly at William with her beautiful alluring black almond eyes. "I've missed you too Finn MacCumhaill (Fin macool) ma bonnie Ettin from the Wolf and wildcat forest... how are yie doin' Wallace?" William replies with glee, "All the better for seeing you Affric." He lowers her gently back to the floor where she does a little spin, swirling her dress around her like a flowering buttercup opening its petals in summer. "Well Wallace, what do yie think?" He smiles and puts out his arms to hold her close, "Come here you..." She falls into his arms and they embrace passionately. Andrew starts to pull at

William's sleeve, "Hey Wallace, we're all going up the toun on some business, will we meet you here later?" William replies, "Aye, we'll be staying down here awhile I reckon." Andrew glances at Affric who smiles back at him. "Aye Wallace, I reckon yie will. We'll be seeing you here later then." William bids his friends away then sits back down beside Affric in front of the fire, where they talk of times past, good and sad.

The inn becomes even busier as the day wears on and is becoming extremely noisy and rowdy. William looks at Affric, "Feck Affric, that Lübeck ale sure is strong stuff right enough... do you want to go outside with me for a wee while? It's stopped raining and I, I... I think I'm gonnae to be sick..." Affric exclaims, "What... you... sick?" William stands up and staggers, "Affric darlin', tha mo feckn ceann loma-làn easgannan..." (My feckn head is full of feckn eels) Affric laughs at the condition of her long-time friend. "Wallace, you've went soft in the head since I last knew you. I just hope yie have no' went soft anywhere else big fella." William, now feeling very dizzy and nauseous, tries to focus as he replies, "I think we need to go outside quick Affric, like I mean, right now..."

William staggers clumsily through the crowd. As he stoops to make his way through the inn and out the door, he bumps into some English soldiers, but they are too drunk to really be bothered, but one of them is the soldier that passed them earlier and he notices William in particular. He watches curiously as William and Affric finally make it to the door and disappear outside to sit down on some beer barrels in the fresh air. The rain has stopped and the breeze coming from the banks of the Tay is refreshing. William exclaims, "Thank feck for that Affric, I'm no' used to being in such noisy places as that, I couldn't hear my own feckn thoughts in there." Taking William by the hand Affric says, "Come away with me Wallace, I've a wee cosy crib by the square midden over there, I think you need to be sleeping off that ale you've been drinking, you can rest awhile with me then yie can meet wie Moray later." William stands up, his head is spinning and his world is revolving in the opposite direction. "I think that might be a good idea." Affric takes William by the arm, throws it over her shoulders and helps the gentle giant to her little Bothy across the square from the Inn. Once inside Affric's Bothy, William drops onto her crib and immediately falls asleep. Affric sits awhile, watching her old-time lover, she runs her fingers through his hair but it hurts her to see him, to be with him once again, for she is realising how much she still loves him. Shaking off her sad thoughts, she quickly undresses and then climbs into the crib pulling warm mantles over them both; then she cuddles up beside him. Affric is feeling the first peace and real comfort that she has known for many years as she lay close beside him.

Back at the Inn, the English soldier is still wracking his brains trying to remember where he has seen William before, he is sure he knows him from somewhere. He moves through the throng and queries the innkeeper, "That giant Scotchman who was sitting at the fireside a little while ago... do you know his name?" The innkeeper thinks a moment then replies, "Aye, he said his name was William Wallace, that's his wagon out there at the side of the Inn." The Englishman thinks he recognises the name, he begins to place it in his head, Wallace... he ponders. Suddenly it comes to him... WILLIAM WALLACE... The soldier quickly rushes over to his three companions and speaks to his Coistrel. (Sergeant-at-arms) "Coistrel, I need to speak with you, its really urgent..." The Coistrel enquires, "Fitchett, what do you want?" Fitchett replies, "I need you to hear what I have to say... it's vitally important." The English soldiers make their way to a quieter corner of the inn, where Fitchett tells the Coistrel and the others his story... "About four years ago when I was last here in Scotland in the shire of Ayr, I was serving with sir Arnold De Ferrier, quartermaster to sir Henry de Percy. We were keeping those warring Scotch heathens apart, when I was with a patrol that was ambushed by an armed gang of villainous brigands, there was over a hundred of them I tell you, but miraculously I was the only one that managed to escape." Intrigued, the Coistrel enquires, "So, tell us what happened?" Fitchett continues, "There was but seven of us with sir Arnold out on patrol near the town of Ayr, we stopped to water our horses and catch some fish to meal, when suddenly we were surrounded by a whole army of Brigand outlaws and they attacked us while we were defence-less. We fought valiantly with what little we had, but we were vastly outnumbered and overpowered..."

"Go on..." says the Coistrel eagerly, "Well sergeant, we fought as hero's to a man, till Sir Arnold and I were the only ones left alive. But we bravely killed many Scotch dogs that day, I tell you, but we were finally overwhelmed. The brigand chief was so impressed that both sir Arnold and I had fought with such courage and outstanding bravery, he decided that he would grant us life and let us go free. But as we mounted our horses, the cowardly Brigand chief laughed, then he stabbed sir Arnold thrice in the back then he cut sir Arnold's head off before I could save him. I hacked my way through the villains with my mace and sword, I managed to reach my horse, barely escaping with my life..." The Coistrel smirks as the two other English soldiers grin at this tall tale. He says, "And the point of your story is?" Fitchett exclaims, "The Brigand chief... William Wallace, he's here..." The look on the English soldiers faces change dramatically. "He's here, right now?" enquires a stern faced Coistrel as he grips his sword hilt. "No," replies Fitchett "But he was here only a few moments ago, I enquired with the innkeeper, who said to me that wagon outside belongs to the Brigand chief, so he must be close by and he must be returning to pick it up." One of the other English soldiers speaks, "Shall I go to the castle and inform Lord Alan Fitz-Alan?" The Coistrel thinks a moment; then he replies "No wait, if we can capture this brigand chief alive, we may be handsomely rewarded for our diligence so soon after arriving into this shit country. At the very least, we will be favoured by those who are ranked above us." The Coistrel pulls Fitchett close, "What does this Wallace look like?" Fitchett replies, "He's a big bastard, about a two heads taller than you and in his mid twenty years I think, broad shouldered and muscular. He's got long brown-blond hair, tied back and long hanging side-plaits with a saffron material tied through them… and he has a rough growth of face hair." Fitchett pauses, then he continues nervously, "He looks like one of those wild Scotch mountain men; he was wearing long boots and party coloured breeches, I think."

Pondering, the Coistrel thinks of what would be the best course of action. He is himself in his forties and has come on this campaign as his last outing before retiring. The Coistrel thinks that if there is a reward for this Brigand, perhaps he could make a substantial amount of money to retire on, if in fact this Brigand chief is all Fitchett has described. At the very least he would get favourable grace from his superiors, for to be an outlaw in Scotland is now treasonous and that is the original mandate for a sergeant-at-arms, to arrest those suspected of treason, and Longshanks had chosen him personally to attend Sir Alan Fitz-Alan. There are only twenty sergeants-at-arms in the whole of England and the personal guard of Longshanks, but he alone had been sent to Scotland. The sergeant feels aggrieved and snubbed by Longshanks and also by Sir Alan Fitz-Alan, who described him in front of his men as only worth half a knight. No... thinks the Coistrel. I will deal with this myself. He turns to his men "This is what I want you to do... You Fitchett, you will wait here with me, for you know what this Wallace looks like. I want you other two outside, now... Take Wallace's wagon and then drive it up to the barracks, then I need you to come back with our troop as quickly as possible. When Wallace comes for his wagon, we'll be waiting for him." The two soldiers quickly finish their ale then go outside where they wait a little while, then they go round the corner and jump on William's bow-wagon and drive it away up to the English barracks near the castle of Saint John's toun. The Coistrel walks towards the inn door with the Fitchett. He says, "I want you to wait behind this door, when you see Wallace coming, let me know." Fitchett replies, "Yes Coistrel." Suddenly two men rush through the door shouting, "FERFICHT.... FERFICHT..."

Everyone roars and begins rushing to get outside the inn and jostling out the door. The Coistrel is bewildered; he asks the innkeeper, "What's going on? What does this Ferficht mean?" The innkeeper replies, "Ferficht? Oh, it means fair fight, it's a bare-knuckle brawl that's about to happen in the square between two of the bargee families. It's called a fair fight as there are no rules, unless your opponent goes to ground or calls enough..." the Coistrel enquires, "Where is this happening, outside the inn?" The innkeeper replies, "Aye, yie can put a wager on it too if yie like. There are eight men from each family going to fight, and it's judged by members from two differing bargee families to be keepin' it a fair and an honourable fight." The Coistrel calls out, "Fitchett, lets go outside, now. I want you to stand on one of those large oak ale barrels and look out for this Wallace, when he comes back to this corner looking for his wagon, that's when we'll capture him." Fitchett swallows hard, for he remembers

Wallace and how well he really could fight. "Coistrel…" says Fitchett nervously "Perhaps we should wait for re-enforcements." The Coistrel looks curiously at Fitchett "What are you talking about? I thought you said he was a cowardly rapscallion? Get up on that barrel or I'll have you skinned alive, now move." Fitchett quickly jumps up onto the oak barrel outside the inn while the Coistrel stands close by, watching the crowds gathering for the Fer Ficht spectacle. After a while, he decides that he too would stand on a barrel and watch the fights while Fitchett keeps a lookout for William.

A great crowd gathers in a large heaving circle to watch the first two bargemen fight. While the scrappers fly at each other with a vicious flurry of merciless blows, the crowds grow larger, jeering, shouting and roaring with every bone shuddering blow struck by each athlete of the Fer Ficht. William stirs with the noise of the commotion outside the Bothy. He sits up and scratches his head, for he can't remember where he is… then he feels the warmth of a naked female body by his side, suddenly a rush of fear sweeps through his body, slowly he lifts up the mantle, then he sighs with great relief in seeing that although Affric is naked, he still has his breeks and boots on.

Curious about the noise and commotion going on outside, William gets up and wanders over to the small window and opens the decayed wooden shutters to see that hundreds of people are gathering in the square, cheering-on what looks to be a big gang brawl. He watches awhile, then he glances over to where his wagon should be "It's gone…" he shouts, "Where the fuck has my wagon gone?" Affric stirs from her sleep, "What's wrong Wallace?" William exclaims, "My wagons gone, some fucker's stolen ma fuckin' wagon." He rushes back to the crib and picks up his léine and Brat. "Wallace," says Affric in a sultry voice, "Come here and make love to me…"

William exclaims "What?" in a state of panic, "Fuck off, Affric I cant… some bastard has stolen my wagon." Affric grabs his arm; in a demanding voice she say, "I said, make love to me Wallace…" William looks at Affric in muddled disbelief. "Someone has stolen ma fuckin' wagon Affric, ah love yie, ah love yie dearly as a friend, but ahm in love with Marion and I could never betray her trust, no matter if folk thought otherwise." He utters, "I cant." Affric spits out her words with venom, "What the fuck do you mean, you can't… and who are you tellin' tae fuck off?" William rushes towards the door shouting, "Affric, someone's stolen my fuckin' wagon ah yell yie." He falls over the crib, picks himself up then runs out the front door, he stops outside and stands bare-chested as he looks to see if his wagon is anywhere in the nearby vicinity. Affric comes rushing out the door behind him stark naked. Some of the crowd turn around and roar with delight on seeing her nubile naked body.

"Fuck you Wallace…" screams Affric. She jumps up and smacks him right across the mouth with her tiny fist. William staggers back, recoiling from the sharp sting on his jaw. He looks at Affric in complete surprise while she continues to curse him. She flicks her hair back, turns and walks over towards her Bothy, picks up a bucket of urine left for the wool-dyers, then she walks back and throws the contents all over him. Affric then marches back towards her Bothy still cursing and slams the door shut behind her. Now drenched in sour smelling piss and utterly confused, William turns and sees a large crowd laughing and jeering at him. Regaining his thoughts, he begins pushing his way through the thronging crowds towards where his wagon should be. As he gains closer to the Inn, Fitchett recognises William, he shouts to the Coistrel and nervously points… "That's Wallace over there, here he comes." The Coistrel responds quickly…

"Get to that corner where his wagon was and detain him, I'll get him from behind, then we'll capture him and take him prisoner." Fitchett stammers, "But…" The Coistrel snarls "Hurry up you fucking idiot, I don't want to lose him in this crowd." Meanwhile, William is still pushing through the crowds as a man on a mission. He's angry that he didn't see that Affric still has feelings for him, they are not the same as his feelings are for her, but he's more concerned that he could not see his bow-wagon anywhere. Eventually he reaches the corner of the inn and stands for a moment looking at the ground where his wagon should be.

"HALT…" Commands a voice close by. William runs his fingers through his hair, not really hearing the voice amongst all the screams and yells of the crowd watching the bloody Fer Ficht. "WALLACE…" says the voice with authority "You are under arrest, in the name of the King." William looks down and sees an English soldier tightly gripping an unsheathed sword and looking up at him. "What the fuck are yie talking about Englishman, what King, and who the fuck are you anyway?" Fitchett says once more, "Wallace, you are under arrest in the name of the King." Confused and annoyed, a befuddled William tries to explain, "Some bastard has stolen my wagon, and it's me you want to arrest?" Fitchett stands before William, shaking… He says nervously, "You are under arrest for the murder of sir Arnold De Ferrier, quartermaster to sir Henry de Percy." Shaking his head in confusion, William exclaims, "Who? What the fuck are you're talking about Englishman? Where the fuck has my wagon gone?" Fitchett is quaking when William feels a hand thump on his shoulder from behind. He looks round to see the tough looking English sergeant staring at him with intent. Without thinking, William throws back his elbow and smashes it into the face of the sergeant; he quickly takes a step forward and boots the unfortunate Fitchett between the legs, crushing his testicles against his pelvis. Fitchett groans, doubles up, staggers backwards vomiting and falls into the crowd. Turning to look for his wagon, William is struck on the face by a heavy fist, knocking him backwards against the inn wall.

The crowds begin to cheer and form a circle around William and the English sergeant, who is already bleeding from the nose and mouth. William immediately rushes him and the two fall to the ground in a violent tussle, they grapple for a few moments when suddenly, a pair of large brawny bargemen lifts William high into the air, then the sergeant too is hauled into the air by another two large bargemen. One of the elder Bargee states non-plussed, "There will be no wrestling when yiez are on the ground, if yie please." The elder bargee wags his finger at William and the sergeant, then says, "You two, keep it fair…" William exclaims, "What the fuck…" as he tries to make sense of everything. The Coistrel has broken his own sword belt when they rolled on the ground and his tabard is flying open, he quickly throws the belts off, spits into his hands and makes a gesture, "Come at me Scotchman… if you have the courage."

The situation is completely surreal to William. He's nursing a hangover; then Affric, who was completely naked in the town square, had punched him on the mouth and flung a bucket of piss over him. His wagon has been stolen, an Englishman who is no longer to be seen wants to arrest him for murder, now another bear of an Englishman wants to fight him… and people are taking bets on the outcome… A jolt of lightning suddenly flashes through William's head as the Coistrel's fist catches him full in the face, bursting his lips and knocking him back into the crowd.

A dazed William is quickly flung back into the human ring, where he sees the Coistrel is now stripped bare to the waist and circling him with fists tense, waiting to gain another opportunity to strike him. The sergeant spits on the ground and beckons William.

Suddenly the sergeant lunges at William with a mighty swing of his fist. William ducks beneath it and slams his fist into the Englishman's ribs then throws a powerful left hook, catching the Englishman on the jaw, forcing the sergeant to stagger back. The Englishman shakes his head then rushes William again and the fight begins in earnest with mighty blows traded between William and the Coistrel. The two combatants fight long and hard, suddenly; the Englishman catches William in a bear hug and lifts him off the ground, crushing his ribs with a powerful vice-like grip. William feels as though his back is breaking, he raises his arms up and smashes his elbows down on the Englishman's head, but it only makes the Englishman grip tighter. William can't breath, he opens his arms wide and with all his strength, he smashes his cupped hands over the Englishman's ears. Instantly the sergeant drops William to the ground, then he staggers back in great pain holding his ears.

William quickly gets up from the ground and strikes the Englishman rapid on the jaw three times then smashes him in the side of his head with knuckle breaking impact. There's a great cheer from the crowd as the two face-off each other, both William and the Englishman are bloody, bruised and ready to continue their epic Fer Ficht bout of fighting. As the two circle each other, William looks at the Englishman, he's smaller but a tough bull-muscled man, well fit for a fight. The Englishman momentarily smiles, William can't help himself as he smiles too. Apparently they are both enjoying themselves in a well-matched scrap. Then the

Englishman glances over William's shoulder and his fighting smile disappears, to be replaced with a look of deep concern. William glances behind to see a disturbance in the crowd that appears to be coming his way when he feels a thump on his chest and he's lifted high into the air. The Englishman has him in another bear hold. William reaches down and clasps both his hands on the Englishman's chin and begins to push hard, but he notices the Englishman is trying to speak…

"Listen to me Scotchman," Growls the Coistrel. William feels the Englishman loosen his grip momentarily, something is very wrong. "Listen to me Wallace…" barks the sergeant. William is shocked, how could this stranger know his name. The Englishman continues, "I'm going to fall back Wallace, listen to me… you must land on top of me, and when you do, hit me hard on the face then run for your life away behind the inn. If those soldiers coming here now catch you, they will surely hang you." Now William is totally confused but his instinct is telling him he has to listen and trust this Englishman, for nothing has made any sense since he woke up in Affric's crib. The Englishman shouts, "Hit me they way you did before, but for fucks sake, this time miss my ears. I'll fall, I give you my word Wallace, we will surely finish this Fer Ficht another day… so do it, do it now, trust me."

Knowing he doesn't need to be told twice, William opens his arms and smashes his hands just behind the sergeants ears, then true to his word, the burly Englishman staggers back, pulling William on to the top of him as he falls, the Englishman whispers, "Now smack me hard and run Wallace, run for your life." William smashes the Coistrel with a loose open fist, jumps to his feet, but he stops and stares at the burly Englishman lying on the ground, he looks at his bruised and battered face, there's a feeling of camradre and that he can trust this stranger. "GO Wallace… what the fuck are you waiting for?" William grabs his léine and brat then makes his way to the back of the inn and runs up the back alleys as English soldiers arrive at the scene, only to see the sergeant getting to his feet. The knight commanding the troop enquires, "Coistrel, what is going on here? We were informed there's a riot in progress and some murderous villain named Wallace is on the loose hereabouts." The Coistrel replies, "No, no, not at all my lord, it's a traditional fight here, nothing more. The Scotch put one of their best fighters against me and I beat him so soundly that he ran away from here like a scared rabbit. I was demonstrating to all of these vermin who their betters are my lord."

The knight appears smugly satisfied. "I was also told there was a brigand chief called Wallace here who is wanted for the murder of a loyal English noble?" The Coistrel replies, "Not that I know of my lord." At that moment, the innkeeper comes rushing over to the knight and begins pulling at his arm, remonstrating. The irked knight enquires, "What is it? What do you want you from me you annoying little man?" The innkeeper replies, "I've just been robbed sir. I have a complaint to make sir about some of your soldiers and a thief sir, they... they stole six of my best barrels of Lübeck ale." The knight enquires, "Have you any idea who they were?" the innkeeper replies, "I don't know who the English soldiers were sir knight, but I do know the name of the rogue who was their ringleader, his name is William Wallace." The annoyed knight barks out an order, "Coistrel... make a report to the captain of the guard, and make sure a warrant goes out for this man Wallace's capture for stealing ale, though I do not know how we may catch him, it would appear that every rogue here who commits a transgression is called William Wallace." The knight continues "And Coistrel..." The sergeant replies, "Yes my lord?" The knight continues,

"Very well done in showing these Scotch villains some stout English spirit. Here, take these few merks and get yourself some ale." The knight hands the sergeant a few silver coins, turns his men and they march back toward the town. The Coistrel walks over to the innkeeper, he says, "I'll make that report myself innkeeper, and I will pay for your Ale and for you to keep your mouth shut, then we will hear no more about this matter nor mention that young mans name ever again… are we agreed?" The Innkeeper replies, "Aye sir, I'll be thanking your good self sir." The Coistrel gruffly commands "Now get in there and get me some hot swatches for my cuts and bruises, and set me up your finest ale, for I have worked up a good thirst scrapping with your young ale thief."

The sergeant sees Fitchett sitting behind ale barrels at the back of the inn, looking deathly white, doubled up and still in great pain from the kick on the testicles he received from William. The Coistrel laughs to himself then goes over and manhandles Fitchett up by his surcoats and roughly pulls him close, "You will not mention that young man Wallace again Fitchett, you will forget you ever saw him, or I swear… I will cut your fucking heart out and eat it myself in front of you. Wallace is no more a brigand chief than you are courageous. Now get in there and fetch my ale, then I want you to permanently disappear, if you know what's good for you."

The Coistrel pushes the badly injured Fitchett along the wall and roughly shoves him through the inn door; then he walks back inside to happily bathe his wounds from his first experience of a Scot's Fer Ficht. He smiles to himself, knowing he won't forget the relentless young opponent, William Wallace. Meanwhile, William is still wandering through the back streets, vennels and pathways in a pointless effort trying to find a way out of Perth and get home to safety. The aches and painful bruising are starting to have a debilitating effect; then he remembers that Moray and his friends are supposed to meet him later at the inn. He doubles back, avoiding English patrols that seem to be everywhere, till he is back behind the inn. Pulling his Brat over his head, he looks around at the buildings for places he could shelter and watch for Moray's return. He didn't want to go to Affric, she is too demented; then he sees some stuke's (Haystacks) in a marshalling yard and climbs on top of the stuke closest to the inn.

A light drizzle rain begins to fall and William wraps himself up to wait on his friends return. The noise of horses and men talking wake William with a start, he had fallen asleep and it's beginning to get dark. He's cold, wet and very sore from his Fer Ficht with the Englishman. He crawls to the edge of the stuke and sees Moray and his friends tethering their horses below him, he slides down the back of the stuke and cautiously makes his way around it, "Moray..." he whispers. Andrew is talking with Scrymgeour and didn't hear William. He raises his voice and calls out "MORAY..." Andrew turns his head and a look of shock comes to his face. "Wallace, what the fuck happened to you? English patrols looking for you, and look at your face? It's a mess." William replies, "I don't fucking know what happened, I went to sleep off the effects of that Lübeck fuckin' Ale in Affric's Bothy, when I came out, my wagon was gone. I came over to see if it was someone that had moved it when some Englishman stopped me and wanted to arrest me for a murder."

Andrew calls on Scrymgeour and MacDuff. There are two others with them. Andrew says, "Wallace here is wanted for murder." Scrymgeour enquires, "Is he?" MacDuff says, "That's not so good Wallace... did yie do it?" William glares at MacDuff; the look is enough of an answer. MacDuff says, "For fucks sake Wallace, you're face is a mess right enough."

William groans, "I think I've got broken ribs." Scrymgeour beckons him, "Here, sit down and let me have a look at yie." Scrymgeour examines William while Andrew makes introduction to the two strangers. "Wallace, this is Patrick Graham of Ceanncardine and this other fella is Hamish MacLellan of Bombie from down in Galloway." Hamish says, "Pleased tae meet yie Wallace, though ah wish for you it was under better circumstances."

William nods a form of greeting. Andrew speaks while Scrymgeour tends to William's wounds. "We heard there's been a warrant issued for your arrest for stealing ale, but you're saying it's for murder?" William replies "Aye, one wee English soldier said it was for the killing of some knight in Ayr, I think he meant the fella that was going to cut my hands off for fishing on my uncles land, do yie remember, I told you about it?" Andrew replies, "Aye, I remember, the bastards." Scrymgeour looks at William, "Wallace your ribs are bruised, but thankfully they're no' broken." MacDuff leans over William and puts his hand on his shoulder, "Wallace, If the English are searching for yie I've a well secure place where you may hide and rest up at Kilspindie, it's a wee bit to the west of here up in the Carse of Gowrie, nobody knows where this place is nor could they find it without local knowledge."

"Naw," growls William, then he relents, "My apologies MacDuff, but my ribs are killing me... I just need to get home. But I thank you." Hamish says, "It won't be the only thing that's killing you if the English find yie." As William slowly stands up, he says "I've got to get out of here now. I need to get across country and back to Glen Afton." Andrew looks at him and says, "You can't ride in your condition." Scrymgeour laughs, "It's a better condition to be riding than swinging from an English feckn rope." Hamish says, "He can travel with us, we have passes from the English to travel west."

Patrick agrees "Aye, yie can get some dry clothes from us Wallace. Clean yourself up and we can leave as soon as you're fit. It's raining and dark so that should keep the English indoors awhile." William looks forlorn, he says "But I don't have a horse, whoever stole the wagon stole every fuckin' thing." Andrew says, "Take Warrior," William stammers "But…" Andrew continues, "Take him Wallace, I've seen how the two of you look at each other ever since you stabled him at Glen Afton. Think of him as an early wedding gift from me to you and the maid Marion." William looks at Warrior, "Moray… I cannot be thanking you enough." Andrew laughs then he replies, "Ach its no matter Wallace. He's a fine stallion, sired by Areion himself, Alexander's old war-horse, and he's a lot smarter than you by a roman mile."

Andrew un-tethers Warrior and leads him back over to William and hands him the reigns. Smiling he says, "Now mind and you take good care of him, he's a stubborn strong-willed hard-headed fuck, temperamental and got a tiny obstinate mind of his own, but I reckon he'll stay faithful to you for life once you master him." William strokes the magnificent broad forehead of Warrior, he replies, "That I will Moray, and I thank you for this." Andrew looks at William curiously, "What are talking about Wallace…? I was talking to the fuckin' horse not you." Everyone laughs out loud, including William. Humour it seems is a great healer and giver of much-needed respite. "Here Wallace," says Patrick. He hands William a large thick brat, "Put this on and lets get out of here, we'll go directly west and then follow the lights o' the golden teeth as far as Culross Ceanncardine. You can stay the night there with us, in the morn you and MacLellan can cross the Forth on the Skinflats at low tide then ride on to ach na Feàrna." Looking at his friends, William says, "I cannot thank yiez enough…" Andrew says, "Ach away with yie Wallace, we are all Céile Aicé here are we not? And what would Marion and Brannah say if I left you swinging from an English gibbet?" Hamish calls out "Come on Wallace, get on your horse and let's get out of here." William shakes hands warmly with Moray, Scrymgeour and MacDuff, then he mounts Warrior. Moray calls out, "I'll send more boxes of homers down to you Wallace, that way we can keep in touch." William replies, "I won't forget this Moray, I owe you..." Andrew smiles as he replies, "Then put in a good word to Brannah for me."

Patrick and Hamish spur their horses, quickly followed by William. They make their way at speed towards Ceanncardine where it will eventually lead the companions to the safety and sanity of ach na Feàrna. "Moray..." calls out Affric as she comes running across the square toward him. "Moray, where is the dirty big bastard? Ah fuckin' hate him..." Andrew catches her by the wrists, "Whoa there Affric, he's gone from here not long since." She screams like a hellish demon and shouts into the wind, shaking her fists, "FUCK YOU WALLACE..." Then she spits on the ground and marches towards the inn while shouting back at Moray, "He fuckin' walked out on me for some noble bitch Moray, fuck him, fuck her, and fuck all o' yiez fancy fuckin' noble bastards." Moray, Scrymgeour and MacDuff are speechless. They shrug their shoulders and don't really know what to say by way of a reply. MacDuff eventually speaks, "You and the Wallace there sure do have a way with the women Moray. Remind me not to go on a double tryst wie you two anytime soon."

The three friends laugh and make their way to the inn behind Affric, when Moray stops and peers into the darkening night. He thinks, '*Take care Wallace...*' as William, MacLellan and Hamish travel through the night, stopping at the Cistercian monastery near Culross Abbey, there they tend properly to William's cuts and bruises then bed down in the Abbey for the night. They sleep till the early dawn, and after bidding farewell to Graham, William and Hamish cross the ferry over the Skinflats and travel westward, reaching the gates of ach na Feàrna by mid-day.

Tired and bedraggled, William and Hamish finally meander through the gates of ach na Feàrna. Malcolm sees them arrive and greets them as they dismount… "William, what's happened to you? And where's the wagon?" Tired, still aching and extremely sore, William replies, "I'll tell you later uncle… Watch out and don't say anything, here comes wee Maw and Margret." Wee Maw sees William and her eyes light up with joy. She wraps her arms around him and says, "William son, your home…" Margret could instantly see that William has been hurt. She enquires, "William, are you all right?" Wee Maw takes a step back and looks at him closely, "Oh William you poor wee soul, what's happened to your bonnie face?" William replies, "Ach, the wagon broke a wheel near the Ceanncardine and I got flung off onto some rocks." Wee maw fusses about him, then she enquires, "Did those rocks have big knuckles?" William and Hamish laugh, then William replies, "Naw, but it sure feels like they did." Then he then makes introductions, "Malcolm, Margret, Granny, this is Hamish MacLellan o' Bombie, he helped me when the wagon crashed over." Wee Maw says, "Pleased to meet yie Hamish o' Bombie, here now, you boy's look awfy hungry, I'll away and make you both some fine scran for yie both."

Margret takes William by the arm and they walk towards the main house, while Malcolm and Hamish stable the horses. William enquires, "How has wee Maw been?" Margret replies, "Ach, she has good day's and bad days." They continue talking of wee maw's health as they make their way to the house. William waits outside till Malcolm and Hamish catch up with him. Malcolm enquires, "I want the truth now William, what really happened to yie?" William sighs, "Awe Malcolm, even I don't know what really happened, but I think the English have issued a writ for my arrest for the murder of an English knight, I think it is about that Knight fella down in Ayrshire a few years back." Malcolm is stunned to hear this information. "Don't say anything to wee Maw or Margret, we'll talk of this later." They enter the house where wee Maw and Margret quickly tend to William then serve both him and Hamish some much needed hot food vittals and nourishments. Later that day Hamish bids farewell and leaves for his Bombie homeland away down southwest in Galloway. William then tells Malcolm of what he knew about everything that had happened in Perth. Malcolm sighs, "Aye son, we'd better get in touch with your uncle Ranald, as a Sherriff he will know how to handle all o' this. It's best you get some crib time too, for yie are lookin' absolutely feck'd son, we'll talk some more the morn when you're well and properly rested."

That night, William lay restless in his crib, he still could not understand or fathom out what had really happened, then he hears a knock on the door and sees wee Maw creeping in with a steaming jug of hot honey toddy. With a big grin she says, "Here yie go son, this will help yie get to sleep and it'll help heal yie at the same time." She pours a wee dram and hands it to him. As William drinks his medicinal craitur, wee Maw gently brushes his hair back, "My my, William, deary me, you're sure a Wallace right enough son. We never need to look for trouble, for it will always finds us." William replies, "It would seem so Granny." Wee Maw tucks him up tightly in his crib, like it was when he was a suckling wain. He laughs to himself as she tends to him with grandmothers care. "Right William me bonnie boy," says wee Maw, "That's you all tucked up nice and snug. And now, now I am going to tell you of the time that your dear grandfather Billy fought wie' the Romans." William looks at wee Maw curiously, thinking Grandpa and the Romans? This should be some legend this one. He smiles, closes his eyes and lay back in his crib, listening to wee maw telling her story. He feels the comfort of the crib and the soothing effect of the hot toddy taking effect. He is so relieved and glad to be home, far away from the madness of civilisation, even more so upon hearing the tall tales of legends past from wee Maw.

He yawns, stretches, then opens his eyes and sees wee Maw and Malcolm carrying platters of hot food into his room. He sits up rubbing his eyes, feeling much better. "Did I fall asleep?" Wee Maw replies, "You've slept nearly a whole day son." Malcolm speaks with a big smile on his face, "There's someone here to see you." William exclaims, "Marion?" Dáibh walks through the door, "Naw Wallace, it's me." A deflated William enquires, "Awe it's you Dáibh..." Wee Maw picks up some clothes he had left strewn about the floor, "I'll be leaving you men to talk." as she walks out the door. Confused, William enquires, "What are you doing here Dáibh? I mean, what are you doing here in Ach na Feàrna? I thought you and Daun had left for Badenoch?" Dáibh sighs, "That's a fine welcome for someone who's just brought your wagon load of salt back for you, and four barrels of Lübeck ale." William frowns, "Don't you mean six Barrels?" Dáibh replies with a grin "Two barrels down for expenses." Before he questions Dáibh about the missing barrels, William is distracted as Daun walks into the room, "Co'nas William," says Daun "It seems you've made a friend in the English soldiery." Dáibh laughs as he explains, "See that wee Englishman yie fought, his name is Fellow's, he's the bare knuckle champion of Edwards army, and he likes you."

William enquires, "I don't know what yie mean?" Dáibh replies, "Well, Daun and me'self went down to the Inn not long after you had left and we met with Moray, MacDuff and Scrymgeour there who were talking with an English sergeant. I have to tell you, his face is no better than yours for a mark o' introduction between the pair o' yiez. He told us what his soldier had told him, but he guessed of the real story. When he met you and yiez scrapped in the Fer Ficht, he said he hasn't enjoyed himself so much in years." William is puzzled, "How did he know who I was?" Dáibh replies, "From the wee English soldier yie crippled, but Fellows sends his thanks and looks forward to the next time yiez meet, oh, and he also sez thanks for his share o' the Ale for saving the rest for yie."

Relief sweeps through William's mind, "But what about me getting arrested for murder?" Dáibh replies, "Fellows took care of it. You'll hear no more about it." William is astonished, "I'm free? No warrants, no writs?" Dáibh, laughs, "Not quite, you're now posted as an outlaw." William looks bewildered, "For what?" Daun replies, "It appears the warrant says that you and some English soldiers stole barrels of ale from the Inn." A bemused William laughs, "So ahm an ale theivin' outlaw?" Daun smiles, "It would appear so." Laughing again, William says; "Jaezuz, how is wee Maw going to make a legend out of that?" Dáibh and Daun laugh too; then they stand up and link arms. Dáibh says, "Me and Daun will need to be going home now Wallace, it's a turnaround visit for us."

"So soon?" enquires William "Aye," sighs Dáibh, "You do know that Daun has a list of chores waiting for me when I get back to Badenoch. I have to build her a new hovel." Everyone laughs at Dáibhs humour; Dáibh continues, "I've left two crates of homers for you from MacDuff and Moray. They say they're for you to keep in contact with them,

Malcolm is giving me two crates of homers to take back with me." William says, "Wait, how did you manage to get the wagon back?" Dáibh looks at Daun then they both grin, Daun explains, "Dáibh and Fellows did it. The English soldiers stole it from you, so we thought we should steal it back…" Dáibh shakes William's hand, "It sure has been great spending some short time with you Wallace's, but we have to be getting up the road to Badenoch, so you stay in your crib Wallace and get your strength back; then we'll all meet up again for the wedding?" William replies with a smile, "Aye, we'll let yiez know when we set the dates, maybe about Beltane we're thinking. Anyways, thank yie both for comin' down and bringing the wagon and salt back down for us…" William laughs, "…and the Lübeck Ale. You two take good care on the road back home, and avoid any English patrols."

Just as she approaches the door, Daun turns and says, "Oh, I nearly forgot." She walks back and takes a small leather pouch out from a side-bag and hands it to William. "Moray sent this for you, to help sweeten up your face." William enquires, "What s it?" he looks in the bag and an expression of delight spreads across his face. Dáibh says, "Haha, it's working on yie already." William exclaims, "It's that vegetable honey." Daun stoops and kisses William on the forehead, then she and Dáibh clasp hands once more, William says, "Thank yie both… for everything." Dáibh replies, "Ach, nae bother Wallace, you just be gettin' yourself fit and fine for when next we meet." William replies, "I will." Dáibh and Daun walk to the door, "Slan, Slan…" says Dáibh as he and Daun leave. William lay back down on his crib, so very much relieved to be free of the serious charges of murder. He begins to feel the weight and stress of the last few days ebbing away from both his mind and body; then he remembers… he licks his fingers then he dips them into the little bag that Moray had sent to him. Pulling his fingers out, he studies with great curiosity the small brown crystals on his fingertips. He licks the crystals off the end of his fingers and a feeling of great pleasure warms his spirits: then he thinks to himself and laughs, "I don't believe this, I'm a feckn ale thief? Now I'm an outlaw… again?"

BAG O' SILVER

Wee Graham runs for all he is worth on his little spindly legs, puffing and panting all the way down the hill from the doocots towards Wallace Keep, "Katriona, Katriona…" shouts wee Graham. Katriona meanwhile, is sitting outside the Keep hand-spinning coarse wool with a broad lap spindle then rolling the yarn against her thigh, she trails it to Auld Jean sitting beside her who is continuing to roll the coarse wool between the palms of her hands into long thin strands to make up rolled balls of yarn for weaving, then they hear wee Graham shouting in the distance. They look over to see him running towards them with his long wild hair bouncing and straggling out behind him, like an extremely old and weathered horsehair mantle in an autumn gale. Katriona and auld Jean laugh heartily at the sight. Katriona calls out, "What is it Dá?" Little Stephen and Caoilfhinn jump up from a great pile of sheared wool where they have been laboriously picking out a flotsam of burrs and dead insects and look out for their funny Grandfather.

On seeing him running towards them, they shout and squeal with joy. Wee Graham finally comes to a halt, breathless and sweating beside them. Jean chuckles, "I haven't seen you sweating so much me darlin' since that night William asked Marion for her hand at the tryst." A slightly embarrassed

Katriona exclaims "Maw?" Wee Graham gasps, "Katriona me darlin, its a message from Stephen." Wee Graham catches his breath, then he continues, "He'll be landing the morn at Invergarvane…" Katriona and auld Jean hug each other with joy, "I can't believe it," says Katriona. "Its true." replies wee Graham. Auld Jean grins, "C'mon Katriona, we have to be getting the place cleaned and ready for Stephen coming home. We have a lot to do and we'll need plenty o' help. Wee Graham, would yie…"

They both turn to see wee Graham away in the distance heading for auld Tam, who is sitting beside a deep water pool. Katriona laughs, "Do yie think Dá might o' known we wanted him to help with the cleaning?" Auld Jean laughs, "More like he's away to enjoy some fine honey-dew craitur wie auld Tam." They laugh and joke about wee Graham as they leave to go into Wallace Keep kitchens to prepare a grand welcome for Stephen's homecoming. Auld Tam is stripping nettle leaves from their stalks and dropping them into a pot for stewing later; then he throws the stalks into a churn of water to soak awhile. He takes out a handful of previously soaked stalks and begins pulping them with a leather mallet to separate them into fine fibre strands. He rolls a fistful of the fibres together, spinning the hemp to make fine lines for use as weaving into nets, snares, fishing lines, bowstrings and a host of other uses. He mutters to himself, "I reckon this day is the day I'll catch that auld feckn salmon with this new line…" Wee Graham agrees as he sits down by beside him...

"Yie could be right Tam." Wee Graham continues, "Great news Tam, young Stephen will be landing at Invergarvane the morn, so he'll be here by the morra eve." Tams eyes light up with delight, "That is great news Graham, it'll fair cheer up the glen when our bonnie Irishman comes back." then he says, "We should be sending a message up to Ach na

Feàrna for William to go down there and pick Stephen up now that wee Maw is well on the mend." Auld Tam stands up and stretches his aching back. "I'll send a couple o' pigeons up after I've finished the hemp spinnin'" Just then, Katriona comes down from the Keep and sits on her father's knee. Wee Graham smiles, "You look so happy me bonnie darlin', Stephen will be home soon enough now."

Katriona hugs him close and says, "I have missed him so much Dá, though it's really been only a wee while since he left us." Tam, still spinning hemp between his palms says, "It was awfy sad news to be hearin' about the passing o' his father though." wee Graham agrees, "Aye, Stephen the elder... I'll miss his visits Tam, he was some man for sure, and it's such a shame he passed before Stephen got to see him one last time." Auld Tam smiles, "I remember when we first met him just afore the battle o' Largs..." They all continue to chatter awhile then Katriona says, "Dá, lets go up to the Keep and sit up there and I'll make us something special from the kitchens?" Tam and wee Graham smile at the thought of food, they pick up all the hemp-lines then make their way back up to Wallace Keep, where they sit down on the promontory to admire the Vista of Glen Afton. Mharaidh comes out of the kitchens with a platter of fresh hot bannocks. An excited Katriona jumps up and calls out to her, "Mharaidh, ma Dá says Stephen's coming home the morn." Mharaidh replies excitedly, "Oh Katriona, this is really wonderful news, it'll be so good to be seeing him back here with us again."

Wee Graham stands up to take the platters from Mharaidh, "Here Mharaidh, let me get those for yie darlin." Setting the platters down, Mharaidh smiles, "You enjoy some precious time with Katriona wee Graham, for I shall wait upon you and your family this day, as you do so often for us, you all deserve to have many moments to treasure as a family."

Auld Jean comes out the doors behind Mharaidh and overhears her words, Mharaidh says, "You too Jean, you rest up with Katriona and wee Graham." But auld Jean prefers to fuss about wee Graham and auld Tam. She says, "Would you two like a wee dram o' honeydew craitur?" Auld Tam looks curiously at Jean, then he replies, "Aye Jean, that would be just fine tá." Wee Graham steps forward and holds Jean by the hand, "I'll get the vittals ma dear, you just have a wee rest there." Auld Jean waves her hands all in a fluster, "Naw, naw... You just sit back down darlin' and rest yourself, let me get it and I'll bring yie a nice wee hot dram too."

Auld Jean turns and notices that Mharaidh is lost in a world of her own. "Is there something ailing yie Mharaidh, for you're looking se' very sad there?" Mharaidh appears as though she's suddenly been woken from a trance, "I don't know Jean, I felt love abound when I came out the door a moment ago, then suddenly, this cold chill feeling came over me and I felt really... odd?" Auld Jean enquires, "Can I get you a wee toddy, or maybe you would like a fine wine instead?" she continues, "Maybe your feelin' a bit strange because the men have been away far too long." Mharaidh sits down, appearing very shaken. "Yes, maybe, I think I'll have a wee cup of milk with some nectar in it if you don't mind?" Auld Jean is concerned for Mharaidh, "Yie look a wee bitty pale Mharaidh, you just sit there and catch yer breath and I'll bring yie some fresh milk and honey." Auld Jean is unsettled in seeing Mharaidh appearing unwell; normally she is always so full of life. Jean then sees her beautiful Katriona glow in the bloom of her pregnancy. "And some hot buttermilk for you ma darlin?" Katriona smiles "Aye maw, I would like that." As auld Jean goes into the kitchens, Katriona sits beside Mharaidh and they begin spinning wool together. Tam looks at wee Graham curiously, "Auld Jean has been a changed wumman these last few weeks Graham, what have you been doin' yie auld rascal?" Wee Graham, happily pulling and beating Tam's hemp fibres has a big grin on his face, "Ach, it was the night William proposed to Marion, later on Jean and me, well… I gave ma darlin a right good Fu…"

"Father…" exclaims Katriona before he could finish. Auld Tam is delighted, "Wee Graham ma man, yie mean yiez both had a good fu—" "TAM." Exclaims Mharaidh. Tam sighs and resumes pulping his fibre, he says, "My my… who would have thought it was still possible…" wee Graham says, "Right you wains," "I want yiez to help me and Tam here to roll up his new hemp line, and after auld Tam sends a message up to William and granny Jean brings out the vittals, we're all going down to the deep pool, where me and Tam are going to show the pair o' yiez how to catch that biggest auld salmon yie ever did see that's annoyed us both for feckn years, and you wains can be helping us." Caoilfhinn and wee Stephen jump up and down for joy. Even at their young age, they know that going with Auld Tam and wee Graham would be much better fun than picking bugs and burrs from great piles of smelly sheep wool. Auld Jean soon returns with wee Jamie, both of them carrying flagons and more hot fresh bannocks, they hand out the refreshing vittals, then they sit together doing the chores and chatting awhile about Stephen and the new baby expected by Katriona.

Auld Tam stands up and runs his fingers through his long shock-white hair. He says, "Here yie go Graham…" he hands wee Graham the hemp fibres to roll and hawthorn hook, he continues, "I am away to write a message and send a couple o' birds up to ach na Feàrna, yie did say Stephen is to be picked up at Invergarvane in the morn?" Wee Graham confirms, "Aye, by the morn Tam." As Tam walks away towards the doocots, he sees a rider galloping towards Wallace castle, he calls out, "There's a horseman ridin' along the north road." Mharaidh and Katriona stand up to see who may be coming towards them. Mharaidh enquires, "Can you see who it is?" Katriona replies, "That looks like Lady Marjorie's white horse?" Wee Graham says, "Aye, its Lady Marjorie all right."

As horse and rider arrive at the corral under the promontory, Marjorie dismounts and runs quickly up the steps to where Mharaidh is waiting. Marjorie is excited, "Have you heard the news?" gaining her breath, she continues, "Cospatrick and Alain, they'll be home in a few days, everything has been agreed at Norham with the English King, now they're coming home." Mharaidh exclaims, "Oh that's such welcome news." Tears begin to flow as the women hold hands, thinking of their loved one's return. Marjorie sits down beside Mharaidh and Katriona. She says, "I'm so relieved and glad that's all over and done with, perhaps now everything can get back to normal in the realm." Mharaidh smiles, "I do hope so, for it has been a terrible time without a King or Queen to hold the reigns of our realm together, perhaps the warring nobles will now see peace is the only life we want, not war, oh but it's so good to hear the men will be returning home." Katriona says, "With Stephen making his way home and wee Maw recovered, William will be back here soon too, and then Alain and the men on their way home… oh, the glen has been so quiet without them tangled all about our feet, it'll be so wonderful to see everyone back home again."

Marjorie smiles at this news, "Then we can expect the wedding arrangements to be next Mharaidh?" Mharaidh smiles with glee, "Marjorie, it will be such a delight to have William and Marion here for the wedding tryst." Katriona enquires, "Would you like some hot fresh vittals Marjorie?" Marjorie replies, "I will Katriona, tá" then she says "Now Mharaidh, are you going to tell me about the wedding arrangements you've planned for the happy couple?" Mharaidh replies "Of course Marjorie, William and Marion have set their hearts on the Beltane for the handfast." Marjorie exclaims, "That's wonderful news." Mharaidh enquires, "Marjorie, would you like some wine or ale to go with your vittals?" Marjorie replies, "I would love some refreshment Mharaidh, I'm so thirsty after that fast ride up here." Wee Graham says, "Right, will yiez tell Tam that I'm taking the wains down to the fishing pool, for this talk o' weddings is not for the ears of ones se' young."

Everyone laughs as wee Graham lifts all the fishing lines and arranges for young Jamie, wee Stephen and Caoilfhinn to hold hands, then he orders them to march behind him as they set out on the fishing expedition in search of the old elusive salmon. Auld Jean and Katriona bring fresh bread, cheese, some casked honeydew craitur and fine wine in Flagons from the kitchens, then the women all sit down for a long and happy afternoon chat.

* * *

A hundred miles south of Glen Afton, De Percy and Lord Cressingham have chosen the most direct route to Ayr town by travelling through the lands of nobles who still remain at Norham swearing fealty to Longshanks. They carefully avoid hostile Gallóbhet country as not to arouse any interest or suspicion from such a large armed English troop moving northwards from the border marches of England. They detour west towards Comunnach Castle and Loudon Hill, where they are to meet a supply column led by Lord Fenwick. After a full days hard riding, they are within morning's ride from Comunnach when they stop and rest both men and horses late in the eve. Cressingham dismounts slowly, as his bulk is beginning to ill fit his saddle. He says, "We will regain our strength and vigour here Percy, it will serve us best if the men do not eat. Let them drink only water and chew on dry fish, as the work we do on the morrow will require hungry pious men to exercise, they know from experience that they will gain great reward of feasting and a well-earned rest upon completion of their blessed tasks." De Percy can hardly contain his excitement, "What say you Lord Cressingham. I anticipate your vast experience over many long years will be a successful tutorage for me in the arts of vigorous peacekeeping, especially upon the new Scotch vassals of our King." Cressingham glares at De Percy then he issues him his orders, "I want you to command the men to make bivouac for the night, do not let them light any fires, I want them removed from any and all comforts."

De Percy looks at Cressingham curiously, "Right away my Lord." Cressingham continues, "And Percy… make note of this, hungry and cold-blood soldiers do very sedulous labours when they're denied sustenance long before their duties, and particularly it is so when they know they will be met with an excess in rewards for doing Gods good work. This method breeds extremely loyal retainers Percy, you would do well to remember this." De Percy replies, "Yes my Lord." The English troop settles in for a chilly evening on the high moors.

As the sun rises next morning, the English troops are cold and hungry, but fresh from their nights rest. Cressingham calls for his horse and speaks to de Percy, "Our scout has done very well it would appear." De Percy replies gleefully, "Yes my Lord, now we may take our rods of guidance to the vipers nest." Looking at de Percy, Cressingham shakes his head; he says, "I will address the men to free their hearts and minds to fastidiously do the work of God and good King Edward. Now Percy, I want you to bring the men together."

De Percy gathers all the soldiers for Cressingham to address. Cressingham mounts his horse and looks at his men with a certain pride, for they have served him well for many years in Flanders, Ireland and Wales. Handpicked for their skills as master butchers, fleshers and slaughtermen, they have also proved to be a source of amusement in times of boredom. Cressingham sits back in his saddle, then he begins, "Men, what we do this day and from this day forth in the eyes of the heathen Scotch and misguided seditioners, may appear a tad harsh, but to free your minds and hearts of any doubts you may have, you shall be absolved from any action you deem necessary by your thoughts and by your swords doing Gods work. What is to be done… is what must be done. We shall spare none the rod, for if these heathen savages think us weak, they may rise up and do evil unto our beloved England."

The English soldiers appear pensive, but all are loyal to a man in the service of their Lord. Cressingham continues, "Good Father Anthony here from the King's bishopric who does accompany us on our mission, requires you all to join him in prayer. After which, the good Father will admonish and absolve you each individually, to bring you closer to God's peace and good grace for what you must all surely endure for the love of our liege lord Edward Plantagenet our King, Overlord Supreme of England, Ireland, Wales and now… Scotland." Father Anthony limps forward and stands in front of Cressingham's horse, clasps his hands and raises his eyes to the heavens; then he looks down while making the sign of the Holy Cross. Father Anthony stands before the soldiers, sermonising assurances of divine forgiveness to the gathering of penitent believers, absolving them all of sin, guilt, blame or earthly penalties and consequence. He then quotes from the scriptures… "By the word of the Lord, he sayeth to all his enemies and non-believers, that I will fill your mountains, your hills and your valleys with your dead. Your rivers will be filled with your people, slaughtered by the sword of God. Then, your land will turn red with the blood of your children and I shall make your land desolate forevermore. Then you will know that I am the Lord, that I alone am the one true God... Ezekiel thirty-five, Amen..." Cressingham makes the sign of the Holy Cross; then he calls out, "All Mount..."

The men mount their horses with clear hearts and minds, with no doubts that the tasks they will soon perform is in the name of God and to protect their blessed king and his righteous Crown. Cressingham rallies all of his soldiers. "Men, you have travelled for a day and a night with only water and dry fish for sustenance. The reason for this is for Godliness and purity of mind. The cause is for the crushing of sedition and blasphemy the pagans of this land have shown to our great King before the very eyes of our Lord God. We shall now go forth into these lands of wickedness and chastise these seditious Scotch for their heathen ways. They have caused you to be deprived of the basest of comforts, and so it is the King and Gods will, that warm food, the pleasures of despoiling heathen women in bondage, shall all be yours as just reward for your forthcoming endeavours and your sacrifice to enact the blessed cause. Carry out my orders with great zeal and diligence men, then these rewards and comforts will be yours for the taking." The men of the troop cheer and hurrah their beloved Cressingham. De Percy mounts then both he and Cressingham canter to the front of their troop, leading them onward towards Comunnach Castle.

* * *

In Glen Afton, Marjorie has long since returned to Comunnach. Mharaidh, knowing that Alain will be home soon, is busier than usual that morning in the kitchens, making the Wallace Keep as homely as possible for his return. Everyday chores around the glen still have to be maintained, with the old men working the fields and livestock, while the women and children collect chook's eggs, bake, salt fish and meat, spin, weave and a host of other necessary tasks, typical of the daily life in the glen. Mharaidh, auld Jean and Katriona go about their chores too, preparing vittals in the Keep kitchens.

"Yeaaach…" groans Katriona "I hate gutting rabbits, it stinks." Mharaidh laughs at Katriona's disgust, she says, "Wait till all the men are back Katriona, I'm sure they will greatly appreciate your hard work." Mharaidh smiles at Katriona, who is still retching while attempting to pull the skin from the body of a rabbit. Auld Jean notices that Katriona is struggling with her chores and thinks perhaps it's best that some fresh air would help her cope with her nausea. She says, "C'mon outside with me Katriona me darlin' girl, we can sit out there awhile and be crackin' some acorns for the stew." They both leave the kitchens and go outside into the fresh glen air, where Katriona looks around at the wild beauty of the landscape. She holds her breath and puts her hands on her stomach, she can feel the baby kicking, she is so exited to be expecting a second child to her beloved Bo' Stephen. Katriona exclaims, "I can hardly contain myself waiting on his return Maw." auld Jean replies, "I know how you feel darlin', I used to feel the same about wee Graham when he used to go away on campaigns in the service of the King, but then one day he stopped going away at all and he's been by my side or under my feet ever since." Katriona laughs, then she looks around the glen, it's bereft of all the young men who travelled to England with Alain. She senses the empty spaces where the men should be doing their work, but she misses most of all the teasing and playful nuisances of her loving husband Stephen. Auld Jean and Katriona watch the children playing and the other women going about their chores, then they smile when they notice wee Graham sleeping of his excess on a great pile of wool, with little Stephen fast asleep in his arms. Katriona peers in the direction Stephen will be travelling in the vain hope he may come home early, then she sees something unfamiliar in the distance, she cannot quite make it out... "Maw, that looks like it's Alain's party is coming home over the southern pass o' the Black Craig." Auld Jean says "That cannae be them home already, surely?" With eyes like a hawk, auld Jean squints into the distance, "There are too many o them, and it's far too early to be Alain or Cospatrick. I wonder who these folks are?"

The meandering pace of the long troop of horse-soldiers with pennants and flags lazily billowing out behind them, doesn't demonstrate anything other than it is a large patrol on its way to Ayr or Glasgow and just happens to have wondered into this particular glen. As the troop gain closer and pass the old men working the fields, the workers hardly pay them any heed, it's not until they begin to notice the unusual style of armour and strange looking symbols on their flags that many of the old men had never seen before that they take notice, they begin to watch these strangers curiously...

De Percy speaks to Cressingham, "With your permission my lord, I wish to explore my excesses this day. I feel that I must demonstrate to both you and your men how a Percy may conduct oneself in the chastisement of seditioners" Cressingham chortles and shrugs his shoulders, there has not been a torture, death or defilement he and his men have not witnessed, or committed during their long campaigns. This mere boy could never impress them. Eventually the

English troops arrive at the corrals below Wallace Keep, Mharaidh comes out to greet the strangers. She says with a welcoming smile, "Good morn' to you all good sirs." De Percy replies as both he and Cressingham pull their horses close to the stairwell, "And a good morn' to you M'lady." Mharaidh signals for the stable boys to come over and tend the horses, then Cressingham and De Percy make their way up to the promontory stairs to greet Mharaidh. Looking at Cressingham Mharaidh says, "If it pleases you my Lord, you look as though you have travelled far, do stay awhile, rest and enjoy the hospitality of a hot meal for both you and your men."

Smiling at the beautiful Mharaidh, De Percy politely replies, "Why thank you m'lady." Mharaidh says, "Please forgive me good sirs. I am Lady Mharaidh Wallace of Glen Afton, my husband is sir Alain Wallace, he's away on royal business, but he'll be home soon. Pray tell me, what brings you through our Glen?" Cressingham replies, "I do thank you m' lady, I am lord Hugh De Cressingham, treasurer to King Edward. And this is squire De Percy, at your service." Mharaidh acknowledges the introduction as Cressingham continues; "We travel to Comunnach on the Kings business." Mharaidh looks at Cressingham, "Please, tell your men they may rest and quarter at the billets over yonder and I will tend to all your refreshments and vittals, and please, you and your squire are most welcome into my home. Follow me good sirs."

Bowing his head gracefully, Cressingham replies, "Thank you for your offer of hospitality Lady Wallace, you are too kind by far." Mharaidh smiles, then she replies, "Only the courtesy I would wish shown to my husband on his travels, I could not do less for you my lord." De Percy pulls a small leather bag from his saddlebags then he follows Cressingham and Mharaidh into the Keep. As they enter the main hall, Mharaidh approaches the great feasting table and pulls a chair out for each of them, "Pray be seated." Cressingham ignores the seat and walks over to sit on a chair beside the great fireplace. Though the fire is unlit, he rests there while De Percy casually wanders around the room looking at everything, as though he is repulsed by what he sees. Mharaidh sits at her usual place at the great table when Percy approaches the seat normally reserved for Alain and sits down. "My husband's seat sir," says Mharaidh. De Percy replies, "No matter, I don't think he will mind that I warm his seat in his absence, do you not think it so... Lady Wallace?"

Sensing a strange and cold attitude from her guests, Mharaidh dismisses her feelings and makes conversation while Cressingham takes out a small parchment roll and studies it for a few moments, then he glances at de Percy. Mharaidh enquires; "Have you travelled far good sirs?" De Percy ignores her polite question and throws a small bag of silver coins on the table. "M'lady." says de Percy, "We would not wish to impose upon your generous and very kind hospitality, we have a hundred souls with us that require fare sustenance. I would pay you well for any cattle, hog and sheep that need to be slaughtered, that my men may dine and gain their strength and vigour once more, for soon I would wish them to be happy in their work, would this suffice?"

Standing up, Mharaidh pushes the bag of coin back along the table towards de Percy. "Sir, pray do keep your silver, as you are my guests I am obliged and more than pleased to make good vittals for you and your men..." Suddenly there's a crash at the door of the hall as wee Graham comes rushing in, quickly followed by Katriona. Wee Graham says, "Ah'm so sorry Ma'am, but ah was fast asleep and didn't hear these fella's coming into the glen." seeing Mharaidh's guests, he enquires, "Would you two fella's be likin' some fine refreshments? Maybe a wee dram or two to take the dust aff yer flaky tongues?" De Percy pulls a kerchief from his sleeve and holds it to his nose, "Good Lord M'lady, but what is this strange looking little creature? And what was that amusing gargling noise that it made just now?" Wee Graham appears bewildered, "What the fuck did he just say Ma'am?" De Percy exclaims, "Ha, the pungent creature does make noises like it can talk, but truly, it does stink awfully." Wee Graham clenches his fists and moves at speed towards de Percy, "Who the fuck do you think yer talkin'..." Mharaidh raises her hand, "Its all right Graham, you go and help Tam, I will tend to our guests." Wee Graham replies as he reluctantly leaves the hall, "Aye Ma'am, ah will, but ahl no be far away if yie be needin' me." De Percy laughs, "I know what that strange little creature is, it's one of French Philip's mangy old poodles from his court; you know, the ones that walk about on their two back legs yapping for morsels and attention."

Cressingham hadn't turned his head, but he laughs at de Percy's attempted humour. Mharaidh speaks to Katriona, "Please, tell auld Tam and wee Graham to cut out enough sheep, cattle, hogs and some game birds for the slaughter then ask auld Jean to be organizing a feast for all our guests right away." Katriona watches the guests cautiously. She is angry at the disrespect shown to Mharaidh and the contempt for her father displayed by de Percy, she replies, "Aye ma'am, will I get the great cauldrons a' boiling for stewing some gruel too?" Mharaidh replies, "Aye do that please Katriona, and make all ready at the long tables, we shall please our English guests with Scots hospitality."

As Katriona leaves the hall, Mharaidh lifts the bag of silver from the table and offers it back to Percy. She says, "Please take this back sir; for you are our guests, there is no need for transaction here." De Percy lays the bag of coin back on the table in front of him, he smirks then replies, "I defer to your kindness M'lady, but I insist..." Mharaidh spends the rest of morning entertaining De Percy and Cressingham, while auld Jean, Katriona, auld Tam and wee graham organize the afternoon feast for their guests. Wee Graham says, "Better keep an eye on these English fella's Tam, for there's somethin' no' fuckin good or right about them." Auld Tam replies, "Ahm on it already Graham, I've sent a couple o' birds up to Malcolm and Ranald, letting them know there's English soldiery here in the glen and to be getting down here quick n' fast." Katriona and the other girls are busily baking bannocks scones and bisckos while making sure that there is food a plenty for all of the English guests.

Mid-day soon approaches and the household food and vittals preparing all morning will soon be cooked to perfection under the masterful eye of auld Jean. She says to Katriona, "Ah hope these Sudrons have a fine pallet and appreciation o' our haggis, stovies and the blackest o' puddins that ever did grace a table. Away and tell Mharaidh everything will be ready in a wee while." Returning to the main hall, Katriona reports to Mharaidh, "All food and nourishment will be ready soon ma'am. Maw is askin' if yiez want to prepare to come to the tables?" Mharaidh replies, "Thank you Katriona, we shall attend in a moment." As Katriona leaves the tableside, De Percy grabs hold of her skirts and pulls her close so that she cannot move away, he laughs, but Katriona says nothing. She begins to flush and anger is evident in her face, but still she doesn't say anything, she just stares at De Percy with utter contempt in her eyes.

"SIR..." exclaims Mharaidh. De Percy laughs and releases Katriona, who quickly leaves the room. De Percy says, "Your bitch maid looks as though she may be about to pup out a Scotch mongrel methinks." Mharaidh glares at de Percy,

"Sir, we Scots do not abase ourselves with a tongue so foul as yours. Please do not disgrace your station while you are a guest in my home." Ignoring Mharaidh's retort, De Percy looks contemptuously about the hall of the Keep. "Your home?" exclaims de Percy, he sneers again "I thought this was your stable M'lady or more likely a hogs midden, surely you cannot live in such foul quarters as this?" Mharaidh is furious, "How dare you sir…" Immediately Cressingham stands up and walks over to Mharaidh, "I do apologise for his rudeness M'lady but it's not really his fault. He was born a bastard and most times he cannot help himself."

Cressingham turns to De Percy "Apologise to Lady Wallace at once you ignorant young fool." Mharaidh is relieved the elder knight has put the sinister behaviour of De Percy in check, but De Percy is livid. Mharaidh and Cressingham watch his face go red and flush with embarrassment. Cressingham is impatient, he demands an apology from De Percy, "Apologise to lady Wallace immediately you inconsiderate fop." De Percy is thoroughly embarrassed by this chastisement, reluctantly he offers an apology, "Do please excuse my behaviour M'lady, I can only think I'm overtired and witless by my inconsiderate behaviour, I meant you nor your maid no offence. Please accept my humble apologies." For a moment, Mharaidh glares at de Percy; then she replies, "Your apology is accepted sir." Cressingham turns to Mharaidh and holds his arm out that she may clasp it as her chaperone, "My apologies too Lady Wallace. Now, shall we gather everyone together? I have a special message to deliver to you and the people of this beautiful valley from my lord good King Edward."

Walking towards the outer doors, Cressingham observes De Percy's behaviour closely, he's curious as to how the young squire plans to carry out his duties, for he has deliberately angered De Percy by humiliating him in front of Mharaidh. He thinks to himself, A good way to stir up his bile. Though he has to admit to himself that he is being thoroughly entertained by De Percy's behaviour. "M'lady," says Cressingham "I would wish everyone resident here in this valley to be present for this speech, it will be given by my young squire De Percy here. I am sure you would agree, he does need practice with his communication, and speaking on behalf of my liege Lord, I am sure De Percy will now be more than keen to demonstrate common courtesy and propriety." Mharaidh, Cressingham and De Percy emerge from the Keep into the early afternoon sun and stand on the stone flag stoop at the front doors. Mharaidh calls over some young boys playing nearby, "Boys, will you be running out and telling everyone that I require them all to be present in the courtyard above the corral. And those that are cooking, please tell them to simmer their duties, as we have Lord Cressingham and Squire De Percy come to deliver a very special message from none other than the King of England himself."

De Percy says, "A moment, m'lady, I require everyone to be present, none of any age would wish to be absent from this speech. I have a sense they will find joy and great salvation upon hearing my words." Mharaidh feels the hairs on the back of her neck stand up. Cressingham enquires, "Exactly how many are hereabouts this day m'lady?" Mharaidh replies, "There are about fifty-five old men, seventy or so women and girls, and over forty children, not counting the herders in the hills and those away to the town of Ayr for provisions." Cressingham replies, "I thank you m'lady," then he enquires, "May we sit down here at this long table? My bones are weary from our long travel and it is such a beautiful view of your valley from here?"

"Of course my lord, I am so sorry, I wasn't thinking. Please be seated…" Mharaidh continues, "Will you please excuse me good sirs? I will be but a few moments, for I must make sure that all will be in attendance for the delivery of your King's message." Mharaidh leaves them both sitting at the table and walks back into the Keep. Cressingham beckons de Percy. "Send instructions to the soldiers at the billets to follow all of these heathens into the courtyard, and make sure the ring of guards is sealed." De Percy replies, "At once My lord." He quickly beckons a soldier, whispers to him, then the soldier rushes away. De Percy and Cressingham talk together as they wait at the long table for all to gather.

Meanwhile, Mharaidh is concerned at the presence of the English. She cannot rationalise what her concerns are, but her instinct is welling up fearful inside her. The sinister foreboding that she felt earlier is flooding back. At that moment, she sees wee Jamie playing with wool spinning sticks in the kitchens with Caoilfhinn and Stephen. Mharaidh waves to beckon Jamie discreetly but with a sense of urgency, thankfully he sees her and runs to her side with little Caoilfhinn. "Jamie," says Mharaidh "Oh Jamie, you must listen to me carefully… take Caoilfhinn and little Stephen out the back door of the Keep. Now you mustn't let these soldiers see you, have you got that? I need you to hide… like it's a special game." Jamie nods. "Good," says Mharaidh, then she continues "I want you to follow the Craig burn away up the hill to the Herders croft, hide Caoilfhinn and Stephen away over at the obhainn in the Glen back. Then you're to take a Garron and ride like the wind to Comunnach castle and tell lady Marjorie there is a large troop of English soldiers here, and that she's to make great speed back here with her men. Tell her I fear something is greatly amiss by the presence of these English… and be careful, you must not let them see you."

Cautiously, Mharaidh walks the children to the back door of the Keep without gaining attention. Jamie, with little Stephen and Caoilfhinn in hand, rush over to some thick gorse bush clusters near the back of the Keep and hide there for a moment, unseen by the English soldiers. Thinking it safe, Jamie cautiously leads the younger children up the blind side of the gully toward the herder's croft. The tension makes Mharaidh's heart beat like a thundering drum as she watches the children disappear safely from sight. Feeling slight relief in knowing the children are now safe, Mharaidh knows it will not be too long before Marjorie will be back with an armed troop from Comunnach Castle. As she turns from the door she is startled, Father Anthony stands silently at the door watching her every move. Mharaidh feels a wave of panic surge through her body; her mind is racing...

What did he see? What did he hear? Father Anthony, a thin-mouthed man with a pox marked face, dressed in a simple black Benedictine coarse habit stares at Mharaidh. She quickly composes herself. He says, "Shall we return to squire Percy Lady Wallace? He is not a person to be kept waiting." Mharaidh is frantic with worry, but she replies calmly, "Of course." As she passes Anthony on her way to the door, she is almost overwhelmed by the odour of stale urine emanating from this man of the cloth. She hurriedly walks ahead of him as he quietly limps behind her. Mharaidh and the chaplain emerge from the front doors of the Keep to join Squire Percy and lord Cressingham outside. De Percy waits impatiently then grins upon seeing Mharaidh approach with Chaplain Anthony. "Splendid, splendid." exclaims de Percy, "I think I see everyone is present, is that correct Lady Wallace. Will you account for everyone if you may." Mharaidh looks around all the faces then replies, "I believe it so." Waving cordially to everyone, de Percy calls out, "Come a little closer."

The old men, women and children shuffle forward till they are all gathered tightly in front of the doors. The English soldiers have everyone penned in and the atmosphere is becoming very tense. Mharaidh notices wee Graham and auld Tam looking up at her, an understanding of something ominous connects between them; they signal to her that they too are acutely aware. Mharaidh feels slight relief knowing that she is not alone in her fears. She knows wee Graham and auld Tam will act quickly should anything untoward happen.

De Percy claps his hands and in a light-hearted tone of voice, he says, "Now Lady Wallace, shall we start with the message before we all retire to enjoy the fine fare your good people have prepared?" Mharaidh is slightly puzzled by de Percy's obvious good manners, and his courtesy. She hears Cressingham cough behind her. She glances at him then he nods for her to respond to de Percy, who is patiently focused on everyone awaiting her reply. Mharaidh reaches out her open hand and replies, "Aye, that would be fine sir." Addressing the small gathering of the household and glen, De Percy begins his speech, "We are now the keepers of our lord King Edwards peace in this realm, and we have been sent here to deliver a message to you all, or should I say, deliver a message to your relative sir Malcolm Wallace of Ach na Feàrna in particular."

The small gathering starts muttering, as some do not speak English, only Dál Riatan or Beurla-reagaird Gaelic, others translate for them. De Percy pauses for a moment and whispers to Mharaidh "Do they speak or even understand English?" Mharaidh replies, "Most do understand good sir." De Percy continues, "Well then… you all may be wondering why I deliver this message to you personally and not to sir Malcolm Wallace directly, but in due course this will become most apparent as to why." De Percy turns to Mharaidh.

"M'lady I find that the rumours abound are true, that this shire is truly blessed with very Bonnie women as you say hereabouts, and you have prepared meal and looked after us exceptionally well this fine morn... M'lady you are the very angel of kind and congenial hospitality."

This unexpected compliment is welcome, Mharaidh smiles, feeling that perhaps her earlier fears were unfounded, "Why, thank you for your kind words good sir." De Percy nods politely in her direction then says, "But I must say to you m'lady, that looking around this gathering I do not see all of you." Mharaidh looks curiously at de Percy; she is puzzled by his remark. Could it be he means Jamie, wee Stephen and Caoilfhinn? She says, "I know not of what you mean good sir, we have sent for everyone, all are here present as you requested?" De Percy takes a step back, "I must apologise m'lady but I did not make myself clearly understood. I will repeat myself anyhoo," Walking directly behind Lady Mharaidh as she faces her kinfolk, De Percy moves slowly up behind her till she can feel his stale breath upon her neck, he says, "I cannot see all of you Lady Wallace... so please be so kind as to remove those filthy rags you think doest make a Lady pretty." A sudden feeling of nausea and panic sweeps through Mharaidh, she turns around as she gathers her senses... "Sir, I do not understand you..." Mharaidh doesn't finish her sentence as an armoured fist smashes into her mouth and knocks her semi-conscious to the ground. Instantly some of the older men and women of the household rush forward to be by her side, but Percy's men brutally club and beat them to the ground.

"Sedition..." exclaims De Percy "We must quell this riotous assembly before it spreads throughout the realm." Triumphantly holding his hand high, De Percy stands proud and addresses the frightened household. "This whore deceives us by offering us false hospitality, she wrongs us and betrays us by sending a boy for soldiers to come to us, for why, I cannot think why? We have been nothing but kind, even offering to pay her for any food we may consume. But we shall match her miserable deceitful ways with punitive measure. Sir Malcolm Wallace will now have the message delivered that my liege Lord does send to those who show us no respect. By her actions, this whore broke the law of our King, and for instigating this treasonous act… she shall be punished." De Percy reaches down and grabs Mharaidh by the hair and violently pulls her to her feet, he pulls her face close to his and sneers as he spits out the words...

"My soldiers pegs need rattled m'lady and rattles a plenty they shall have this day. You should thank me Lady Mharaidh Wallace, for you and the female of your species will have the joy of real men and not some mountain animal. Now remove your rags…" Auld Tam and wee Graham watch this madness with the steely eyes of old campaign veterans. Tam has noticed that a young English soldier nearby is distracted while watching the abuse Mharaidh is suffering at the hands of de Percy.

Auld Tam nudges wee Graham and sees that he too is ready and prepared to move, these two old soldiers will save Lady Mharaidh, or die in the attempt. Whatever happens next, it will cost these English soldiers dearly this day; for anything and everything that auld Tam and wee Graham have ever learned about the arts of war, will all be brought to bear on the English in moments. Suddenly, De Percy slaps Mharaidh brutally across the face, knocking her back to the ground, he grabs her by the hair and shakes her violently, "Take your rags off now you filthy whore of Babylon, or it will be worse for you." Mharaidh is totally stunned and bewildered, her eyes are swelling up, blood runs from her nose and mouth, but she remains defiant. De Percy screams in her face, "Then don't say that I didn't warn you, you Scotch whore." He nods to one of his men at arms who then opens door of the Keep, a soldier walks out dragging the lifeless body of young Jamie along the ground by his leg; the soldier throws Jamie's body onto the steps beside Mharaidh. She sees that Jamie's throat has been violently cut, with his head remaining attached to his body by a mere sliver of flesh. The unimaginable shock amongst the gathering is like a thunderbolt hitting them from the sky, Jamie's foster mother Aileen screams hysterically and runs to gather the lifeless body of her wee boy. As she bends over to cradle him, the English soldier who had dragged Jamie out the door of the Keep draws his sword, with one sweep of his weapon the English soldier beheads the distraught woman. Panic and screaming erupts from the captive inhabitants and fills the glen with the sound of an almost unearthly high-pitched crescendo as Aileen's head rolls along the stone-flagged floor,

The English soldiers begin to brutally slash and stab with sword and lance into the crowd till everyone is huddled in a corner of the courtyard. Tears run down Mharaidh's face as she stands barefoot and shivering in front of the Keep, her mind almost gone, fraught with desperation and concern as to the whereabouts of Caoilfhinn and Stephen. She hears voices in the distance when a sharp flash and shocking pain shoots through her head as she is knocked to the ground. As she lay semi-conscious, Mharaidh could hear the pitiful sobbing of women and moans from her wounded and dying kinfolk. She hears de Percy's voice. "Before God, you have all been tried and found guilty of sedition and treason, we shall now hear the word of God spoken through the mouth of father Anthony." Her head spinning, Mharaidh drifts into unconsciousness. Father Anthony limps out of the castle doors, holding little Stephen and Caoilfhinn by the hands. Katriona screams "STEPHEN..." Immediately a soldier grabs her then pins her arms behind her back and brutally clamps a hand over her mouth. Unable to move or speak, tears flow as Katriona is forced to watch...

There is silence as Father Anthony holds a crucifix high and prepares to quote the scriptures. He kneels and looks to the heavens, "It is Gods will... The lord sayeth that any man who is captured they shall see their little children dashed to death before their very eyes, their homes will be sacked and their wives shall be raped, then they shall be run through by the sword, for I will stir up the Medes against Babylon and no amount of silver or gold will buy them off. The armies of the lord will shoot down the young people with arrows and the soldiers of the lord will have no mercy on helpless babies for they will show no compassion for the children... they shall all be damned... Isaiah thirteen, Amen."

Making the sign of the Holy Cross once more, Anthony nods towards the English soldier who had brought Jamie's body out of the Keep, the soldier steps forward and raises a heavy iron war-mace above a bewildered Stephen's head, Mharaidh stirs and sees Aileen and Jamie's bloody bodies lying beside her. She reaches out... momentarily, Mharaidh and the soldier with the mace glance at each other... then he grins, she realises what's about to happen... Mharaidh screams "NO..." but in a mighty arc, the soldier brings the mace crashing down on little Stephen's head, dashing his brains and blood all over Mharaidh, little Stephen shudders violently, topples over and falls to the ground, shaking uncontrollably in his death tremors. Katriona is helpless as she witnesses the brutal murder of little Stephen, her screams are muffled and her body convulses at the scene before her.

Panic and screaming erupts once more from the folk of the glen when the soldier brutally dashes little Stephen's brains with the mace once more, he then picks up Stephen's shaking body from the ground and hurls the body high into the air and over the heads of the glen folk, spraying his lifeblood and brains asunder. Cressingham chortles as he drinks from a flagon. The assault placed on Katriona's senses are overwhelming as she loses consciousness. Suddenly, Old Jean breaks free from the cordon before wee Graham can stop her and she runs towards Mharaidh, a soldier blocks her path but she smashes a fist into his face, knocking him back. Another attempts to strike her with his sword but she deftly catches the blade with her bare hands, twists it to the side then grabs the soldier and throws him bodily over the promontory down into the corral below. She reaches out to grab little Caoilfhinn when two English soldiers block her with halberd axes. De Percy calls out to her...

"And what do you want you old witch?" Auld Jean ignores him. With tears streaming down her face and blood gushing profusely from the deep wounds in her hands, she reaches out to hold and shelter Caoilfhinn. De Percy instantly draws his sword and runs his blade through her chest-wall, burying the sword up to the hilt and piercing through her back. Auld Jean groans and falls to her knees. De Percy puts his foot on the side of her face, pushes, then pulls his sword back out, releasing a torrent of blood as Jean falls over dying.

Raging beyond ken, wee Graham screams insanely as he pulls out his sgian dhu and rushes forward, double-slashing a young soldier across both eyes, blinding him instantly. Wee Graham sidesteps another soldier about to attack him, grabs him by the waist and swings round low behind the soldier and viciously stabs upwards and repeatedly into the Englishman's groin, his keen blade easily cutting through the soldiers arteries and scrotum. Other English soldiers quickly move in on wee Graham, but he uses the blinded soldier as a shield, he rush-shoves forward behind his shield towards his beloved Jean and Mharaidh. In the ensuing chaos, auld Tam pulls out his gutting knife; grabs the spear of the soldier standing next to him and pulls back hard, causing the soldier to fall forwards into Tam, who deftly spins him around and cuts the soldiers throat from ear to ear. Auld Tam turns swiftly and blocks a sword blow with his forearm and plunges his blade downwards into the neck of another Englishman, blood sprays everywhere. He moves forward, avoiding a spear thrust while ramming his blade deep into the face of another soldier, he pulls it back out and slashes the spear soldier across the throat. Tam duck's under a sword swing then sinks the keen blade into the soldier's groin, twists the blade, pulls it out and strikes up like a skewer, the blade easily sinks deep into the soldiers throat and in below his tongue.

"STOP THEM…" screams De Percy in a panic. An English soldier lunges forward to spear wee Graham, who quickly pulls his human guard aside as the spear glances wee Graham's head and plunges into the face of the soldier he is using as a shield. The spear soldier tries to pull his weapon back out of his comrade, but wee graham leaps on him like a howling wolf, stabbing the soldier mercilessly about the face, eyes and throat. Tam sees a soldier with his sword arm raised to strike wee graham, he moves forward and plunges his gutting knife deep into the soldiers armpit, the soldier screams in pain then Tam stabs him so hard up under his chin, the knife blade goes up through the soldiers mouth and into his brain. Tam forces his blade up with all his strength, lifting the soldier clean off his feet, but he snaps his blade as it enters the soldier's skull. Suddenly, a mace strike from behind fells Tam, stunned by the impact, he reaches out, grabs the soldier and pulls him close, stabbing the broken end of the knife deep into the soldiers eye socket, screwing it inwards with all his strength. It takes four Englishmen to subdue auld Tam and beat him to the ground where they plunge their swords repeatedly into auld Tams chest and body.

Meanwhile, wee Graham is fighting like a rabid wildcat. He dives at the legs of a soldier, holds on tightly while cutting through the soldiers hamstrings and stabbing the inside of his thighs, shredding the unfortunate soldiers femoral arteries and saphemous veins. Wee Graham rolls away from the falling soldier then stabs another repeatedly about the kidney's then he springs up at another and slashes him across the throat. Suddenly Wee Graham is grabbed firmly by his hair, he spins around and slashes his blade through the soldier's wrist, cutting the artery then stabs the soldier repeatedly in the jaw and neck, wee Graham sees his next target as the English soldiers are failing to subdue this little man of total war. Sensing his opportunity, wee Graham rushes directly at De Percy who is fast retreating to hide behind Lord Cressingham. Graham manages to grip De Percy by the face as a soldier grabs and holds firm wee Grahams knife hand before he can strike de Percy, another soldier plunges a sword deep into Graham's back, then another soldier hacks him below the knee, breaking the bone and almost severing the leg. As wee Graham falls to the ground, he grabs the leg of a soldier who is raining blows down on his head, but wee Graham is relentless, he bites deep into the soldier's thigh and stabs him repeatedly about the genitals. The flurry of merciless blows from all the soldiers with their swords and maces finally subdue wee Graham, yet, despite his severe wounds, he is still struggling to get free and fight on.

Driven by extreme incensed hatred and defiance, wee Graham sinks his teeth into the hand of a soldier, drawing blood, but he is severely attacked till finally, he is beaten senseless to the ground. Cressingham shouts out to his enraged soldiers, "Halt, hold him firm men… wait… I said wait, do not kill him." Cressingham stands up and casually wanders over to look at wee Graham, who is now being pinned to the ground. Cressingham smiles, "Ah, much is the pity, it's too late for the other old one… but this one here, he deserves a heroes death, bring him to his knees."

The English soldiers drag the bloodied and dazed wee Graham to his knees. Through a misty haze and nausea, he defiantly spits at De Percy while Cressingham takes out his sword and hangs it above wee Grahams head. He places the sword tip gently between wee Graham's collarbone and throat then very slowly, he begins to push the sword deliberately downward and deep into wee Grahams body, taking great care not to kill him. Cressingham continues to sink the blade methodically down into wee Graham's chest, stopping only when the sword tip touches wee Grahams heart.

Cressingham smiles, then suddenly, he plunges the blade downwards, Wee Graham jerks upright, eyes wide-open, crystal clear and looking to the sky, his body shudders as Cressingham swiftly pulls the blade out of wee Graham's body, spraying blood high into the air. The soldiers release wee Graham: he rests a moment on his knees as tears roll down his bloody cheek. He looks at Jean, then to Katriona. He shudders again, then falls over, his eyes are completely focussed on the lifeless body of his dearest love auld Jean as his blood pumps profusely from his wounds, spraying all over the boots of de Percy, much to his profound annoyance. Cressingham states with great satisfaction, "A Praetorian death for such a noble warrior." He wipes his blade clean of blood and walks back over to his seat at the table.

Wee Graham, auld Tam and auld Jean have succumbed close to their beloved Mharaidh, they had fought to the death as true guardians of the Aicé. The soul and spirits of auld Tam, wee Graham and their dead kinfolk are now released to be free of the earthly pains and cares of this world, now gone to a better place. While the English soldiers brutalise the surviving clanfolks into submission, a flock of wild geese fly overhead, as though they are gathering for the sole purpose of collecting the newborn spirits to carry them west to the land of eternal youth, Tír na nÓg,

De Percy had panicked and everyone had seen it; he quickly tries to compose himself as Cressingham approaches and speaks to him quietly, "You have just lost us five good men dead and eight badly wounded De Percy, and by the hands of two old Scotch beggars and his whore. You had better regain your authority, or I will… Now pull yourself together, be calm and continue as if nothing has happened, or the men will laugh at you from which you will never recover, now take back control." Seething with anger, De Percy quickly regains domination of his nerves, he must now regain the good impression towards Cressingham he had been so carefully nurturing these last few days and try to regain any respect that Cressingham's men ever had for him.

De Percy begins by addressing the frightened Wallace household of Glen Afton. He says, "Now you see resistance will not affect our endeavours? It now appears that we must have an even greater example meted out so that you Scotch may understand our severe but necessary measures." De Percy reaches down and pulls Mharaidh cruelly along the ground by her hair. She sees little Caoilfhinn, bewildered and weeping uncontrollably, seeking safety by hugging tightly to the leg of father Anthony, hiding her face away in his cassock to shelter from the evil she is witnessing. Mharaidh reaches out to her daughter, but De Percy stamps down hard on her hand, pinning it to the ground. Father Anthony caresses Caoilfhinn's hair gently, all the while smiling at Mharaidh with an air of cruel satisfaction. Suddenly De Percy yanks Mharaidh up violently by the hair, "Listen to me whore, if you want this flock of sheep to breath a little longer, then do as I say…" De Percy twists Mharaidh's hair tighter, forcing her high onto her toes. He stares into the hazel eyes of Mharaidh and speaks to her quietly… "Now m'lady, I require you to remove your rags, I want to see all of you. If you do not, I will execute all here very slowly, as I have days yet to wait on your husband's return, so I shall be in no haste."

Katriona appears to recover from her faint, but is witless and in a daze. Mharaidh sees blackish blood running down between Katriona's legs and covering her bare feet. De Percy calls out to Katriona, "You… house-whore… come here, quickly damn you. Help this lady whore to remove her rags, and the rest of you, I want all of you stripped naked, every man, woman and child." The women and children cry and weep hysterically in fear of what the English may do next. Cressingham beckons De Percy and whispers, "Set the sexes apart and separate children from their parents, when they see each others vulnerability, it weakens any resolve to resist." De Percy turns to face the household and calls orders to the soldiers, "Separate the men women and children; strip them all of their rags. When they are all naked, take the men to the kailyard, for I am sure you men of God need some relief with your lances and horse-boots this day. We must be of a good appetite when this work is done. But first, let them see the naked body of this fine Lady of so-called Scotch nobility."

Turning to face Lady Mharaidh, De Percy slaps her viciously across the face, breaking her nose and splitting her lips. "Woman, understand me, this is not for your pleasure or our titillation that I do this to you, but if you do not make speed, I shall deliver punitive justice on young Katriona here." With tears rolling down her cheeks, Mharaidh begins to undress, Katriona appears as though her wits have gone as she helps Mharaidh remove her clothing. Her clan weep and cry out for mercy as they witness her abuse. "Oh do hurry up." says De Percy impatiently. It is not long before Mharaidh and Katriona are both naked. They try to hide away their vulnerable nakedness by cowering and covering themselves with their hands, but De Percy orders two soldiers to force Mharaidh and Katriona's arms tightly behind their backs and bind them securely, then he pulls Mharaidh's hair again, forcing her face toward the sky. He reaches down between her legs and begins defiling her. Powerless to resist, Mharaidh spits in his face. De Percy laughs aloud then runs a finger through her spittle and licks it from his finger. He grins at her, amused; then he turns his attention to the frightened naked household before him and smirks. Mharaidh sees her opportunity; she lowers her head onto de Percy's shoulder and nuzzles him gently, much to his surprise.

Suddenly, Mharaidh sinks her teeth into his neck. De Percy screams and cries aloud, trying desperately to tear himself away and push her off, but Mharaidh clings on, biting deep into his neck. Soldiers try pulling her off, but she holds on, biting ever deeper, despite the blows raining down on her head, a soldier comes in from behind, sticks his fingers into her eyes and pulls her head back with all his might. The searing pain causes Mharaidh to release her grip, but she has ripped a mass of bloody skin from de Percy's neck.

De Percy tries to stem the blood pouring from the wound but the burning pain makes him jump about and run around in circles screaming for help. The soldiers laugh heartily while Cressingham walks over to De Percy and grabs him roughly by the face with one hand and pushes his head away to the side… he laughs and say's, "Oh it is just a mere flea bite Percy, you will live, unfortunately." Cressingham calls over to a soldier standing nearby… "Rip some of the material from that sow's dress and wrap it round this poor little girl Percy's neck wound." Cressingham looks at De Percy with contempt, then he turns towards the cowering weeping people of the glen. "Men, take these peasants to the corrals. I want to show these women here how much we English do rather enjoy our sport. When you get there, put the old men in the centre of the field then bind the women's arms fast, bind all of them, for who knows what pestilence they may carry in their claws and teeth."

While the soldiers brutally herd the three family groups down to the corrals, De Percy, almost beside himself with fury, pushes away the soldier who is tending him and holds the cloth to his own wound; he then storms over to where Mharaidh is laying. As she looks up at him in a daze, De Percy viciously kicks her in the face, knocking her senseless. De Percy again grabs Mharaidh by the hair, pulling her semi-conscious body close to him. When he hears her groan, he stops for a moment and senses the floral scents in her hair…

"Ah, it would seem that you savages may wash after all, and you my fine lady, you will soon wish that you were already dead, for I will make you pay dearly for your assault on one of England's finest soldiers of the Lord and good King Edward…" he barks out an order, "Bind this whore by the neck and drag her to yonder tree over there and secure her. I want her to watch the amusement her old men will now provide for us." Cressingham watches De Percy closely; he is amused and heartened to see the young squire making an attempt regain his composure. De Percy holds a kerchief to his bloodied neck and walks down to the corrals, where he immediately commands, "Send in the lancers and skewer the old cretins, but only once each mind you," De Percy continues, "I also wish to see the skill of flail and mace used in their miserable dispatch. The bravest of warriors who does dispatch the most with the flail alone will have first choice of these Scotch whores to rattle his peg in later this night." The horsemen enthusiastically spur their horses on and gallop into the corral with their lances dropped to begin the slaughter. Many old men take only deliberately inflicted flesh wounds and fall to the ground, where the destroyer hooves of the English cavalry trample and crush them underfoot. Others are cruelly bludgeoned by mace and axe. The wives, daughters and young women, wail at the sight of the butchery of their beloved fathers, husbands, brothers and sons. Finally, the English soldiers dismount and cruelly murder the remaining survivors with the flail. De Percy cries out, "Oh such mirth dear Cressingham, look, see how they wriggle when kissed by the blessed flail. Such pleasure we owe the Saracens for their mentoring of the Christians." Cressingham laughs, "Well really Percy, it was by example of the Papal Question the Saracens learnt that trick."

They both lift and drink a cup of wine each as they sit and observe the last of the wanton butchery, observing till naught but bloody heaps of gore adorn the corrals as the blood-soaked English soldiers walk triumphantly from the field of battle. Cressingham stands up; he says, "Gather onto me my brave soldiers. For I say to you all that you have excelled in your duty, now you may take to the feasting. And as for you de Percy, I say your father whomever he is, he would be proud of your work here this day. As a reward, you may take first choice of the women and children to unlock that dry rattle in your peg. Fine work young sirrah, fine work indeed." Cressingham is stoutly pleased by the delicacy to which De Percy is executing his duty, despite his amateurish mistakes. Though he had found it highly amusing to see the young fop scream and panic when lady Mharaidh had attacked him. "I must say to you too de Percy, I did have my doubts about your measure, I still do, but you do muse me greatly... and I feel that your temperament is well suited to peacekeeping the Scotch. Tell me young sirrah, what is your pleasure with the women?" De Percy sighs, "Well, there are some old hags who no peg would dare try to rattle or extract pleasure from, not even a Scotch peg I warrant you. But they should satisfy the basest of the men's instincts." They both laugh heartily, though De Percy is greatly relieved he has once again redeemed himself in front of Cressingham and his men. Calling out to a guard, De Percy says, "You there...I want you to fetch some of the men then go and hang those old hags from the bough's of yonder tree over there, take those witches that shall not be getting a pegging later this night. And only hang them by the hair of their heads, I want them to witness the evil doings of these traitors when they receive their just punishment for this day's rebellious sedition." Cressingham chortles, "My my de Percy, it would seem that there is absolutely no end to your enthusiasm and vigour, or your colourful imagination."

Nearby, Mharaidh regains consciousness, only to find she gagged and is bound naked to a tree, her face is extremely swollen from the beatings and her body covered in cuts and bruises... her once proud beautiful hair is now simply a mass of tugs clotted with blood. De Percy feigns sympathy as he walks over to her and looks into her eyes, "Now you see what happens when you Scotch heathens betray an English guest, do you see now what you have forced me do?" A Soldier approaches de Percy, "Sir, there are fourteen hags left, I fear the bough's may break from the weight of the witches." De

Percy glares at the soldier, "Some of your men are Smithfield butchers are they not?" The soldier nods positively, "Yes my Lord." De Percy continues, "Then I require you to incise the witches from cunny to teat. Let their entrails spill out to lighten the burden of the poor oak bough's. And slice off their eyelids too, dowse the sockets with kitchen vinegar, or piss if need be. I require their eyes to be open to witness all." The soldier immediately turns to carry out de Percy's command.

Father Anthony limps towards Cressingham and De Percy with little Caoilfhinn clinging to his hand, believing him to be keeping her safe from harm. "My Lords, if I may be so bold, I say to you that these heathen children here are born sinners, with your blessing I shall take them and verily I shall chastise and punish them in order to please our Lord God. I shall administer unto them appropriate and suitable justice for their sins, in that, they may be granted Gods peace as sinners, absolved and redeemed when they stand before the gates of heaven." De Percy grins, aware of the particular redemption nuances Father Anthony has in mind. Cressingham says, "I have witnessed such lessons before by priests upon children my dear Anthony. Indeed, a peculiarly lustful sermon it was too… but sadly, t'was not to my taste. But of course, you may take these heathen children to do with as you please." Father Anthony can hardly contain himself at the thought of the forthcoming applications and chastisement of the children of the glen. He thanks Cressingham and De Percy profusely, blesses both of them, then he hurriedly limps away to gather together his young flock.

Cressingham turns to de Percy, "Order our men to unbind the younger serving girls, but tether their ankles together as you would bind a feisty filly and slice through each heel to prevent any of them even thinking about running away, then let them serve us such fine fare as they have prepared for us this day, we should not wish to be appearing rude or ungrateful as guests of this household." De Percy replies, "At once my lord…" he hesitates; then he enquires "My lord, before we feast, I would like the men to remove the heads of the field sport and place them in little piles, cover them in pitch oil, but not to light them yet. I propose this eve that we shall have Scotch lanterns to light up this dark and evil place while our men are full and hearty rejoicing in doing Gods work this eve."

Looking at de Percy, almost in admiration, Cressingham says, "De Percy, your infinite pleasures and boundless spirit does provide me with great amusement. I rather fancy that Lady Wallace will surely benefit immensely from my peg this night." De Percy replies, "But of course my lord, please do take her, for I have plans for young Katriona and I will of course be busy myself. There are also a couple of young boys nearby I rather do fancy too." De Percy wants both women, but thinks it prudent and best served to be pleasing Edwards Master treasurer and bring Cressingham closer to his side. De Percy barks out an order "You men, I want you to take these two haggard witches and wash them thoroughly, they should be somewhat presentable to please Lord Cressingham and I later this eve." Cressingham almost thanks to de Percy, "Well done Percy, you command my men so well, but I advise you thus, do not get too enamoured with such temporary authority, for they will cut your throat in the blink of an eye should you slight me, or if I wish it so. Now come de Percy, we must dine and discuss this eves entertainment."

All through the remainder of the night, rapine and savagery continues. The horrific screams of women and children being tortured, abused and defiled, could be heard on the boundary hills, now manned by English sentinels who wait patiently, like nighthawks who hunt a sunset prey.

* * *

An early morning mist rises above the canopy of the Wolf and wildcat forest when Alain and his men pull their horses to a halt on the Boarsback crest of Auchenbroch. They can see in the distance, the peak of the Black Craig and further beyond, the tip of Loudon Hill. Alain and his Brother-in-law Sir Tam Halliday had left the Norham conference early with their men of the Glen Afton and Corriechd Gallóglaigh and had been riding hard and fast all night, with no stops for a lengthy rest. Alain looks at Halliday and says, "The men and horses need to rest awhile." Halliday replies, "Then I must be leaving yie Alain, I have to be travelling east from this point anyway and my men are anxious to get home to see their loved ones." Alain looks around and sees that his men are exhausted and very tired. "I understand Halliday, I think maybe I'll keep on going too, we've only a few hours left o' some hard riding to be reaching the Afton glen, I'm sure glad we departed Norham early though, as I've no' much o' a taste for all that nobility and their fine ways."

Halliday puts his hand on the shoulder of his kinsman, "It's been too long that our families have been apart Alain, this year will be different, and with young William to be wed in Lanark it'll be a grand occasion to bring all the clan up from Corriechd to see yie all. All of those years that I spent abroad serving foreign Kings were good, ach but, at the end of the day there is never going to be a place called home other than this land of out forefathers. Will you be telling wee Maw that I'll be bringing Dorinn up to meet her and the rest of the family very soon?"

"Aye, ah'll tell her," replies Alain, "She's talked a lot recently about how much she misses Dorinn, and wee Maw, she's no' getting any younger." Halliday laughs, "Aye, ah know that feeling in ma bones only too well Alain. It's a long enough time passed since we all sat together beside the slow runnin' waters o' the Annan flow, so ah reckon a return Fèis after the wedding will most certainly be in order." Alain nods his tired head in agreement. "Ah'll speak with Mharaidh when I get back, or if ah get back, for if I don't leave now, I think me and ma men will fall asleep here sittin' on our horses for a week."

Halliday laughs again, then he replies "Mind yie give my love to wee Maw, Mharaidh and the rest o' the clan." Alain replies, "I will Halliday, and you give my love to Dorinn, for we've missed yie both for awe these years yie have been away soldiering' abroad." The two kinsmen shake hands, "Aicé speed yie Alain…" Halliday smiles, then he and his men set off in the direction of Corriechd. Turning his horse, Alain addresses his men… "Clansmen, I for one intend to ride on for Glen Afton. Those of you who wish to come with me, mount now, and those who wish to rest here awhile, we'll tell your families that you'll not be a long time behind us." Though all of them are desperately tired, nobody wishes to remain behind. They mount their horses to follow their Chief on the road towards their homes and families.

* * *

Rain falls heavily like heavenly tears of sorrow that morning upon the fields and homesteads of Glen Afton. Cressingham, having spent the night in the bedchamber of Alain and Mharaidh, wakes. He lazily looks over at the battered body of Mharaidh, lying motionless on the cold stone floor beside the bed. He calls out, "Guard…" A soldier immediately enters the room and glances at the wretch lying naked on the floor. The soldier shudders at what he sees, Mharaidh has been severely assaulted and is covered in bloody bruises.

He can also see vicious looking bite marks about her thighs, breasts and face; its obvious Mharaidh has been horrifically abused. There are also deep welts all over her body and thick black blood pooling between her legs. Her face is a bloody swollen mass as a result of several beatings. Cressingham sits up and drawls, "Take her bloody carcass and throw it to the hogs... No wait, is she still breathing?" The soldier quickly checks her body for signs of life, "She breathes my lord." Cressingham barks an order, "Then take her away and bring her to her wits man, for I have entertainment planned for her husband to witness upon his return. Now, take her outside for she is stinking the place abominably."

The soldier grabs Mharaidh by the hair and drags her outside and throws her to the ground at the front doors of the Keep, he binds her hands tightly to the door rings then goes in search of ice-cold buckets of water to bring her out of her unconscious state. Cressingham, brazenly wearing Alain's night mantle, comes to the front door, yawns and pisses on Mharaidh as he enjoys the view of Glen Afton, then he notices a rider galloping fast towards the Keep. A sentry calls out "I think it's our boundary sentinel my lord." Cressingham waits at the door as the scout arrives, dismounts and runs up the steps to greet him, "My lord... the Norham treaty has concluded, Alain Wallace left early, he is but a few hours ride from here with a retinue of forty or fifty armed men." Cressingham calls for De Percy who is nearby, he immediately comes running over, "What to do my Lord?"

As they walk back inside the Keep, Cressingham calls out to the guard "Rouse all the men, today we lay waste to this pestilent place and leave Gods work to be finished by the Crow." De Percy enquires, "My lord, what shall we do with all the women and the girls?" Cressingham replies curtly, "Cut their throats and be quick about it." De Percy issues an order to his men to start killing the surviving folk of Glen Afton. The command quickly passes throughout the glen, much to the delight of the younger soldiers who relish in their apprenticeship duties, hoping to impress the veterans with their brutal skills. "Where is your wench? Enquires Cressingham, "Have you got rid of her yet?" De Percy nods his head, "Yes my lord, I disposed of her earlier this morning." De Percy laughs as he makes light of Katriona's demise. "She now simmers with the stew in the large cauldron outside the back of the kitchens. She was so cold in temperament I grew oh so tired and weary of her weeping. I thought that a little time in the simmering cauldron would warm her senses, but alas my lord, I fell asleep and she is now but mutton I fear. But I did have her child cut out so that she could at least see the little brute before she succumbed." Cressingham chortles, "You have a flair for doing Gods work in this land of Philistines Percy." De Percy replies "Why thank you my lord," He continues, "In fairness to the little Scotch brute yearning to be near its mother, it now cooks in a little pot beside her." Cressingham stares at De Percy in sombre curiosity, almost in disbelief. An indignant De Percy splutters, "I am not completely heartless my lord."

A Soldier standing nearby sniggers, De Percy glares at him "Why are you still standing there?" The Soldier nervously replies, "The children my Lord, what are we to do with them?" Cressingham looks at De Percy, "You deal with this." De Percy replies, "Dispatch them all with haste… then I want the men to cut off the women's breasts and lay them on the top bars of the corral, after all my good man, the returning husbandry of Afton may need to suckle on something of their loved ones after such a long journey. Cut off the heads too, pitch and light them then throw the carcasses into the hog pens, its time the beast of this place fed is on fine Wallace meat.

There is no need to be uncouth and thoughtless doing God's work, we must demonstrate some measure of benevolence." Cressingham beckons de Percy, "Walk with me." The two men enter the Keep where Cressingham calls for his wardrobe and dresser. While he waits, he speaks to de Percy. "We have a hundred men here Percy, well ninety or thereabouts due to your incompetence. I want all the men strategically placed on route to this shit-pile, when Alain Wallace and his men return here, my men will know what to do. The archers are to be allowed only two arrows each, they costs money you know. When the Scotch gather at the corral, the bowyers are to take down all of Wallace's men's horses first, then his men, by the time it's all over, I want our archers to have no arrows left in their quivers, if two hundred arrows cannot dispatch an unruly mob of forty-odd Scotch simpletons in a corral, I'll have every fifth man here castrated, flayed and hung, then I will have you flayed... do you understand me?" De Percy is taken aback, but he has clearly heard his master's orders. "I do my lord, your plan shall be set out immediately." Cressingham scowls, "And one more command that shall be obeyed de Percy... Alain Wallace is not to be harmed." De Percy is angered, but he knows Cressingham will certainly have him flayed if he is disobeyed, for he is feared for this particular calling mark. De Percy replies, "Yes my lord, right away my lord."

*   *   *

It's not long before Alain and his men ride through the southern gateway to the glen as the sun finally breaks through the grey clouds, it cheers his heart to see Glen Afton bask in the mid morning sun. As they slow down and bring their sweating, panting horses to a walking pace, Alain says to wee Graham's nephew Andrew on a horse beside him, "We'll soon be home now young fella." Andrew replies, "Aye Chief, it'll be grand to be home and put our feet up at our own fires." Cheerfully, they wander down the south road towards the corrals below the Keep, but they halt just far enough away, sensing something is very wrong, they notice small piles of what looks like charred animal carcass in the fields, suddenly, one of Alain's retinue calls out, "Those are bodies lying in the runrigs." Another exclaims, "That's our women hanging from the boughs of those trees..." Another points, "Look... those are bloodied heads on the field stakes..."All good order immediately breaks down in utter confusion as the despairing Gallóglaigh set to gallop the last half-mile to their Keep and Balloch's. "WAIT..." shouts Alain while quickly surveying and assessing the appalling scenes, but his men are blindly rushing forward; his horse gets barged aside by passing riders. Frustrated and confused, Alain quickly spurs his horse to a gallop while trying to catch up with his men as they scatter-gallop down the drove road and in through the gates of the corrals, they are met with a maelstrom of tracer arrows. Two or three arrows strike each man, save Alain, who is clearly identifiable by his coat of arms.

As each man and horse falls dead or wounded, English soldiers emerge from doorways lofts or from behind Wagons to dispatch the fallen men with lance or sword while others surround Alain, leaving him armed but unable to respond or help his men. More soldiers appear and quickly examine every body, cutting throats or dashing brains with mace or axe, in a matter of moments, all of Alain's fifty men and boys lay dead, including young Andrew Graham. English soldiers quickly encircle Alain, he spins his horse around to kick and fight, but none will come close enough, suddenly everything goes deathly quiet, the soldiers look up to see the Keep doors slowly open. Alain looks up at the Keep too and sees Cressingham and De Percy walk out towards the edge of the promontory. He is horrified when he sees behind the two Englishmen, Mharaidh and little Caoilfhinn being aggressively pushed forward by armed soldiers, they are both bound, naked, badly beaten and appear terribly abused, so much so, Alain barely recognises them. Desperately, he glances all around the corral, kailyards and Keep grounds, where all he sees are the defiled and mutilated bodies of his friends and family strewn asunder... He closes his eyes when seeing hogs tearing at human flesh... his mind spins as he tries to make sense of everything he sees and the sight of his beautiful wife and daughter... then he hears a distant voice through the mists of screaming chaos in his head... "Alain Wallace...?" says De Percy. Alain tries to focus on this Englishman who grips his beloved Mharaidh firmly by the hair and holds a dagger at her throat. De Percy orders, "Dismount, disarm, and come forward," Alain sits motionless while observing the horrific scenes before him. His mind races thinking of what he can do, but can find no solution. De Percy jabs his blade deep into Mharaidh's throat, forcing her to cry out. Alain's heart is beating like a manic drum pounding in his chest; his senses are nauseous and spinning. De Percy shakes Mharaidh violently by the hair, intimating he will push the blade through her throat if Alain does not obey.

Slowly and cautiously Alain dismounts. He drops his weapons and walks towards the steps that will lead him up to his loved ones, and perhaps somehow save them from this madness. As soon as he places a foot on the first step he's quickly overpowered and secured by the soldiers who force him to his knees, there they viciously beat him to the ground and keep on beating him till he is semi-conscious. His struggle is futile, he's manhandled; stripped naked and roughly bound with auld Tams hemp line so brutally, the lines cut deep into his flesh. The English soldiers savagely pull Alain up and force him onto his knees where he is securely bound and gagged, quelling anything he may attempt to shout out or say. Alain never takes his eyes away from his dear wife, he can see she is looking at him too... her eyes plead for Alain to wake her from this horrific situation, but he can do nothing. Tears fill his eyes as he observes and prays for this to be his own hellish nightmare. His mind frantically races, he desperately tries to think of a way out of this situation. Fear, love and anger confuse his thoughts, then he notices de Percy's dagger, Alain looks at the blade... he is mortified when he recognises it and to whom it had belonged.

De Percy, now quite certain that Alain is bound securely, pushes Mharaidh to the ground and pulls little Caoilfhinn in front of him, suddenly, he pushes the point of the dagger into her throat and slices the blade forward, opening her windpipe and jugular while taking great care her blood doesn't splash onto his boots. Alain screams in shock and terror seeing this unimaginable act of barbarity enacted upon his child, vomit fills his throat and mouth at the shock and terror of his witness, while his muffled screams and struggles amuse Cressingham and de Percy. Alain weeps as he watches little Caoilfhinn gasp, his beautiful child clasps her tiny hands to her throat, her eyes plead with her father to stop the searing hot pain... but he can do nothing to help her. Caoilfhinn topples over, gasping for breath through the gaping wound in her throat. De Percy picks the child up by the leg and tosses her dying body over the promontory to land on the ground beside Alain.

Mharaidh wails like a demented banshee. De Percy walks behind her; grabs her by the hair and drags her down the steps to where Alain is held fast beside the body of little Caoilf-hinn, still trembling and shaking in her death throes while looking desperately at her father. De Percy kicks Mharaidh behind the legs and brings her to her knees. "Do you want this whore of yours to live Wallace?" Alain, half-blinded by tears and blood, nods his head. De Percy and the soldiers laugh. With Mharaidh's arms still tightly bound behind her, De Percy holds her firmly by the hair and forces her knees apart, he arches her backwards over his thigh. Alain is almost deranged by the enormity of the situation, De Percy sneers, "You still want this whore after she has satisfied the pegs of real men?" Alain pleads as best he can with his eyes, pitiful muffled noises are heard coming from behind his gag as he screams to spare his beloved Mharaidh, his Anam Chara. Cressingham, who is standing nearby in a poise befitting a despotic Roman Emperor, holds up a writ and calls out in a thick baritone voice, "Wallace..." Alain looks up in absolute terror, crazed with fear for Mharaidh. Cressingham continues.... "Alain Wallace and the Wallace tribe of the Black Craig, Glen Afton, ach na Feàrna and those of Kilspindie, the Machars and Rhinns of Galloway, you have been have been charged with sedition, rebellious and wanton thoughts against your rightful King, lord Edward Plantagenet. You are all hereby tried before a court of your peers and found to be guilty this day. You are to be summarily executed forthwith."

Glancing at De Percy, Cressingham nods his head. De Percy yanks Mharaidh upright, pulls her head back then slowly and deliberately he slices her throat open from ear to ear. Immediately unnatural sounds of hissing noises are heard as a fine spray of blood pulses from her gaping throat... Alain screams and struggles to break free of his bonds, but to no avail. The unearthly noises coming from Mharaidh's throat continue for a few moments longer till she falls over in front of Alain, she desperately looks into his eyes as her mouth gasps and gapes for air it cannot purchase.

Alain is forced to watch his loved ones pain and terror in their demise, while the death rattles of Mharaidh and little Caoilfhinn make great amusement for Cressingham and his men. Cressingham glances at Alain, he speaks quietly... "You shall meet her soon enough Wallace, and when you meet your brother Malcolm some time soon in your heathen hell, you may then thank him alone for our pleasures these past few days." Cressingham closes on Alain's ear then he whispers, "Before your day is done Wallace... we are going to flay your wife and your daughter in front of you as we would skin paltry rabbits, then we will use horse-boot nails to pull their skins tight when we pin their hides to those oak doors of that stinking pile you call a home. I want you to watch this duty we perform, for what education would you have if you did not witness the punishment for sedition. Then Wallace, we will take great care in flaying you alive when all is gone before you." De Percy barks out an order, "Cut off his eyelids, for this seditious Scotch dog must not miss any of the entertainment we shall be providing for him."

*   *   *

Endless hours pass as the English soldiers slowly remove the flesh from the bodies of Mharaidh, and Caoilfhinn. The terrors wreaking havoc in Alain's mind have driven him near to insanity. His eyelids incised and body in great pain, with strong hands gripping his head, he is forced to witness every detail of the skinning and barbarous defilement of his loved ones. Alain prays through the mists of terror that he may die soon and join his family. De Percy concludes the skinning and the nailing to the doors of Wallace Keep, the flesh remains of Mharaidh and Caoilfhinn. De Percy calls for the men to throw the inner carcass to the hogs while he walks back to deal with Alain, he kneels and looks closely into

Alain's face, he ponders awhile, then he says, "I think we shall set you free now Wallace." Unable to really comprehend what De Percy had said, Alain hears more words in some distant place, "Cut his bonds." He vaguely feels his wrist bonds being cut, but his arms flop down by his sides, there is no strength left in his muscles due to the circulation being deliberately withheld for so long. Alain sits for a few moments in a world between heaven and hell; his mind clears a little, enough to know that when he feels any strength return, he will kill de Percy. Suddenly Alain hears a movement behind him, but before he can react, Cressingham thrusts a dagger through his throat, missing the major arteries and carefully piercing his windpipe. Cressingham pulls the blade back out, leaving two small cut-holes in Alain's throat gasping for air. De Percy approaches Alain with the blade he used to murder Mharaidh and Caoilfhinn; then he kicks Alain over onto his back. As Alain falls to the ground, in his hellish nightmare the only sound he can hear is the open throat rattles of his lungs gasping in air, then Alain hears Cressingham's voice somewhere in the distance...

"Squire De Percy shall post a proclamation to the doors of this place, stating that in order to quell treason and sedition by lawful means, the proceeds of trial, guilt and execution of this rebellious pack of miscreants was fair, just and necessary..." Cressingham walks forward with father Anthony by his side. He makes another declaration "Men, I now want this Wallace carefully flayed, he must be kept alive and conscious at all times during the entire process. Be very conscientious and diligent; then I want his hide nailed beside his lady and their brat to the doors of his hovel. As is proper, Alain Wallace and his filthy brood shall be waiting at the door for their next guests to arrive. And when they do arrive, they will most surely be encouraged to reject any notion of sedition that has brought this particular Wallace tribe to an end." Cressingham's men cheer and applaud their lord and master, knowing that his personal satisfaction will bring them great rewards. Alain feels the dull sensation of his body being manhandled then being pinned to the ground... Unable to close his eyes, he watches as a group of English soldiers sharpen their butchery knives on whetstones while others stand around drinking ale, laughing and guffawing while looking down at his body. He sees two young looking soldiers being taunted by the older ones, then the youngest one stoops and reaches between Alain's legs and grip his manhood, then the instant agony from a severe burning pain in his groin shoots up his spine, crystallising his mind beyond description. His awareness is entirely alerted to every nerve-end in his body, the terror and suffering is compounded by the emerging white-hot pains of razor sharp knives slicing into him as they begin to meticulously peel his flesh from his body as one unbroken pelt... the excruciating pains engulf Alain.

After an eternity of immeasurable suffering, the blessing of the great sleep beckons. Alain knows that very soon he will be by the side of his loved ones. Cressingham and De Percy's men move delicately as the last piece of flesh is removed from the muscle. They all laugh seeing the body twitches and eye spasms from Alain's living, breathing carcass. De Percy steps forward with sword in hand and raises it high in the air. Alain Wallace is now freed from all earthy pains as De Percy holds high the fleshy skull of Alain Wallace of Glen Afton. De Percy stands proud and triumphant as he calls out, "And so ends another treacherous brigand chief and his outlaw band..." Silence follows. De Percy had expected a great hurrah... but nothing is heard, the English soldiers show no reaction at all... Cressingham then steps forward, raises his open hand, then he says, "Well done men, you did good work this day." The soldiers joyously cheer and hurrah Cressingham, so pleased that Alain Wallace has been successfully skinned alive for their master… De Percy is shamefaced and livid that all the men have ignored him, he skulks away unnoticed to hide behind lord Cressingham's large frame. Cressingham though, is now bored with a familiar scene of flaying, he gathers all the men to the corral in front of Wallace castle. He says, "Soldiers of Christ… Father Anthony will now hold prayer to absolve you all for your diligent duties this day, that none may ever feel remorse upon reflection."

Father Anthony walks forward; he looks to the heavens then he looks down and notices blood on his boots while making the sign of the Holy Cross. "I see that some of you wish to keep those young heathen sluts as your personal concubina, but this you cannot do, for these whores are using their womanly wiles and cunning to try and bewitch you, but men, the lord doth sayeth…These heathen whores, do not listen to them. The Lord your God is testing you to see if you love him with all your heart and soul. Serve only the Lord your God and fear him alone. Obey his commands, listen to his voice and cling to him. The false prophets and Sabine whores here will try to lead you astray, they must be put to death, for they encourage rebellion against the Lord your God while keeping you from following the path of the faithful, you must execute them to remove the evil from among you… amen."

While his soldiers nail Alain's skin to the doors of the Keep, Cressingham addresses the men who have taken some of the Glen girls as their own. "Take them away and kill them, quickly, now move. You have my word, there will be plenty more of these Scotch whores for you men elsewhere, have no doubts about that." Cressingham and De Percy turn and walk into the Keep. They enter the grand hall to meet with their faithful spy and scout, Cressingham says, "There is a bag of silver on the table for your troubles. Meet me in Ayr two weeks from now, we may need you for other of the King's Business." The scout thanks Cressingham, lifts the bag of silver from the table then leaves. Curious, De Percy enquires "Other business, what business my lord, I was not made aware of any other Kings business? I have won your confidence have I not my lord?" Cressingham replies, "No Percy, you most certainly have not won my confidence. You have much yet to do over many years before you may presume that. But I do warm to your excesses. Anyhoo, now we shall soon be closing on Castle Comunnach to warm our feet at another's fire." De Percy enquires gleefully, "More chastisement my Lord?" Cressingham replies, "No Percy, this is a friend of our lord King Edward." Cressingham smiles at De Percy, he thinks, Perhaps one day I may even like this repulsive little Percy bastard...

THE PIZZLE

On the southern banks of the river Clyde, William has taken warrior out on a long early morning ride-out past the Ynchinnan fish landings, through the great coppice willow fields and away to the bustling smithy village of Gobhain. He scarcely believes his friend Moray has gifted him such a proud and handsome beast as Warrior. He canters along the winding bridleways on the banks of the Clyde for many hours as far as Glasgow, till eventually he returns to ride through the gates of ach na Feàrna, the ride-out with Warrior has greatly lifted his spirits. It's been only days since he returned from Saint Johns Toun and he's feeling much better, with his bruised and sore ribs healing quickly, though it is a stark reminder of his narrow escape from English justice... again. He also can't help thinking of the English soldier he had fought in the Fer Ficht, then curiously, the Englishman let him escape from garrison soldiers intent on arresting him and then the same Englishman stymied charges made up against him. Laughing as he washes and brushes down Warrior, he thinks, I'm still wanted as a feckn Ale thieving outlaw though...

At that moment, wee Maw comes out of the kitchens and calls out to him, "C'mon son, yer scran is ready." William replies, "Tá granny, I'll be in when I finish grooming Warrior." He slides his hand down the left foreleg of Warrior, squeezing along the back of the leg, testing the strong tendons just above the pastern, "Hup..." he commands. Amusingly, Warrior raises his feathered foreleg. William catches the hoof, pulls it backwards, then with a hoof-pick, he pries out dirt, little stones, manure and anything else lodged in the shoe. He checks the frog for injuries and any sign of cracks, grease-heel or thrush, happily he finds Warrior to be clean and healthy. He feels good about the companionship of Warrior, for the stallion is everything that any rider loves in a horse of character. William takes a soft damp cloth and gently wipes around Warrior's eyes and muzzle, cleaning away any dirt and chaff that's accumulated after their morning ride. Next, he examines Warrior's eyes for tearing and his ears for any lodged seed heads, insects or dirt.

Running his eye keenly along warriors back for rainrot, William examines the skin for any sign of fly warble or ringworm, then finally, he wipes around the dock and tail head. "Perfect." sighs a delighted William. Malcolm, who is mucking out the stables with Sandy nearby says, "You and Warrior have fair taken to each other." William replies, "Aye, he's a wonderful horse uncle." Malcolm walks over and strokes the long jaw of Warrior. "He's a bonnie steed right enough, such large handsome eyes, fine body lines, well-muscled loins and a noble well-arched neck." Warrior pricks his ears up and raises his head as if he knows he is being admired, and rightly so is the expression in his eyes and posture. Malcolm examines Warrior's muscle lines and runs his hands over his back. "He's an Iberian cross and a Persian wind drinker William, you can see it in the deep well-angled hips and laid-back shoulders... and look at the long level broad croup and naturally high tail carriage." Malcolm pauses to admire Warrior, "Aye William, would you look at that now, thick strong bones and good hoof walls.

He's definitely from Areion's bloodline, Alexander fair knew all about his horses. Did yie know that he raised them all from foalhood specifically for the arts of war?"

"Naw." replies William, who is enjoying watching his uncle go over Warrior like a little boy with a new toy, Malcolm steps back beside William and gazes at Warrior. William grins while listening to his uncle's learned interest, he enquires, "What's an Iberian?" Malcolm hasn't noticed the cheeky grin on William's face while posing the question. "Ach," sighs Malcolm knowingly; "Many folk have different thoughts on that, but for me... I reckon the finest Iberian comes from an ancient Carthaginian stock bred with a Vilano, that's a fine sturdy horse from the Pyrenees mixed with Saracen or Barbary bloodlines." Malcolm certainly knows his horse breeds, thinks William. Malcolm notices a bit of a blank look in William's face, he smiles then continues, "An Iberian we think off here, comes from a Moorish kingdom called Andalusia. Anyway William, what's Warrior like to ride out?" William teases Malcolm, "Like the wind uncle, he's light to the touch, a soft-mouth, sensitive on the reign, and almost serene on the gallop, like pouring the finest o' coo cream, so smooth..." Malcolm exclaims, "Right William, that's enough." William laughs, "Would you like to ride him out uncle?" Malcolm grins, "William me boy, I thought you were never going to feckn ask." He continues, "Since I lost auld Janus to the malady o' the gut twist, there has ne'er been a horse like him..."

Wee Maw calls out, "COME AND GET YOUR SCRAN OR IT'S GOING INTO THE DOGS." Her loud voice startles Malcolm and William, who laugh at the shocking resonance of a great big voice coming from such a tiny petite frame as wee Maw. She gives them both the infamous Look then she brusquely goes back inside the house. Malcolm says,

"You'd better put Warrior in the far corral before we go in, if you don't want to be lose him by the way those mares are looking at him." Warrior pricks his ears up and begins walking towards the mares corral, Malcolm exclaims, "Would you look at that," William smiles, "Moray told me he was a smart horse, I reckon he must have a Wallace attitude too."

They both laugh as they walk Warrior to the secure stallion corral then close the gates behind him. Malcolm enquires as they walk back towards the kitchens for wee Maw's scran, "Do you know how much it would cost to buy a horse like that?" William replies, "Naw no' really, an ordinary half-decent horse would be about five Merks at most? So then maybe, twenty Merks?" Malcolm glances at William, "Try again." William replies, "Well, he is no' a glue pot, and the most I have ever known a horse to sell for was fifty merks, so I reckon say maybe… a hundred Merks?" Malcolm laughs, "Try five hundred Merks and more for one of Alexander's stud breed stallion's." William is utterly surprised; he gasps "WHAT?" Malcolm explains, "Aye that's right. When they sold off Alexander's stable at auction, I went to see if I could buy one of them, but the cheapest horses started at five hundred Merks." William exclaims, "That's nearly ten years wages uncle." Malcolm continues, "Aye, then your friend Moray must think a great deal of your friendship." William can hardly believe that Moray has gifted him such a beautiful horse, and at such a cost?

William shakes his head in disbelief. "I'd better be checking with Moray in case my brain was addled during the fight, just to make sure that he did gift me Warrior and I didn't just dream it." Malcolm laughs at William's sudden uncertainty, "If young Moray is anything like his father, you'll have no concerns there. I know lord Moray well from the Royal courts and Garda Rígh, I can tell yie, he is a proud man of his word."

"Malcolm… Malcolm…" a voice calls out nearby. Malcolm and William turn to see young Sandy the stable lad running towards them. Sandy hands Malcolm a couple of small tightly wrapped notes from the pigeon lofts; Malcolm quickly reads through the first note, "There's a skreev here from Tam down at the Glen Afton. He says your father will be coming home soon from Norham and that the treaty has been settled." William says, "I can't hardly wait to see Dá and show him Warrior. He'll be pleased, or a wee bit jealous maybe, Oh, and by the way, I've something tell everyone… Marion and I want to be married before the coming Beltane, so, I need to talk to me Dá and Mharaidh about it soon anyways, feck ah'd better tell wee Maw as though she is the first to find out, so don't say anything yet." Malcolm looks at William with an expression of pleasant surprise, "She's not, is she?" William considers what Malcolm could mean, then he realises, "NAW…" he laughs, "We just want to get married as soon as we can, because there's no one else we want to spend our lives with." Malcolm laughs, "Ah was just checking to make sure, for yer a Wallace after all." Malcolm opens and reads the second note from auld Tam,

"This is good news too, Stephen will be arriving at the Invergarvane longshore the morn by the looks of it, auld Tam is asking if yie'll take horses down and pick him up." William says, "That's great news uncle, ah'v missed Stephen about the place and it'll be sure good to be seeing him again, and he's gonnae be a father again too." Malcolm smiles, "I'm pleased to hear that William, she's a bonnie lass Katriona, well suited to yer mad Irish friend." Malcolm knows the bond is strong between Stephen and William, as close as the best of brothers could ever be. Malcolm says, "I was sad to hear of the loss of his father." William agrees, "Aye, I cannot think what it must be like to be feeling his pain." Malcolm continues, "Well, he's needing you to take horses down and to be waiting for him. And when you meet with Stephen, will you both come back up here, I need yiez to take the salt wagon down to Glen Afton for your father for he's almost no salt left, and if he's home by now or home very soon, you'll be needing all o' that salt down there before yiez start the fall season hunts for the preservin." William replies, "Sure uncle," Malcolm continues, "There's another wagon to go down that Stephen can drive, its full o' iron workings that Alain needs for his smithy and a few other vittals, including three barrels o' that Lübeck ale." William enquires, "Are you coming with us?" then he enquires curiously, "Just hold it there uncle, what do you mean, three barrels?" William considers that Malcolm and wee Graham may be in collusion. "Well," says Malcolm as he scratches his chin, "One of the barrels was leaking, so I had to put it into several wee fragile churns to save it or yie would o' lost it entirely."

"But…" exclaims William. Before he can finish, Malcolm slaps him on the back, "Ach, William, am just jesting with yie, but ahl be thanking you just the same for your generosity, ah just knew yie wouldn't mind." William laughs to himself at the continuing loss of his infamous Lübeck Ale that has him marked as an infamous Ale thief. Then he remembers, he had forgotten to pay the Innkeeper. He laughs to himself as they walk towards the house, William enquires "Will you be coming down to Glen Afton with us?" Malcolm replies, "I was thinking of going down some time after noon this day, but ma auld horse is lame… my, and ah do miss my bonnie Janus." William enquires innocently, "What are you going to do about getting another good horse, the auctions?" Malcolm simply smiles at William… William smiles back, but Malcolm keeps on smiling, William is beginning to wonder what's wrong with Malcolm? He feels awkward, thinking what the ailment could be that's causing this unusual expression on Malcolm's face. Then it occurs to him, he exclaims, "Awe naw, naw… Feck naw… awe for fucks sake uncle." Malcolm continues his inane grin… William laughs then he says, "Ach, all right then. But mind and be extra careful, he's an expensive horse to replace if you hurt him." Malcolm laughs… "YOU TWO?" shouts Uliann, "YOUR VITTALS ARE GETTING COLD." Malcolm exclaims, "By the feckn Aicé William, Isn't Uliann beginning to sound so much like wee Maw? Come on son, we'll better get our vittals eaten or wee Maw and Uliann will be feeding us Warrior for our supper."

By mid-morning, William has saddled and tacked two bright Connemara's for himself and Stephen and loaded up a packhorse with everything to keep him warm and nourished for a few days. He notices Malcolm canter Warrior around the main yards of ach na Feàrna. He watches with pride Warriors poise, carriage and general demeanour. He thinks… What a beautiful horse. Malcolm canters over and pulls up beside him then dismounts. "William me boy… this is the most responsive horse I've ever ridden, he's definitely from the same stock as Janus." William strokes the long black mane of Warrior, "Well… you take good care o' him for he can get a bit jittery at full gallop and he spooks real easy too, aye, and he responds best first thing in the morn' when he's thoroughly washed, brushed down then hard pressed and pushed to work. And mind this too, he can be a right stubborn touchy bastard." Malcolm appreciates William's sensitivity, "Don't fret son, I'll take good care of him." William glares at Malcolm "I wasn't talking to you… I was talking to Warrior."

Malcolm is not amused hearing William's comments. For a few moments there is a stony silence between them, then they both burst into laughter. Malcolm laughs out loud,

"Aye William, you're sure yer fathers son right enough."
William grins, "I'm only jesting yie uncle, that's what Moray
said when he gifted Warrior to me or me to Warrior I still
don't know which is which." Malcolm smiles, "Aye, he's a
beautiful to ride, I think we will take good care of each other
most likely." Malcolm continues, "Well William, we had
better get ready to go."

Malcolm and William hook up their packhorses to trail
for their ride-outs and checking all the horse-tack when wee
Maw and Margret come to see them off. Wee Maw holds
Malcolm by the hand, "Be giving our love to Mharaidh and
the family when you get down there to Glen Afton son, and
mind, both o' yiez take care, for there is no' just bandits
roamin' about out there, there are English patrols everywhere,
and I hear they are bein' very strict and heavy handed with
everybody wie that martial law." Malcolm replies, "We'll be
fine Maw." She turns to William, "And especially you William,
you're young and folk are always wanting to be fightin' with
you. I want you to be taking the old drovers roads away over
high Kilmaurs to Invergarvane, and keep your head down...
don't be reacting to anyone who might cause yie trouble."
William replies, "I will, I mean I won't granny. When I meet
with Stephen we're coming straight back up here to pick up
two wagons then we'll head down the back roads to Glen
Afton." Wee Maw looks at William and grins, she says, "And
to finalise the details of your tryst with the bonnie maid
Marion I hope?" William smiles "Aye granny, that's the first
thing that I'll look to be doin'."

As he leans over to hug wee Maw, she whispers, "I want
to see some grand-wains very soon William, so you two
get busy." He stands up looking indignant, then exclaims,
"Wee Maw..." He laughs as wee Maw embraces him, "Take
care William, I love you dearly son." William replies,

"Ah love you too Granny." He embraces Margret then he and Malcolm warmly embrace too. Malcolm says, "You listen to your granny me boy, and you be keepin' well away from any signs o' trouble, for these are dangerous times." William replies, "I will uncle." William mounts his horse then turns and walks towards the gates of Ach na. Feàrna, he turns and looks to see wee Maw Margret and Malcolm wave goodbye, he waves back to them then spurs his horse on and canters out through the gates. With a great sigh, Malcolm puts his arms round Margret and wee Maw then he says, "I sure hope he keeps away from trouble, for he has had a tough time of it these last few years." Wee Maw wrings her hands with concern, "More like I hope that trouble keeps away from him." Malcolm agrees, "Aye, you're right there Maw."

Malcolm clasps Margret gently by the hand as they walk towards Warrior. She enquires, "Why didn't you both travel awhile together then part ways in Glasgow?" Malcolm replies, "William is going up to Leckie mòr's place up at Carlibar to deliver a message for me, then he's going to Crosbie to pass Leckie's message replies on to Ranald. From there he'll head down the coast road to Invergarvane. That's a quiet road so he'll be fine. Me… I'll be stopping off in Glasgow awhile to talk with Bishop Wishart, then I'm going straight through Ruthers Glen and on to Glen Afton after that." Wee Maw, who's listening, says, "I think you both should o' travelled together, Ahm feelin' that there's something bad in the air with all these English troops pouring into the country, and our own folk are no' yet back from Norham. You mark my words son, there will be big trouble in this realm very soon." Malcolm says, "I hear yie Maw." But he too has deep concerns, more than he cares to admit, especially since he was forced to stand down with all other commanders of the Garda Bahn Rígh upon the supposed '*invitation*' of Longshanks.

Malcolm thinks, For the good of the realm? He smiles to allay wee maw's fears. "Maw, there's stability in the realm now that we have a peace keeping army in Scotland. When there's a new Regent back on the throne, we'll soon be back to normal."

Spitting on the ground, Wee Maw mutters, "We already had peace Malcolm, we don't need the English tellin' us how to manage our own affairs. The Romans, Saxons and Norsemen tried that and we did all right without their help thank you very much. So you tell me son, what makes today different from our entire history of being a sovereign realm?" Malcolm replies, "I don't know, I can't answer that, nuthin' ah suppose." Wee Maw curses, "It's those there Feckin Normans and their famishin' feckn greed, that's what's makin' the difference." Margret and Malcolm are surprised to hear wee Maw curse. Margret exclaims, "Maw, I have never heard you curse… ever." Warrior, standing nearby, shoves his big head between Malcolm and Margret to look at wee Maw; his ears prick up as though he too had heard her curse for the first time. Malcolm laughs, "Would yie look at Warrior, even he appears surprised." Wee Maw sighs, "Ach," she waves her hand and turns her head in disgust, "Ach ma bonnie wains, I just wanted to hear what it might sound like myself. You have to try everything once in this lifetime son, and wouldn't those duplicitous Normans fecker's make their own mothers curse."

Malcolm and Margret laugh at wee Maws second outburst of cursing, "Maw, yie certainly know how to change a situation for the better, ah reckon a lifetime in the court o' Alexander and ah'v still so much to learn from you." Wee Maw smiles, "Aye ah know, that's true… yie have learned near everything yie know from me son, but ah'v no' let yie know everythin' ah know… yet."

"Anyways," says a slightly bemused Malcolm, "I'd better get goin', I think Warrior here is also anxious to get goin' too." Wee Maw says, "Come here you…" she embrace's Malcolm with the love of a mother and son so richly woven between them. She says, "Now you take real extra care, and don't you be falling off that big horse, for you're no' as young as you seem to think yie are anymore." Margret puts her arms around Malcolm and gives him a romantic kiss. He hugs her close with a passion, she giggles and whispers in his ear "And you hurry home Malcolm Wallace, for I'm late…"

Malcolm hasn't really noticed what Margret had said at first, then he leans his head back and looks at her, he notices her cheeks are glowing like a setting autumn sun and her eyes are sparkling like tiny diamonds. Malcolm is slightly perplexed, "It's me that's going, but its you who's late?" Wee Maw nods, smiles and shrugs her shoulders innocently. Malcolm exclaims "Aye..?" His great eyebrows rise up with sheer delight. Margret says with glee, "Three moons now." Malcolm lifts Margret and swings her around, so overjoyed… "Put her down you daft big lump." orders wee Maw "Sorry, sorry…" exclaims Malcolm as he places Margret gently back on the ground, he exclaims, "Really?" Margret smiles, "Really." He calls out to his stable lad "That's it, we're no' going Sandy… unbridle the horses." Wee Maw growls, "SANDY… Don't you move if yie know what's good for yie." then she gives Sandy the Look. "What's wrong?" Enquires Malcolm, "Don't you want me here?" Wee Maw replies, "You've got that right son. Now you and Sandy be getting' on your way, for yie don't know how long we've waited to be free o' men in this household for us to get it back into a proper order." Malcolm smiles and embraces Margret; then she says with a twinkle in her eyes "Take care *'Father'* and hurry home." He grins then says, "You take care too, Maw…"

Malcolm mounts Warrior while Sandy sits on another horse waiting with a packhorse in tow. They turn their horses and ride out of Ach na Feàrna towards Glasgow. Malcolm is feeling absolutely elated at this unexpected news from Margret. Lost in his thoughts, time passes quickly, and it isn't too long before both he and Sandy are approaching the old Mungo Bridge to cross the Molendinar River and take the road leading up to Grey Rock castle and Glasgow Cathedral. They sit awhile at the bridgehead, watching streams of English troops crossing the bridge to make their way up to the castle to take control; other troops cross to the west to take possession of the enormous Ruther's glen castle, home to Scotlands great Parliament. Malcolm waits with Sandy until they can cross and follow the road up to Glasgow Cathedral safely.

Eventually they arrive at the Cathedral near to the doorway of the sacristy. Chancellor Lamberton, a young man about the same age as William, comes out the doors to greet Malcolm and Sandy. "Malcolm, it's so good to be seeing you, it's been awhile. What brings you here to seek Saint Mungo's peace this fine day?" Malcolm dismounts and tells Sandy to feed and water the horses; then he replies, "Good day to yie too Lamberton, I've come across to see if Wishart has returned from Norham yet?" Lamberton frowns, "No, not yet, but he'll be back here soon, with good news I hope." Malcolm sneers, "Bring back good news from Norham Lamberton... Yie reckon? Nothing good for Scotland will come back from that place." Looking furtively around him, Lamberton says, "Come into the sacristy Malcolm, it'll be much safer to talk in there." Malcolm exclaims, "Safer?" Lamberton beckons Malcolm to follow. They enter the sacristy, where their conversation will be private and they can discuss the state of the realm in detail. They talk awhile and find they have much in common between them. Lamberton says, "I don't agree with the nobility and the church hierarchy Malcolm, it would appear the nobles have risked everything for a bag of gold each." Malcolm replies, "Not all of the Nobles." Lamberton continues, "Malcolm, for the last few years Wishart and I have suspected that many of the clerics introduced by the English Bishop Bek have been manipulating our ancient records and all our historical documents." Malcolm enquires, "To what end, for what purpose?"

Wringing his hands in frustration, Lamberton replies, "We don't yet know, but we do know something is greatly amiss, though we cannot yet lay proof of our suspicions, for its mainly Saint Andrews and it's satellite priories that's affected. That's where most of our ancient history are kept, but we find we can no longer gain willing access, though I personally believe it's mischief to Scotland's disadvantage. We cannot prove anything or put forward any credible cause or theory, but even if we could do this, who do we tell... who?" With a look of concern on his face, Malcolm replies, "Many of the Garda bahn Rígh have also been suspicious and sympathetic to your train of thought Lamberton. It appears that so many of our faith leaders are now lost to us, replaced with a new breed that appears to show more loyalty to thrones abroad."

Lamberton looks out the small open window at the large numbers of English troops arriving to garrison the castle. "This feels more like an invasion than peacekeeping Malcolm, I cannot understand why the nobles have ordered our armies to stand down and forced our men of office to resign, only to be replaced by an army of English clerics, magistrates, sheriffs and governors." Malcolm sighs, "No one outside that clique of Norman nobles who attend the signing of the Ragemanus can understand this madness. Wishart, Moray, Comyn, I mean, what are they thinking? If anyone could have stopped this it should have been those proud men?" Lamberton's head drops, "I cannot understand their thoughts Malcolm. Please forgive me, and I say this in your confidence, but when I press Bishop Wishart, he prevaricates or distorts the truth as I know it to be, he does so logically and with an arrogant authority, yet scrupulous delivery. When I remonstrate, he calls his reasoning politic. He truly believes that this English army is Scotland's only hope of remaining a sovereign realm," Malcolm says, "Sometimes I think my brother Alain has the right idea, he's a Breitheamh Rígh of the ancient order of Céile Aicé, living happily and contented enough with the sunrise in the morning. His only fear is that his family would ever live a day in melancholy or malady and he cannot remedy their ailments."

Lamberton nods his head in agreement, then he says, "I truly believe in God Malcolm, but it gnaws at my spirit when I see the common man who lives in abject poverty averting his eyes, bows, scrapes and trembles as he is passed by a man of God, dressed in his fine black and purple robes. Or how that same common man cowers in the sight of the crucifix that looms over him and his children in the midst of their village. I also see how the church instils fear and commands the common man to willingly suffer for what he doesn't truly understand, all to keep Gods self-appointed gatekeepers in ermine and wine. The bishopric are no different to my way of thinking, than the English king who now imposes the same style doctrine upon our realm, by using the law of fear, punishment and damnation upon the common man if he does not bow to him in servitude?" Malcolm smiles, "It sounds as if your faith is a little shaken Lamberton, but you're right, who would want to be a god-fearing man? Perhaps Alain has something again in that it is more natural for a man to be earth loving rather than God fearing."

"Perhaps," sighs Lamberton. He looks curiously at Malcolm, "It sounds like your own faith is being tested too, whereas my faith in God is strengthened and grows ever stronger, even though Bishop's no longer see faith and happiness as the true path, they say it must be suffering and servitude to be instilled in the flock. There's many of the calling that would reject the Bishops theory Malcolm, for there is great discontent abroad. If the common man wishes to have faith in God and have happiness and joy because of this faith, then his only fear should be is to lose the faith that brings this happiness to him and his family. I would willingly sacrifice myself for that to be the true religion and calling of our realm."

"Ha Lamberton," laughs Malcolm "Now I hear a very young Wishart in the delivery and concerns in your words." Lamberton continues, "Malcolm, those good men and women who have true faith, the truly devoted, I see they are fearful and cower in the shadow of the church when they scramble past in search for a crust of bread or a drop of milk to feed their hungry family, all because our food resources have been decimated by the English who now take everything like a swarm of biblical locusts, and taxing everyone like the money-lenders of Judea. They leave nothing for the local population and these thefts are supported by our higher clergy." Malcolm says, "Sadly that is true."

Lamberton continues, "Every day Malcolm, I see hundreds of grey faces with blackened eyes hereabouts, men, women, children with bellies swelling with hunger begging for God's help. These poor wretches say they no longer have any hope of salvation, only a fear of starvation and destitution. We distribute all the food and sustenance we have, but it is not enough. The poor would lick the leather off the Bishops or an English Knight's boots who pass them by just to gain a little nourishment. Yet they still have hope in their hearts for the church to save them, this thought is planted by clerical tricksters who preach, *'Follow me, give me your alms and God will bless you, God will save you, refuse me and you'll burn in hell for all eternity.'*

Listening intently, Malcolm says, "I truly do understand what you're saying Lamberton, but I also believe that Wishart fights for the independence of the Scottish church, and he will not succumb to the demands of Longshanks' split tongued Bishops and the Churchmen of England. I'm also certain that Wishart must know that these men Bek has planted here in our Monastic libraries are burrowing into our ancient records like a plague of avaricious paperlice." Lamberton sighs, "Malcolm, I too would wish Scotland to remain independent, where men and woman can worship in their own way in their own homes with a church that brings them light and happiness not fear and damnation." Malcolm shakes his head, "These days it would appear idealistic and dangerous thoughts you are having Lamberton, but not impossible, for that was a dream shared in the days of my youth." Lamberton says, "I fear it will surely be impossible if the tyrannical Church of England places its boot upon our necks as English soldiers now do to innocent Scots." Malcolm looks at Lamberton curiously, "Lamberton, there's soon to be a meeting of the Céile Aicé hosted by Abbot Bernard in the precincts of Kilwinning Abbey, it's regarding all of these matters. I would like you to consider attendance, as there will be extremely important people there that I'd like you to meet, and they you I believe."

"I'm intrigued," exclaims Lamberton, "Tell me more?" Malcolm continues, "This is for your ears only… Bernard the Abbott of Kilwinning, Duns Scotus, Laurence de Ergadia and many other imminent theologians have constructed our realms first written constitution for the benefit of Scotland's entire community. It's a radical proposition of a common peoples governance, whereby, the common people will own the land and the King shall be elected by the peoples representatives to rule over us by agreed laws and statutes, prior presented by a peoples parliament, it's called the Declaration of Kilwinning. One hundred of us who can have an effect on the governance of our realm will sign this Declaration, to be delivered to His Holiness in Rome if Scotland falls foul of that Norham tryst with the devil. We will declare our cause as the Communitas de Scottus to His Holiness, that we will elect our own monarch to reign on behalf of the people as a King or Queen of Scots, not of the land, for the people shall own the land as a citizen's right. We will not be subjects subjected to the whim any imperialist Crown authority, but a land where we enact laws that is the will of the people based on the ancient Laws of the Feinechus, governed by the people for the people."

Lamberton stares at Malcolm as though energised by this declaration and commitment of the one hundred Communitas. He ponders, the law of the Feinechus… the freemen. Malcolm continues, "Lamberton… can you imagine a time when all the people of this land are citizens not subjects… never again would we be having our hopes, ambitions and freedoms thwarted by the blood feuds of royal siblings, power-hungry claimants or rival foreign kings, this is our alternative proposal to what is happening to us now." Lamberton stands a moment in silence; he stammers "It… It's unheard that a realm may govern itself with but a King or Queen elect? This will be seen as heresy and a threat to the very pillars of Gods chosen blood of Christendom as the blessed princes of Rome." Malcolm replies, "Not so my dear friend, for His Holiness requires all Princes of Rome to be loved by the people, not hated. What we propose is radical, idealistic perhaps, but what choices have we, continuous tyranny and war?" Lamberton replies, "God bless you Malcolm, I beg that you may consider me for any assistance that I may bring to the Communitas at this meeting, for this may be my true calling. If Duns Scotus is your religious mentor and he being our most highly respected secular cleric, then I will openly stand with him, the Céile Aicé and the Communitas." Malcolm puts his hand on the shoulder of Lamberton. "We would welcome you."

Lamberton is obviously pleased, he says, "Malcolm, I would be most honoured to humbly serve Scotland thus." The two men continue talking and discussing awhile about the precarious dilemma that faces the church and the sovereignty of Scotland, till it's time Malcolm makes good to complete his journey to Glen Afton. They leave the security and privacy of the sacristy to the outer doors and stand on the steps as Sandy brings the horses. Malcolm mounts Warrior then says, "We will speak with Wishart soon Lamberton, I am truly grateful for our time spent together this day." Lamberton replies, "And I too my friend." Malcolm says, "I shall keep you informed of all developments good friend." Lamberton says, "Travel safely and in Gods peace." Malcolm calls out, "I'll seek you out by my return from Glen Afton, after I have spoken long on this subject with Alain and the council of the Breitheamh Rígh. Farewell my friend."

Warrior senses to walk on by his own initiative, Malcolm smiles at the acute understanding Warrior already has of his body movements. The very nature and spiritual harmony shared between Malcolm and Warrior is refreshing after such intense deliberations and deep concerns shared with Lamberton. He turns and waves farewell, then both he and Sandy wander away carefree as they leave Saint Mungo's Cathedral, lost once more within their own particular thoughts. Soon they reach the rolling heights of the Kilmaurs ridge, where Malcolm looks back and can easily visualise the legendary blue winding tail of the Abhainn Chluaidh Dragon, inspired by the lazy meander of the river Clyde. Malcolm and Sandy are both enthralled watching the flow of the Clyde, gracefully easing its way to the west coast from the heart of Scotland. The silvery sparkling blue sheen that fascinates them is coming from the sun reflecting off the water surface, akin to reptilian scales with differing shades from green to blue, making the dragon's tail seemingly come alive. Malcolm feels enriched looking westward across the Clyde panorama, with its lush green forests and rolling hills stretching towards the sea to the magnificent great mountainous backdrop of the highlands standing like sentinels over his homeland.

"A truly beautiful dear green place in my heart." sighs Malcolm. Warrior's ears prick up and he raises his head as though he too shares in the infinite beauty and timeless panorama before them. "Come Sandy," says Malcolm, "Lets get going for Glen Afton." They walk the horses slowly south towards their destination, with Malcolm enjoying the companionship of Warrior. He laughs thinking… And Sandy's companionship too… Malcolm and Sandy walk the horses awhile, till they eventually pause at the summit of the Ardochrigg pass and see the stunning Southern vista opening up before them. "Sandy…" says Malcolm, he points toward an old volcanic rock that stands high in the centre of the great Clyde valley. "See that sole hill about twenty odd miles or so sticking through the forest canopy?"

"Aye." Replies Sandy. Malcolm continues, "Well, that there's called the Loudon Hill, I'm going to run Warrior there to master his grit, you make your way down there behind me in yer own time and I'll meet with you at the top of the

Loudon when you get there, its no' se' far to Glen Afton after that." Sandy grins seeing such boyish excitement in the eyes of his mentor, he replies, "I'll see you down there then?" Malcolm soft spurs Warrior, who immediately kicks at the earth below him and breaks into a fleet perfect long-pace gallop. Before long, Malcolm is thrilled as Warrior moves like he is gliding along on the wind, galloping over rough and even ground with no change to his gait or pace. Malcolm clicks his tongue, Warrior's ears prick up and his pace gets noticeably faster as the two spirits fly as one union of souls, soaring like birds of prey while thundering through the forest road towards Loudon Hill.

The extreme confidence and experience of Warrior in this mixed terrain causes Malcolm to consider that perhaps Warriors confidence is greater than his own, he pulls Warrior to a slower paced gallop, then finally he brings the gallop down to a handsome well-paced canter and it's not long before they approach the landmark Loudon Hill, where Malcolm brings Warrior to a walking pace then finally to a halt.

The proud stallions nostrils flare wildly while gasping in great amounts of air, the sweating horse has soaked Malcolm's saddle and foamed the leathers. Malcolm cools the sweating Warrior by walking him slowly round the west face of Loudon Hill, then as a last run, he charges Warrior up a loose winding path till they reach the summit of Loudon. Malcolm is buoyed from the exhilarating ride. As he pats Warrior's neck, he looks around to see that the vista before him is as breathtaking as that of Clyde valley. He views the small peaks of Galloway in the southwest and then across the shires of Ayr to the firth of Clyde, where he sees the mysterious looking grey mountain tips of the islands of Arran, Cumbrae and snow-tipped mountains of the northwest and beyond. 'This is my Scotland...' thinks Malcolm as he and Warrior rest.

He unties a large bladder filled with cold water and drinks copiously, then he pours the cool refreshing liquid over the head of Warrior, who shakes his head from side to side, his ears flopping as he enjoys the cool unexpected reward. At that moment, Malcolm hears horses travelling up the pathway he had just ridden.

Knowing it couldn't be Sandy arriving so soon, Malcolm stands high in his stirrups and sees eight armoured riders approaching with their lances dropped pointing straight at him. Malcolm is unarmed and the feeling he's getting from the body language of these riders is they are probably not going to be friendly, but he ignores his instincts and prepares to be civil. He can see now by their armorial bearings that they are English. "SPY…" calls out the lead rider. Malcolm looks at him and laughs, "My name is Sir Malcolm Wallace, and I'm not a spy Englishman. I am travelling to Glen Afton to see my brother Alain Wallace and his family. I've simply ridden up the Loudon head here to enjoy all that can be seen at my peace." The English riders talk amongst themselves, but Malcolm can't hear nor gain what they are saying. He enquires "Why is it you would call me a spy in my own country Englishman, when you are only here in Scotland as peacekeepers?" The soldiers ignore Malcolm's question, they lift their lance tips high and begin to pull their horses away when one of them turns around and says curtly, "Follow us Scotchman, if you know what's good for you…"

Malcolm reluctantly follows; he knows he has no real choice. As Malcolm and Warrior walk-on, they quickly catch up with the troop, four troopers at the rear pull aside to let him pass by then they close in behind him. With the entire troop now surrounding him, they make their way back down and around the side of Loudon Hill. Malcolm is wary, but for the moment, he must acquiesce. He looks south and sees

Cumno castle away in the distance, then not far beyond, the gateway to Glen Afton and peak of Black Craig. The soldiers escort Malcolm around the steep southeast side of Loudon Hill, when they pass the last gorse cluster and crag, Malcolm's heart sinks, he sees down beside the Loudon burn about hundred English soldiers with fires bivouacs and a general quarters field camp set up in the meadow.

The mounted soldiers lead Malcolm to the centre of the camp, where a small pavilion in particular has been erected for some noble personage. Two tough looking soldiers stand guard outside the pavilion entrance. "Wait here Scotchman." Commands the lead trooper as he dismounts and walks over to the guards of the small pavilion, he speaks to them briefly, they raise their halberds and let him enter. After a few moments, the soldier re-appears, followed by a young looking squire and a portly knight, both lavishly dressed in well-padded surcoats and colourful tabards. Malcolm recognises the coat of arms on the squires tabard representing the house and arms of the De Percy family from Alnwick in northern England, but he doesn't recognise the coat-of-arms on the large portly knight.

As the two Englishmen approach him, the stout knight declares, "I am Lord Cressingham you rapscallion. Why do you come here and disturb my peace, who are you and why do you spy on us Scotchman?" Malcolm watches both of them closely as they stand arrogantly in front of him. Malcolm replies, "I am sir Malcolm Wallace of Ach na Feàrna. I merely travel peacefully to see my family in Glen Afton sir, and I ask you, why do your men close down my freedom?" Cressingham and De Percy share a furtive glance. De Percy looks at Warrior and puts his hand out to stroke his mane. "What have we here?" Suddenly Warrior lunges forward, biting at de Percy's face. Cressingham and De Percy jump back and shy away from Warrior as he whinnies, snaps and bites at them. It takes all Malcolm's strength to bring Warrior under control. Malcolm commands, "Whoa Warrior…" Cressingham exclaims, "A mean spirited beast I see, someone has trained this stallion for fighting in battle, and by his cut and poise this is a breed far beyond the wherewithal of someone like you, Guards…" Commands Cressingham…

Instantly Malcolm is grabbed from behind and manhandled to the ground. The chaotic scene startles Warrior; suddenly he rears up on his hind legs, flays wildly and kicks out at the soldiers. Some rush forward and try to catch his reigns. Several soldiers pin Malcolm firmly to the ground while others surround Warrior, but the horse kicks, rears and lunges at the soldiers, trying to bite at their faces and necks. It appears Warrior is attempting to protect Malcolm from assault. De Percy screams, "Archers…. shoot the beast." An archer looses an arrow, narrowly missing Warriors head, but it sticks high into his neck. "NO…" shouts Cressingham, "That beast is worth more than all your weight in silver."

More soldiers rush forward to try and capture Warrior, two of them make a dash and catch Warriors reigns. They try to pull his head down and hold him firm, but they struggle to hold on to this powerful thoroughbred stallion, reared specifically for war and the chaos of battle. Warrior rears up and kicks forward unexpectedly, breaking both legs of the soldier clinging to the reigns, the stallion quickly turns his head and bites the second soldier in the side of his face before he can get out of the way, Warrior rears up, pulling at the soldier with such force and power, he rips a large part of the soldiers face away, then he brings his front hooves crashing down on the head of the soldier with the broken legs, killing him instantly. Warrior breaks free of the cordon and runs in circles causing mayhem, kicking, bucking and biting at the soldiers, who quickly realise it's impossible to capture a horse that's been trained to fight in battle. Warrior charges wildly through the strung-tied English corral, breaking the light tethers and stampeding all the other horses throughout the camp.

"KILL HIM..." shouts Cressingham, two archers immediately loose their arrows that strike warrior on the rear flanks, causing him to bolt and career through the bivouac tents of the English soldiery ripping many down. Suddenly he turns and gallops directly at the archers but falls and slides sideways, scattering the archers in all directions. Warrior quickly rises and bolts for the path to gallop away up and around the west side of Loudon Hill and out of sight. There is utter chaos and devastation left in Warriors wake. Cressingham and De Percy return to where Malcolm still lay pinned to the ground by six burly soldiers. Cressingham says. "You must be a horse thief Scotchman, you could not afford such a mighty beast as that stallion, nor could you have trained him in such arts." He continues "Bring this horse-thief to my pavilion where I shall put this Scotchman to the question,"

Two guards roughly haul Malcolm back onto his feet. Cressingham turns and nods at his men, immediately the guards release their grip of Malcolm. Cressingham says, "Walk with me sir Malcolm Wallace... if that truly is your name." Bewildered, but still cautious, Malcolm is keen-eyed and observes his surroundings while walking the short distance to Cressingham's pavilion, with four soldiers close behind him and others watching nearby. Malcolm is shown to a seat at a campaign table full of rich food and wine where he's ordered to sit. "Please, do indulge me." says Cressingham as he sits opposite Malcolm. De Percy sits at the side of the table and waits patiently, he knows Cressingham is about to demonstrate the skill of the question, and he's always eager to learn more from this knight's macabre trade. Cressingham enquires, "Sir Malcolm Wallace you say, then may I introduce myself, I am King Edwards treasurer in Scotland, lord Cressingham, and this... well this is squire de Percy." Malcolm replies, "Aye, then why do you and your men treat me this way lord Cressingham, I but travel to see my family and I am now held here against my will? None of this needed to be if you had simply shown me the common courtesy of a welcome." Cressingham replies, "Why my dear Malcolm, surely you must see things from my point of view, we are camped here peaceably in this strange and unfamiliar land, then you are caught on that hill spying upon us, next, that damned stallion wrecks my camp and kills two of my men without as much as a by your leave, so how could I know who you are? You could be a savage assassin or deranged brigand from those despicable Wolf and wildcat forests, sent here to cause trouble for us as peacekeepers."

Malcolm enquires, "You know that's not true and now you know who I am, I'm free to go?" Cressingham replies, "Not yet, for you must satisfy me that you are who you say you are? Is that not a reasonable request?" Malcolm knows immediately Cressingham is a clever man by leaving him no other real option but to agree to stay, though he keeps watching for an opportunity to make an escape. Cressingham enquires, "You say that you are the commander of this eh... what did you call it?" Malcolm replies, "I didn't say my lord, but yes, I am the former commander of the Garda Bahn Rígh, the queen's bodyguard, but how could you have known that?"

"Ah, quite." replies Cressingham "Then you will be familiar with the names of all your senior knight commanders, officers and captains then? Could you name but a few for me?" Malcolm is in a quandary, how could Cressingham have known he was a commander of the Queens guard.

As he ponders over his situation, he looks down, and gasps…
He focuses on the unique dagger hilt in de Percy's sword belt.
He quickly regains his composure, looks up and says, "Lord
Cressingham, I will tell you everything you would wish to
know, if you would have your squire here answer me one
simple question, honestly and faithfully. If his answer be
truthful, I will surely know, and you shall also know the
truth, for if it is a lie that is carried in the conviction of this
squires voice… you will know and you will also know I speak
the truth, then will I be free to journey on?" Supping from a
wine goblet, Cressingham is amused, for he hadn't expected
this reply. De Percy appears puzzled; suddenly he jumps
up from the table and backhands Malcolm viciously across
the face. Malcolm immediately moves to attack him but the
guards quickly hold him back. Cressingham says, "Percy,
this is no way to treat our guest, now sit down… sit I say."

Cressingham looks at Malcolm and considers this
opportunity to gain the names he needs. Letting Malcolm
go free may be prudent, and by giving him this false sense
of security it would also mean Malcolm will trust him to
keep his word in the future, Malcolm would be his to use
or to kill, whatever and whenever he chooses. Cressingham
replies, "I am interested to hear the question you may ask my
squire, who's honest answer would allow you to divulge all
you know, yet, is this question really so simple?" Malcolm,
his face still stinging from the assault by de Percy, smiles, "It
is an honest question my Lord, simply requiring an honest
answer." De Percy objects, but Cressingham raises his hand,
"Sit down I say Percy you annoying fool, you are disturbing
my thoughts." Cressingham continues, "I find the converse
with sir Malcolm here deeply intriguing. I wonder what
answer could possibly set him free to become our informa-
tive and dearest friend, yet your answer may also confirm to

me what I have thought all along, that you Percy, you really are a despicable lying bastard." Once again Cressingham is deliberately setting a rage in de Percy. He will wait and watch for any mistakes, lies or otherwise De Percy will undoubtedly make. Cressingham sits back and begins eating and drinking leisurely while watching both Malcolm and De Percy closely. The situation is becoming unusually interesting for Cressingham, this Scotchman who wants to ask only one question, and providing he receives an honest answer, he will reveal names much sought after by Longshanks.

This moment has everyone curious, though De Percy looks as though his confidence is badly shaken by this unusual request. A broad grin sweeps across Cressingham's face as he slams his goblet down onto the table... "Wallace, I have made up my mind... you have a wager, I agree to your terms." De Percy immediately remonstrates, "But my Lord..." Cressingham sneers, "Oh do shut up Percy. You're snivelling and grovelling like a whiney bitch pup does you no favours at all in front of this noble Scotchman; see how my men all laugh at you. Now Sir Malcolm, I give you my word as a Lord of England's royal court, that you may ask De Percy one question, and if we both agree that his answer is a lie and pending your delivery of names that will truly confirm to me who you really are, then you will be free to leave us and continue on your journey."

Considering his situation, Malcolm knows he is now committed, he leans on the table, clasps his hands and looks directly at Cressingham, then at de Percy. In a calm voice, Malcolm enquires, "Tell us de Percy? How come you by the dagger that you carry there in your sword-belt?" For a moment, the simplicity and innocence of the question is highlighted by the confused reaction from de Percy, which appears to be utter disbelief and consternation.

Tension mounts in de Percy's face as the enormity of the question dawns on him, and what his answer may reveal. De Percy is clearly at a loss, caused by this unexpected question, and it's becoming glaringly obvious he is desperately searching for a credible answer. Cressingham is greatly amused at such a simple question producing such an animated response from his squire. He sits back in his chair, knowing that something is clearly going on between De Percy and sir Malcolm. He is thoroughly enjoying being entertained by this curiously brief exchange. De Percy stammer's "Why... I, well I..." Cressingham laughs at de Percy's flummox; then he demands, "Answer him you half-witted fool, what could be making it so difficult for you to find your tongue?" De Percy looks as though he is going to cry or run away rather than provide an honest answer to Malcolm's question, then he blurts out, "It was a gift from my father." Cressingham and Malcolm knowingly glance at each other, "He lies," sighs Cressingham, "Though I'm not entirely surprised."

"It is Wallace here who lies," screams De Percy, "He dares to insinuate that I am a liar?" Malcolm shows no reaction as Cressingham speaks, "Do sit down Percy, sir Malcolm didn't call you a liar, it was I who called you a liar, and quite clearly you are a liar." He smiles as he places his goblet on the table, then he looks at Malcolm, "You were correct sir Malcolm, we both know that he lies, for he's simply a bastard who cannot help himself." Cressingham sups some more wine then says, "I really am quite fascinated sir Malcolm. Please... you may continue to question Percy, no doubt he has many more lies to tell us... this is quite fun you know." Allowing himself a confident smile, Malcolm enquires once more, "I ask you once again de Percy, where did you get that dagger?" De Percy stares at the table, his face turning purple, frantic with desperation. Everyone within earshot is now intrigued by this simple question and the failure of De Percy to answer truthfully. The atmosphere turns fraught with the tension and state of panic emanating from de Percy. "Well?" enquires Cressingham impatiently, "And make it the truth this time Percy, for we shall all know..." De Percy says nothing by reply; though his head looks as though it is about to explode, such is the tension etched his face. Malcolm speaks, "There are only two of these dirks ever made Percy, and I know who has the other one." Cressingham, now becoming extremely irritated, crashes his fist onto the table...

"ANSWER HIM YOU YOUNG FOOL." The shock of Cressingham's demand causes an instant response from de Percy, he shouts wildly into Malcolm"s face... "All right Scotchman, I will tell you, I took it from the body of Alexander when we ended his miserable life... yes, your so-called King. He squealed and cried for mercy like a pathetic little girl, like your brother and his bitch wife did and all the other vermin we left to rot in that glen of yours... how do you like that now Scotchman?" Cressingham is visibly shaken by de Percy's outburst, Malcolm too is completely taken aback, he can't believe what he has just heard, no one can believe it, it is too incredible to be true. Cressingham mutters in complete disbelief, "Regicide..." Everyone within earshot is shocked into a stunned silence in reaction to de Percy's incredulous revelation. "MALCOLM..." hails a voice from the distance. Cressingham quickly turns round as everyone looks up the Loudon Hill where they see the silhouette of a horseman, a packhorse, and what looks like Warrior on the skyline...

"GET AWAY FROM HERE..." screams Malcolm, Cressingham quickly nods at four archers, who immediately nock and loose at their target. Sandy, who is watching from the hilltop, is unsure of what's happening as Malcolm appears to be dining with these English knights. Baffled by Malcolm's warning, but before he could react, an arrow strikes him, instantly penetrating his arm and piercing through his rib cage and plunging the barbed arrow tip deep into his lungs. Almost simultaneously a second arrow strikes him in the throat, then a third and fourth go through his thigh, pinning him to the saddle. His horses bolt and flee over the back of the hill and out of sight. Malcolm seizes his opportunity while everyone is looking up the hill, he pulls Alexander's dirk out from de Percy's belt and quickly stabs at de Percy, who moves slightly, the blade enters his body just above his collarbone and out his back. Percy staggers backwards screaming in pain. Malcolm turns and slashes the nearest soldier across the throat then plunges the blade deep into the same man's chest. Cressingham shouts in a panic…"Kill him you fools."

Catching a glimpse of a sword blade coming directly at his head, Malcolm deflects it with his forearm, the blade cuts deeply through the muscle, but he pushes the sword aside and barges into the soldier, stabbing him many times about the neck and face with the dirk. He turns quickly to see if there is any escape route, but is instantly struck on the back of the head.

Reeling from the pain, Malcolm sees De Percy and lunges at him, but the back end of an axe smashes into his wrist, breaking the bones and causing Malcolm to drop the blade, he's struck again on the back of the head and falls over in semi-conscious agony. De Percy quickly picks up the dirk and strikes out at Malcolm, who moves a fraction as the keen blade narrowly misses his throat. De Percy viciously stabs him, driving the razor sharp needle-point blade through Malcolm's cheek just above the jaw, smashing through his teeth, almost severing his tongue, the force of the strike pins his face to the ground. De Percy pulls the blade out of

Malcolms face and prepares to finish him off, but Cressingham for all his bulk and size, moves in quickly and kicks De Percy viciously below the chin, knocking him onto his back. Four English soldiers quickly pin Malcolm to the ground where he lays in terrible pain. Raging, De Percy quickly gets up and runs over to a horse where he rummages about in a saddlebag then pulls something from the bag and runs back over to the prostrate Malcolm. He throws two objects like two oily leather skull caps to the ground in front him. De Percy screams hysterically "How do you like the fine work of your Kings blade now Wallace?" He rips the bandage from his neck revealing a vicious looking bite wound. He screams "Your brothers whore did this to me before I sliced off her breasts with your kings wonderful dagger… what do you say now my truth-seeking Scotchman?"

The intense pain in Malcolm's arm and face is near causing him to pass out and not quite grasping what's been said. Spitting blood through the haze of pain, he stares at the objects lying on the ground before him. De Percy kneels beside Malcolm's face, lifts and shakes the two objects before his eyes then rubs them roughly into Malcolm's face, he pulls them away screaming… "So you say you're a Wallace? Then you must recognise these?" Malcolm groans in agony and tries to raise himself while Cressingham observes the crazed de Percy, listening intently to his insane ramblings. "Enough…" commands Cressingham. Soldiers pull Malcolm up from the ground and sit him back on the seat. De Percy continues to shake the loose leathery objects in Malcolm's bloody face, "These are the tits of lady Mharaidh Wallace, would you like to kiss the whores teats one last time?" De Percy leers, "Ha, my fine honest Wallace… Where are your trick questions now…?" Malcolm groans in agony and despair, he's unable to move, held fast by the strength of the soldiers holding him down, he can't speak as his near-severed tongue is swelling up inside his mouth. The unimaginable pain and terror of the moment and de Percy's outburst are racing through Malcolm's mind. Trying to escape is all that is keeping him conscious… and a burning desire to kill de Percy. Cressingham calms the situation, "De Percy, you are bleeding profusely, take your shift off that we may get the surgeon to tend your wounds, now go to my pavilion at once, I will deal with you in a moment, first I must deal with this rogue." Cressingham looks at the soldiers and points towards the back of Malcolm's knees.

The soldiers immediately beat Malcolm mercilessly till he is barely conscious. They then proceed to strip him naked and bind him securely with ropes, two soldiers pull and twist Malcolm's arms behind his back and tie his wrists together, another soldier pulls his legs together and sits on his legs gripping his ankles firmly, another stands in front of his prostrate body and pulls his arms forward, forcing his face further into the ground. Another soldier grips his arms too then they pull his arms forward with all their strength, a sickening crunching sound is heard as both Malcolm's shoulder blades are dislocated. Cressingham orders his soldiers to stay their torment as he commands another soldier to pour ice-cold water on Malcolm's head. Malcolm screams as the shocking pain from his wounds, beatings and dislocations race through his body like white-hot irons. A soldier binds a long piece of material tightly around Malcolm's bloody mouth, muffling his screams. Through the mist of pain, Malcolm watches as Cressingham picks up Alexander's dirk and walks over to him. Cressingham looks at the blade in admiration. "A blade for a noble King indeed…" He stoops over Malcolm and viciously plunges the blade deep through the back of Malcolm's knee, then he jerks it backwards, slicing through ligaments and tendons. He repeats the painful procedure on the back of Malcolm's other knee. A satisfied Cressingham looks down on Malcolm "Now you won't be running away Malcolm, as my men have a special treat for you." The soldier holding Malcolm's feet together, takes out a dagger and sticks it through the flesh between the Achilles tendon and the bone in Malcolm's ankles, he twists it then quickly pulls it back out, then he forces a long piece of rope through the bleeding holes and ties Malcolm's ankles tightly together. Malcolm can scarcely remain conscious as the shocking searing pain races through his entire body. "Over there." points Cressingham.

The soldiers drag Malcolm along the ground till they come to a tall broad oak where they throw another rope over a bough, tie an end to the knotted piece that binds Malcolm through his ankles, then they haul him high into the air until his face is level with theirs. They secure the rope by tying it around the base of the tree and stand back watching Malcolm swinging in slow circles while racked with indescribable pain. His naked body hangs upside down, trembling and shaking uncontrollably with the agonies of his wounds. Malcolm tries to focus as he sways below the bough of the tree, but even his powerful muscular frame cannot free him from this cruel and tortuous bondage. He focuses on the face of a soldier who is laughing at him, when suddenly, an arrow rips through the soldiers skull then another thumps into his back. Malcolm sees another soldier struck by a number of arrows. As they both fall dying underneath him, the other two soldiers spin round to be met by three arrows each in the chest. Malcolm watches vaguely through his blood-filled eyes, he sees someone running over and violently cutting open the throats of the soldiers who had bound him moments before. The pain in his body burns fiercely in every nerve and fibre of his being like a million white-hot irons, but he may be being saved. That singular thought momentarily alleviates the intense shocking pain. Someone has come to save me, thinks Malcolm. He thinks long enough for him to have clarity and hope.

As Malcolm hangs and swings in slow circles, all he sees occasionally are Cressingham, De Percy and more English soldiers walking towards him. Cressingham is enraged by the incident caused by de Percy, but he says nothing for the moment. He stops a distance away and orders his soldiers and De Percy to wait there while he continues on alone. Cressingham walks up to Malcolm, who is suffering in excruciating pain. "I know you cannot speak Wallace, more is the pity, but I do know you can hear me. I have not finished with you yet, for I must have my pleasures too. It was most unfortunate for my soldiers there, but what they heard cannot be for the ears of anyone but myself and my King; I do trust that my little demonstration does show to you that my disposition is even handed."

A guard calls out, "Lord Cressingham, there's a large body of men and wagons making there way here from the south east." Malcolm prays it could be someone who will stop this torture or that Cressingham will kill him quickly, but Cressingham is distracted, "De Percy, come here, now..." De Percy, having just seen what happened to the personal guards of Cressingham a few moments ago, tentatively approaches the enraged English lord with his head held low. Cressingham says, "You young fool Percy, how come you by Alexander's royal dagger? It's true what you said isn't it." De Percy could not find a reply and pitifully shrugs his shoulders. Cressingham looks down at him, "I do not know what I should do with you? Methinks I should cut your wretched throat here and now to be done with you."

De Percy weeps, "Please forgive me my lord, I thought nothing of it at the time, after we disposed of Alexander, we were returning to our mounts when I saw the blade lying on the ground. I knew I could not leave it there, that's why I picked it up and kept it." Cressingham rages, "You should have destroyed it or left it with the King you idiot, but instead, you wear it as a badge of incredulous stupidity, and then you put our King at risk to accusations of Regicide... What do you think our lord will do to you when he finds out about this folly?" De Percy replies, "He will have me put to the sword my Lord."

"Put to the sword?" exclaims Cressingham, he laughs out loud, "Our King would have your tongue ripped out and your body broken over many years of endless torture, and the same would be placed upon your family by association for treason. I had thought, indeed I am still considering the question of putting an end to your miserable life right here and now, then sending your worthless body home a hero, saying you were unfortunately killed during the capture of this dangerous felon, Sir Malcolm Wallace." Cressingham presses his bloated face next to de Percy, "You will tell me now Percy, who led the assault on King Alexander, for you do not have the wit for such a duty yourself?" De Percy instantly blurts out. "It was sir Humphrey De Courtney my Lord..." Cressingham sneers, "You witless fool, now I know everything, and the ease in which I extracted this information makes you now a constant risk to me."

Cressingham taps Alexander's blade against his hand as he ponders over de Percy's fate. Eventually he speaks, "I will grant you this one folly de Percy, but now your soul belongs to me. Now get out of my sight. Go back to my pavilion, do not speak to anyone between here and next we meet. I want you to watch from the Pavilion all that shall be dealt to Wallace here… for this shall be yours if I hear you have uttered a word to any… do I make myself understood? Not one word." Dropping to his knees, De Percy weeps profusely, in gratitude he kisses Cressingham's feet, just then, a knight and group of soldier's rides towards them, "Get up Percy, and leave me while I decide what to do with you, as I am still in a flux of consideration." At that moment, the approaching knight calls out, "My Lord…" Cressingham replies, "Lord Fenwick, welcome my good fellow."

Sitting upon his horse, Fenwick observes the scene curiously, "What to do lord Cressingham, Is this a seditious Scotchman you have swinging from that bough behind you?" Cressingham replies, "A brigand and a murderer I have apprehended by the name of Malcolm Wallace my lord. He killed six of my men and wounded many others before I subdued him in single-handed combat. I was about to chastise him, will you join me for some amusement?" Dismounting, lord Fenwick approaches, "This damned country is all brigands and foul murderers my dear." Cressingham bids his retainers approach and look to the comfort of Fenwick, "I have been travelling for days from Newcastle, we carry provisions for sir Henry De Percy to make him comfortable in these awful lands. Lord Percy is to assume his titles as the Warden of Galloway, Ayr and Justiciar of Dumfries."

Cressingham smiles, knowing he now has his own spy in the rival De Percy camp. "Lord Fenwick, what shall we do with this ragged fellow hanging here, what is your pleasure?" Reaching out, Fenwick grabs Malcolm by the face and looks into his eyes. Malcolm groans as black blood oozes through the rags binding his mouth. Fenwick replies, "Yes, I do think some sport would be a welcome distraction after such a long and an oh so wearisome journey." Cressingham replies, "My thoughts exactly lord Fenwick, but first, may

I invite you to dine?" As lord Fenwick's baggage train arrives at the foot of Loudon Hill and begins to make camp, the two knights walk back up to the pavilion and sit at the feasting table, where Cressingham invites Fenwick to dine with him before they set to sport with Malcolm. Fenwick says, "I hear that you are to be the king's lord high treasurer in Scotland me' lord Cressingham, in charge of taxation and collection I believe?" Cressingham replies, "I am my Lord, we are to bide our time awhile in this realm and get to know the wherewithal in response to our just imposition of martial law." Fenwick enquires, "And what of their King when he is chosen?" Cressingham laughs, "Forgive my obvious pleasure in your enquiry dear Fenwick, but if Moses himself were to be the next King of Scotland, he would have to climb mount Plantagenet to get permission for his ten commandments."

"You are a wit," guffaws Fenwick "If our Liege lord Edward is next to God, then you must be next to Moses when God instructed him to kill every Midianite woman, boy and non-virgin female. Although the virgins here are to be shared equally amongst our soldiers as a proper use of these Scotch creatures methinks." Cressingham grins, "I shall certainly be a little more lenient on the Scotch than Moses was on the Midianites, for where then would my tax revenues come from? And I do fear there surely cannot be many virgins in Scotland, therefore it is there I believe that the biblical comparison sadly must end."

Fenwick sniggers at Cressinghams reply, then he says, "I understand this peacekeeping duty will be most tedious, though it must serve to be the most frugal and rewarding elimination of a sovereign kingdom I have ever known. For this reason these Scotch heathens do not deserve to rule themselves, especially when they cannot even hold their own piss without offering it up to the highest bidder."

Cressingham laughs as Fenwick continues, "My dear Cressingham, I feel the need for some sport now that we are hale and hearty." Cressingham replies, "How careless and thoughtless of me my lord." Cressingham stands up, "I had almost forgotten about the fox awaiting his chase, what shall we do with him?" Fenwick replies, "Execute him?" Cressingham smiles, "Then I shall carry out your wishes at once my Lord. But perhaps I may make a proposition… some sport with Wallace first my lord, I have an idea that you may be greatly entertained by my special, eh… methods?" Rising up from his seat at the table, Fenwick enquires, "Why, I think that is a splendid idea. What do you have in mind?" Cressingham and Fenwick amble over to where Malcolm is hanging, his face now swollen twice it's normal size, coloured black and purple with the blood settling caused by hanging upside down for so long.

Fenwick enquires, "Is he still alive?" Cressingham examines Malcolm closely, then he replies, "He is very much alive my Lord. I have seen them hang like this for five days or more before they succumb." Cressingham casually swings Malcolm around in circles then grips his head and pinches his cheek, "You are still alive Wallace, aren't you?" Fenwick claps his hands and exclaims, "Oh good lord Cressingham, how exciting, I can hear the devil groaning." Cressingham calls out to a soldier standing close-by and issues him an order, "Soldier, fetch my prize pizzle." then he speaks to Fenwick, "I have been perfecting the art of the flay lord Fenwick, do you partake at all?" A curious Fenwick replies, "No, what is it you intend to do?" Relishing his forthcoming pleasures, Cressingham says, "It's an exhilarating sport my lord, to take as much skin from a wretch as you may without killing him." Fenwick appears impressed, "That must take a great deal of skill Cressingham, oh sirrah, I do admire your delicacies."

The soldier soon returns with Cressingham's prize pizzle. Fenwick enquires "And this leather thingy really made from a bulls peg?" Cressingham replies "It is." as he unrolls a long leathery whip that has been soaked in coarse vinegar. He throws the tail of the whip high and lazily behind his head, then flicks it forward to where it makes a crisp sharp "Crack" like clean dry hand clap.

"Good God man…" exclaims Fenwick, "It's about eight feet long. I am certainly looking forward to this demonstration Cressingham. I have seen this spectacle only once before when I was but a squire on the crusades." Proud and in his element, Cressingham explains, "I first discovered the art of the flay in a book I read when I was a youth on a visit to Rome, apparently the Romans found it to be invigorating for the spirit, and also a way to severely chastise without the early expiry of the chastised." Cressingham casually flicks the whip forward and cracks it. "The skill is to relax and savour the moment of administration, rush, and you may kill the wretch. Do you know dear Fenwick, that it's entirely possible to half a man in two with less than a hundred strokes. I know, for I have mastered it many times." Fenwick replies "How fascinating." Stepping forward, Cressingham punches Malcolm in the ribs, instantly Malcolm groans. "Did you hear him Fenwick, now we shall awaken him with the sting as we remove his flesh." Cressingham calls out to a soldier, "You there, remove that rag from around the prisoners mouth, he needs his mouth free to sing this particular song."

The Soldier quickly removes the rag that binds Malcolm's mouth, he immediately takes in great gasps of air. Other soldiers from the camp and baggage train begin to surround the spectacle. They wager on how many strokes it will take for Cressingham to remove the surface skin from the torso, legs and head of Malcolm while keeping him alive and conscious.

Cressingham steps back a distance, far enough that no blood will splash on him when he administers the first of the flay, moments pass as Cressingham lines up Malcolms torso, then he throws the whip tail forward along the ground. "Hold him steady…" commands Cressingham. A soldier steps forward and stops Malcolm from swinging. Now, as a hanging deadweight, everyone waits… Cressingham pulls back on his pizzle then whips it forward, the tip instantly cracks off Malcolm's back, taking out a deep bite of flesh with its contact as Malcolm lets out a blood curdling scream. Fenwick's eyes light up with excitement, "I see what you mean Cressingham, very exciting, thrilling even…"

Again Cressingham whips Malcolm's back and Malcolm releases a primal scream. Cressingham and Fenwick are greatly amused. Cressingham spends long deliberate time whipping Malcolm, till half his buttocks, back, chest and the rear of his skull is stripped of flesh. Cressingham is sweating profusely with his excretions… he looks at Fenwick, "Would you wish the pleasure good sir?" Fenwick replies with obvious excitement in his voice. "May I? My God Cressingham, the thrill of it all, you were right about this being an invigorating spectacle, I must investigate this more." Cressingham smiles, "The secret is to keep the objects screams to a high pitch, when he starts to dull down, it is best then to leave him awhile or he may expire. Do you know dear Fenwick, that you can do this for days on end upon the same object, it is a great pastime for the alleviation of boredom, and the screams are good for the humours of the spleen."

"I say Cressingham, this is truly exciting." Fenwick attempts his first whip and cuts a deep gash across Malcolm's ribs, the soldiers all cheer Fenwick on as he makes another attempt, only to cause another deep gash across Malcolm's face. "Finesse my dear Fenwick, Finesse…" Cressingham advises,

"You must employ finesse to fully enjoy the thrill of the wretches song." Concentrating, Fenwick whips Malcolm once more, this time Fenwick meets with success, the piercing scream from Malcolm matches previous screams extracted by Cressingham. Fenwick is ecstatic, "I did it, I did it… Cressingham my dear, such fun…"

Time passes by till Malcolm's skin is completely flayed from his back, legs and ribs. He hangs in such excruciating pain that it could never be described in words. Cressingham and Fenwick agree to rest awhile and decide to walk back to the pavilion for refreshments. "My word," says Fenwick, "T'is such a pity that we must going by the morn Cressingham, for I do believe you have a convert to the pizzle in me." Fenwick continues, "I do hope you don't mind my Lord, but I have ordered my archers to use that Scotchman for target practice, if that meets with your approval of course. He is your prisoner after all." Cressingham replies "No, no my lord Fenwick, he is your prisoner to do with as you will. I cannot take this honour alone. I do believe our lord Edward will be extremely pleased that you personally apprehended and eliminated one of his most seditious and treasonous opponents in this cursed land." Fenwick is taken aback and looks at Cressingham, completely surprised and delighted. He taps the end of his nose then says, "By God sir, I shall not forget this magnanimous gift Cressingham, you have my deepest gratitude good sir." Cressingham waves his hand frivolously, "Oh my lord Fenwick, think nothing off it, he was only a vermin Scotchman. There will be many more for the pizzle in this land, I warrant you."

They both laugh then chatter as the final sport is played out on Malcolm. English archers begin firing arrows into his body from a distance. As each arrow buries itself deep into his body, it's accompanied by great cheers, jeering and whistles from the watching English soldiers.

Eventually, Malcolm passes from this life to a better place; long before the archers have tired themselves abusing his earth bound body. Fenwick looks up and notices the lifeless body of Malcolm hanging in the distance, "I think we should leave him hanging there as a deterrent to other Scotch scoundrels passing this way Cressingham, don't you agree? Though I rather think that Scotchman swinging there like a hung hedgehog should have at least thanked us before he expired, for it cannot be a life worth living in this forsaken province for poor wretches such as he. What kind of life could he have had that is worth any account to a civilised man." Cressingham guffaws at Fenwick's comment, "I concur my lord."

They cheerfully dine while watching the sport continue on Malcolm's lifeless body. Cressingham continues to foster good will with another of Longshanks' much-favoured member of the English royal court. A short distance away, De Percy sulks and nurses his wounds while watching Fenwick enjoy the privileges that should rightfully have been his upon the demise of sir Malcolm. He sneers at the thought Cressingham has so easily duped Fenwick into taking the responsibility for the killing of sir Malcolm Wallace... he thinks, *'That's not a good claim to be making when in a foreign realm, knowing relatives of the victim will be honour bound to seek you out for blood vengeance. My foolish Lord Fenwick.'* De Percy laughs at the thought, but he knows that he has much to do to gain back the good humours of Cressingham, he also knows that he has much to learn from this intelligent and shrewd political strategist. He is also acutely aware that his life is now at the mercy and whim of Lord Cressingham. *'No, I will watch Cressingham closely and learn. Every Scotchman who dares to cross me now will pay dearly for this day's chastisement.*

And I won't forget it was caused by a Wallace, I will not forget that name… Wallace.'

FIRES OF DARKFALL

William walks along the Invergarvane longshore as two of Morrison mòr's Blue Angel Birlinns drop their sails and begin manoeuvring on the tide swell to close in on the beach. He gazes at the backdrop of the Kintyre Peninsula and Rathlan islands as they reach across to compliment the mainland coast of Ireland on the horizon, creating an all-shimmering natural aquatic theatre in the early morning sun. William has not slept and spent much of his time since dawn in remembrance of all his many friends who'd died on the Duibh hill looming behind him... He sits down on the sandy beach, peacefully enjoying the solitude and serenity, the silence broken intermittently by the occasional squawking cry of a seagull, the cackling of a beachcombing crow or shrill whistle of a lapwing peewit, accompanied by a choral backdrop of repetitive washing sounds caused by the tide swell pushing ashore, then dutifully retreating in a synchronization and rhythmic beat to the splashing of one hundred oars rowing each of the Birlinns.

Looking up, William sees the Birlinn oarsmen pulling furiously, long and deep, all in order to speed up the last few yards to push each bow of the sea-greyhounds high over the loose shingle and onto the longshore beach. Brushing himself down, William approaches the longships as showers of roughly tied packs and bags are thrown ashore from each

Birlinn, followed by a variety of crewmen and traders hastily disembarking. It's then William sees Stephen standing on deck with Morrison mòr shaking hands. Stephen turns and jumps from the Birlinn and cheerily waves to William. Morrison mòr nods towards William who returns the gesture in kind. Stephen shouts out gleefully, "How are yie Wallace?" William replies, "Feckn great for having you back with us Mac ua h'Alpine."

The two friends meet and greet with the warm embrace of bonded brothers. Many others barely notice them, such is the rush to go their various ways into Scotland and far from the place of landing used by Scots and Irish alike for over a millennium. William helps Stephen pick up and carry his kit over to where the horses are tethered. He enquires, "How was the wake for the passin' o' your father." Stephen replies, "Holy feck Wallace, the wake be-Jaezuz, I was so feckn drunk and for near a week I tell yee. But sure now, that's me Dá sent off safely away to a far better place than this." William enquires, "And what about Ròsinn and wee John, how are they doin', will they be coming over the water soon?" Stephen replies happily, "Would yie credit them, haven't they a little bleedin' family of their own now, two wee fella's and a bonnie wee girl."

"Feck," exclaims William "Wee Maw will be happy to hear this news." Stephen continues, "But I've to be telling you that they're going off to Flanders and the Low Countries soon, wee John has found good work with a Flemish wool trader, he sez he will write you when they arrive there safely." William sighs, "Wee John off to Flanders, ach well, he always did have a want for adventure, though I never thought it would be with a wife and family in tow. Anyway Stephen, do yie have any other kinfolk still left alive over there?" Stephen laughs, "Apart from me dear auld Maw, oi do, but I was the only genuine bastard that me fadder ever had." Both of them laugh as they strap Stephen's kit onto the back of the packhorse. Stephen enquires, "Have you been waiting here awhile?" William replies, "Naw, I arrived here last night. I had hoped you'd be across sooner rather than later though, then I thought you might even be a couple of day's yet, so its great you came in this morn." Stephen picks up the reigns of the horse William has brought for him, "Get on your horse Wallace, for I have a wonderful woman that will be dying to see me." William mounts his horses and pulls up beside Stephen. "If I were you Stephen…" Looking at William curiously, Stephen enquires, "If you were me what Wallace me boy?" William laughs, "I wouldn't be sitting here talking to me, I would already be over that hill on my way to meet ma darlin." William spurs his horse and canters along the beach towards Turnberry Castle; then he turns north towards Ach na Feàrna. Stephen gallops after him, dragging the packhorse and catching up after a few miles, then they both slow down to a walk.

"Why are we heading this way Wallace? I thought we would be going over the Duibh hill above Invergarvane, then northeast to Glen Afton?" William replies, "We've to go up to Ach na Feàrna first and pick up salt and vittal wagons then take them back down to Glen Afton" Stephen appears extremely disappointed… "Fuck Wallace, do I have to go too? I need to be seeing Katriona. I have this awful feeling in me gut that she needs me… I just want to get to me woman and put me lovin' arms around me darlin' then hug her the only way this man can hug his woman; if you get ma meaning." Looking at the serious innocence etched in Stephen's face, William says, "Feck it Stephen, I agree with yie. When we get near to Turnberry, we can cut overland to the abbey of Crossraguel, I'll go on up to Ach na Feàrna from there and you can head over the Carrick to Glen Afton. I'll get a couple o' the boys from Ach na Feàrna to drive the wagons down for I'd be the same as yourself if it were ma bonnie Marion that I'd come home to see." Stephen grins, "Yer a good man Wallace, sure I am just pure champin' at me own bit to be seeing me darlin' and wee Stephen." William says, "She must be missin' yie so Stephen, she was so heartbroken when yie left for Ireland, but ah reckon wee Graham and auld Jean would keep her mind busy while yie were away." Stephen says, "I've missed her Wallace, I never thought I would ever feel like this, but sure now, I'm feckn glad I do, it's a great feelin' to have the love of a very fine woman. William nods thoughtfully then he replies, "It sure is Stephen; it sure is."

Travelling along enjoying each other's company, Stephen says, "It's a funny thing isn't it, one day you're free to do what you want wit not a bleedin' care in th' world, then you have a family and everything changes. Having a wife and family sure is the most wonderful disaster inflicted upon any man." William sighs, "Ah, that reminds me ya auld stud yie…" Stephen looks at William curiously, "What are yie talking about there Wallace?" William laughs, "Katriona and you having another wee Mac ua h'Alpine in the making, you kept that one quiet." Grinning from ear to ear, Stephen replies, "Ach sure now, I just couldn't be helping me'self now could I? It's a terrible affliction for a man like me with too much virility for me own good, an over-abundance o' manliness some would call it." William laughs, "Well keep this to yourself Stephen, but me and Marion won't be far behind yie."

"Naw… not you and the bonnie maid Marion…" A smug William replies, "Yup." Stephen laughs, "Well feck me ya durty big feckr. Then it's congratulations to you ma virile brother. Does anyone else know yet?" William replies, "I think wee Maw is on to us, but no-one else. When I get back to Glen Afton we're going to ask her Dá to wed us on the Beltane."

Stephen shakes his head in amazement and with the sheer joy of being back in Scotland to hear such welcoming news. He enquires, "How many moons is she?" William replies, "About five by now she says," William grins thinking about his love as Stephen's face lights up, "That's about the same as me and Katriona, is that not just a wonderful thing?" William enquires, "Stephen, when yie get over to Afton, If Marion is there with Mharaidh and Katriona, will you tell her I'm bringing a big surprise with me that I bought for her when ah was last up in Perth. Oh, and if yie see Brannah, tell her Andra Moray is asking after her, and ah mean he's asking for her if yie know what ah mean." Stephen replies, "Sure now, that I will," Stephen ponders, "So what's this big surprise yie have for Marion?" William grins, "Yie will never guess." Stephen replies, "What did yie get her, a diamond the size o' yer big head?" William laughs, "Naw, it's even better than that…"

Stephen is curious, "Tell me Wallace, the suspense is doin' me nut in?" William replies with pride, "I bought her a big barrel o' Lübeck Ale." Stephen exclaims, "What the… are yie feckn mad Wallace." William continues, "Naw Stephen, I have a cunnin' plan behind ma madness, I thought it would be great idea to sweeten up her auld fella to get him ready for us askin' to be wed about the Beltane." A bemused Stephen looks curiously at William, then he exclaims, "Ah don't believe ahm hearin' this… yie've bought bonnie Marion a barrel o' fuckin' Ale as a weddin' gift? Are yee feckn… naw, oi already know the answer to that, yie really are mad. But Ale Wallace, what were yee thinkin' me dense, lovable brother?"

The two friends meander up the drove road chatting about the loves in their lives, when William stops and exclaims, "Fuck Stephen, you wouldn't believe what else has been happening since you left for Ireland." Stephen enquires,

"Aye… Like what?" William's face darkens, "The English are back here in force this time and putting garrisons in all the towns, castles and ports o' Scotland. Apparently they're here as peacekeepers until we've got a new King or Queen, and that'll be when the King o' England decides who that is." Stephen looks at William, this time with a depressed expression and a deep serious frown on his face, "And you Scots actually believe that?" William replies, "Its no' us ordinary Scots Stephen, it's the church leaders and most of the nobles… they seem to be saying that without the help of the English, we're fucked." Stephen sighs, "Naw, now you Scots really are fucked, how could yiez be so feckin stupid as to invite the feckn English back in? I'll wager that the most of those fellas that agreed to all o' this shite are Norman. Och Wallace me boy, I've seen how they behave in Ireland, you have too, Jaezuz, I feckin warned you didn't I, and I know you know I know I did." William smiles, "And ah know yie know ah know yer right."

Exasperated, Stephen replies sternly, "I know I'm bleedin right, didn't I feckn warn you what would happen here Wallace? And this will be just the start of it." Stephen shakes his head, "When the Normans raped and plundered their way through my Ireland, they feck'd our Breitheamh laws like they had never been. The fact is these English and Norman settlers want to live like they're little bleedin' kings over what they call us savages. The bastards are oblivious and ignorant of our ancient circumstance Wallace, these feckn Norman princes don't realise they are as much amenable to our ancient Breathaimh laws as the lowest of the people that they think to lord it over, and then they call us their subjects, simples or bleedin' villains? Oi don't fuckin tink so. I reckon trouble will no' be far away ah tell yee, this is a disaster in the makin." Listening quietly to Stephen, William knows the Breathaimh laws are still the unspoken rule of the Céile Aicéin the remote corners of Scotland. He has studied them and knows well the detail and minutia of all the Breitheamh prescriptives, though the Norman law of feudalism in Scotland has long since usurped it generally. Stephen is showing unbridled frustration as he continues, "Our ancient's governed all our Breithiúna prescriptives for more than a thousand years." William shakes his head, "Aye, and the feckn priests now try to tell us that our ancient laws never existed." Stephen spits on the ground, "If our people ever did go to war, it was for the sole benefit of the Clan or kingdom, not for an individual's greed or aggrandizement. If folk transgressed, the sentence would be in accordance with the law of the people. These feckn Normans respect no law ceptin' that which satisfies their greed. Wallace me boy, these feckrs will stop at nuthin' to obtain land and they'll use bloody force upon anyone to gain territorial possessions and at any cost, particularly the cost of our own people. Our bleedin' existence means nuthin' to them." William can hear the pain of frustration borne from experience in the words of a fellow Cruathnie.

"So Stephen…" he enquires "Did you have any problems from De Burgh or his men when you went back home?" Stephen smiles, "Now there's a man of interest… Did you know that after your last debacle in Scotland with that little civil war yiez had, those fella's Robert Brix, Richard and Thomas de Clare of Thomond and that group o' Scottish nobles who formed the Turnberry Pact… didn't they not just come across the water and join wit De Burgh to fight our chiefs?" William enquires, "Yer feckn jestin me?" Stephen replies, "Naw, they did, and it was not long after they defeated their own Scots kinsmen on the isle of Manaan, and wouldn't you just believe it? They then handed the island over to the feckn English King as a gesture o' good will..." William exclaims, "Fuck off Stephen, that's Scotland's main trading Island in the west. They cannae do that?" Stephen drops his head, "Well they did I'll be tellin' ya, Manaan now belongs to Edward of England." Gloomy thoughts invade the peace of the two young friends as they ride along in silence, suddenly Stephen sits up in his saddle wide eyed with an enormous smile, "Oh Wallace, that'll be reminding me, do yie remember that bastard son of old Phelim O' Connor, young Dermott?" William replies, "Aye, What about him?" Stephen replies, "Well Wallace, he's asking after you, he misses that fine bow strength of yours and he's wondering if you wouldn't mind to be coming back across to Erinn, for he's set to be having another adventure against de Burgh and he has a place for you if you want it?"

William ponders, "That might be a thought, especially if the English are set to be making life in Scotland as miserable and dangerous like the last time they were here." Stephen laughs, "Well Wallace, sure now, you can't be going back to auld Erinn and then get caught." William looks at Stephen curiously, "Feck Stephen, you just asked me if I would go back, then you say that I can't be going back?" Smiling as they ride along, Stephen replies, "The only work you Scots fella's are allowed to be doin' in old Erinn now, other than in bonded servitude, is for an English or Norman Lord. The English and the Catholic Church in all their wisdom, have colluded to make another new law to put you lot down over there, they declare that any Scotch, be they man woman or youth, are now to be deemed heretics. The Justiciary in all of Ireland has made laws prohibiting any Irish to associate or work with a Scot, if any Scotchman or native Irish seek confederacies, the offending Scot and their Irish employer are to be put to the question then imprisoned and put to

more bleedin' questions." William exclaims "Questioned...
yie mean tortured don't yie?" Stephen replies, "Aye, but
they call it questioned or imprisoned now." William laughs,
"Imprisoned?" Stephen laughs, "Aye, that's the words they
want recorded in the annals of auld Ireland, yie know, to
make them look civilised for posterity. But they will still
torture you, have your prick torn off by hungry dogs, pluck
your eyeballs out, cut your nuts off, then hang you up to bleed
out, the English Lords call it *'imprisoned'* in my Ireland. Aye,
those Norman bastards sure have a wordy sense o' humour."
William laughs, "If that's imprisoned, what the feck would
they do to us if they said that we were condemned?" Stephen
says, "Aye, for some reason they're sure desperate to keep the
Irish and Scots apart, maybe they fear what might happen
if we all ally together..." William replies, "Maybe we should,
could yie just imagine the amount of shit that would drop
down the inside legs of English armour if that ever happens."

They both laugh at the thought; then William enquires,
"So, what of De Burgh Stephen, now that I know I can't go
back to Ireland." Stephen replies, "Well, do yie remember
old Dermott's O'Connor's sons, Conchobar and Rory?"
William replies, "Aye, how could I forget those two lovable
bull-headed murderers? Those two boys are right mad feckrs,
but I really like them... so what about them?" Stephen grins,
"Conchobar and Rory were so bleedin' sick that every time
they and other Irish chieftains went to pay their taxes to
de Burgh, he would force them to go on their knees, then
he would pull their beards before he would allow each
one to speak, and all just to be amusing his English guests
and his friends." William sighs, "Fuck... Old King John of
England sure lives on in de Burgh right enough, the dirty
bastard." Stephen says, "Ach Wallace me boy, it wasn't just
the beard pullin' that had set Rory and Conchobar off."

William enquires, "What did set them off then?" Stephen replies, "Do yie mind o' those two women De Burgh murdered up near Domhnach Daoi?" William replies, "Aye, ahl never forget it." Stephen continues, "Well, the younger one o' the women de Burgh murdered, she was their wee sister Cloda." William groans, "Awe naw…" Stephen sighs, "Awe fuck aye. Well I'll tell yee, Rory and Conchobar set about raising a mighty federation o' fighting O'Connor's from Connacht and Offaly, wit Turlach mòr's men o' Athlone, then they all joined wit' the Northern UíNeil's and the Geraldine's o' Kildare… all the clans that have a right good blood feud goin' wit de Burgh, they feckn hate the red earl and his Irish sympathiser's wit' a vengeance… Now, Dermott's boys have gathered near on a thousand madmen, all armed up to their back feckn teeth wit a fightin' fury in heir hearts."

"Jaezuz Stephen, I learnt a lot from Rory and Conchobar, it sounds like they're going to have some fine hop over there." Stephen laughs,"Hop he sez… Sure they've been hopping all over de Burgh for a about a year now, and they've pushed the red Earl and his English forces out o' Trym on the Boyne; then the boys made a most perfect alliance with Manus O'Connor's very own madmen. All of these collective Gallóglaigh brethren were rejoicing so bleedin' well, it caused de Burgh to retreat from Roscommon to be hiding away in the deepest dungeons of Clanrickarde near Mayo."

"Fuck me," sighs William "Rory and Conchobar are doin' the do' then?" Stephen replies, "Aye, and the pair o' them are doin' it all over de Burgh. The last news I heard was that young Rory had stormed the castle of Tiaghquin and his brother Conchobar laid waste about Dunmore; then they both marched on Ard'Narea and the Ballintogher fortification settlements, after which they burned them down to the ground I might add, the lucky feckrs are havin' a whale of a time. They're now happily chasing de Burgh, the Normans and all o' those fine Englishmen away from east Connaught and back into the Dublin pale." William enquires, "So where is De Burgh now?" Stephen replies, "The big Norman shit managed to escape from Mayo, then a friend of yours King Edward, he sent more troops from England and Dublin to aid de Burgh, but they couldn't dislodge the grit of the merry men of the O'Connor alliance, so De Burgh is now set about busily rebuilding the castles of Aird-Craibhe, Benn-Fliada and the castle o' Sligo to be hiding away in."

"What are the O'Connor's, Geraldine's and O'Neill's doing now then?" enquires William. Stephen exclaims, "Would you bleedin' believe it, they went home happily defiant. And get this me foin Scotchman, they went home contented with their plunder and so very well satisfied in themselves that no de Burgh or any feckn priests will be coming soon with the holy cross in one hand and the hangman's rope in the other no more." William sighs, "Stephen, we could do with all those fine fella's in Scotland right now." Stephen replies, "Ach you never know Wallace, maybe some day they will come a' visitin'. They said if it gets too hot over there, they be thinkin' that a visit to Scotland would be just fine and bleedin' dandy."

As they ride along, William enquires, "Did you ever hear anything about that young Elizabeth lass, de Burgh's daughter?" Stephen replies, "Apparently she's been forgiven, but only after it was confirmed that her twang was still in tact." William laughs, "That's one way to put it." Stephen laughs, "Here's another way to put it. It was confirmed her wee kipper had not been ripped asunder by that young fella Robert "THEE" Bruce, wasn't that his name?" William laughs, "Aye, Robert thee Bruce." Stephen says with a grin, "Well Wallace, as it so happens… Thee Bruce's old fella Robert Brus of Carrick, he's one of de Burgh's strongest allies, so it would appear that all is well between her and him now." William says, "I don't think de Burgh would have too much to say after we left him." Stephen grins, "I tink it was nearly a year before he had anything to say at all, mind you, it would have been a bit difficult after we left him with his mouth wrapped around the back of his head, oi'm sure me bleedin' foot still hurts from that day. But it was good thing when we graced him with a Scots kiss wit such fine Irish brogan leather and so much free time to be thinking of his rude behaviour." William laughs, "Aye Stephen, he should actually be thankin' us, for we revealed to him that he really did have the luck o' the Irish that day."

The two friends laugh, then Stephen says, "Aye, lucky for him that we didn't bury him alive on that shore... yie could say he had the luck o the Irish to get off Scot free." They both laugh at the banter, then William says "You could also say we left him speechless," Stephen quips "And at a loss for words..." The two of friends laugh heartily as they near Crossraguel. "Wallace me boy," says Stephen "Now it's for you to be telling to me what' else has been happening to this sad little old country without me foin company in it, what's wit ya?" William thinks awhile then he laughs to himself, "Fuck me Stephen, you wouldn't believe what else's happened." Stephen pulls his reigns close as they cross a burn, "If you're involved Wallace, then I will sure believe it; no matter how unbelievable it is." With William smiling to himself as they ride along, Stephen becomes curious, "Like eh, are yee going to tell me Wallace, what is it would I not be believing?" William cheerily replies, "The English have declared me to be a wilful sinful drunken wretch, a vagabond, a waster and now it's official on all the wanted writs... I'm an ale thieving outlaw." Stephen exclaims, "What th' fuck," he reigns his horse in to a stop and grins at William, "Well done me inferior Scots brother, I always new you had the making of a good outlaw in ya… but how the feck did all this come about? And you being an honourable bleedin' Ale thief to boot, oh, oi'm so feckn jealous." William nudges his horse to walk-on, but Stephen isn't satisfied, "Wait up Wallace ya durty Ale theivin' feckn outlaw yie… tell me how it is you came about earning such glorious merit and distinction as to be entered into the annals of history as a feckn ale thief, and all of this without me good self there to guide yie, well done me boy, oi'm so proud o' yie? Right enough, now, there's a noble profession and fine enterprise to be aspiring too, and I've only been away a few weeks?" William tells all to Stephen about his adventures and misadventures as they make their way over the Ayrshire hills.

It isn't long before they approach the south wall of the nave to the wondrous Cluniac abbey of Crossraguel. Stephen remarks, "Fuck, that seems like it was a quick journey." "That's because I couldn't get yie to feckn shut up." laughs William. They dismount and let the horses graze awhile as they wander around the stalls and busy trader wagons surrounding the industrious little abbey. William says, "I don't want to stay here too long Stephen, I need to be getting back to Ach na Feàrna if I want to be seeing you all before dusk sets in Glen Afton this night." Stephen agrees, "I'll be going to head out me'self now Wallace, for the bonnie lass needs me more than she knows, I just have this gnawin' feelin' in me bones…" William says, "Do yie not mean yie fancy a gnawin' feelin on yer bone?" Stephen laughs, "Ach Wallace now that's a fine romantic thing to be sayin, and ah must admit, it does sound good." The two friends laugh as make their way back to the horses and mount. William says, "You take the packhorse with you, its got kit I need down there anyway." Stephen secures the packhorse to the back of his saddle and turns to face William, "Ach, it's sure been great to be back and to be seeing you again Wallace." William puts his hand out and they both shake by gripping the wrists, "Mac ua h'Alpine me brother, I sincerely wish I could say the same about you." Stephen frowns… then they both laugh. William continues, "Will yie tell ma folks I'll be down as soon as I can." The two friends bid each other farewell and set out in different directions for their final destinations.

A few hours later, William approaches the last milestone to Ach na Feàrna. As he canters along he's thinking how happy he is now that Stephen is back and how much he enjoyed the conversation and craic with him. Soon he'll be seeing wee Maw, knowing that he'll get well fed and to be telling her the news about wee John and Rosinn, then he'll leave as quickly as possible to make it down to Glen Afton before nightfall. He thinks about some of the things that he and Stephen have talked about, it warms his heart and brings a grin to his face. He also thinks about Stephen and Katriona having another child and wonders if it will be another boy or girl, would they call it wee Graham regardless? He laughs to himself, '*Fuck… what if Stephen's wain is born with ginger hair, who would get the blame?*' William stops laughing when he considers… '*What if Marion has a wain with ginger hair; who would get the blame then?*' As he wonders along he laughs at the thoughts, though he knows if it's a boy, he would name him after his grandfather Billy, if it's a girl then Marion would choose, for a wee girl would still be an Aicé in his eyes. William grins at the absurdity of his thoughts then he spurs his horse to a gallop the last few hundred yards to Ach na Feàrna.

As he canters through the open gates, he brings his horse to a sudden halt, something is making him uneasy, there's nobody at the gates. He looks around the place, there doesn't appear to be anyone anywhere, not even anyone working the fields near or around Ach na Feàrna. He feels a cold chill running through his mind as he tentatively walks his horse into the yards. He notices unfamiliar horses tethered over at the main house, he continues to walk-on through the eerie silence, there is absolutely nobody nor any livestock to be seen? He thinks *'Where is everyone... there are no chickens, no hens, goats, oxen or cows?'* William looks over to the horse corrals; there are no horses, nothing... It's as if everyone has left in a hurry. He walks on slowly and cautiously through the Ach na Feàrna Balloch homesteads, till finally he arrives beside the strangers horses at the main house, where he recognises there is one horse that belongs to his uncle Ranald, the others are stud stallions belonging to men of station. Suddenly the main house door opens, Aunia and Uliann run outside crying and weeping. William quickly dismounts where they grasp at him and hold him tightly "Oh William..." they cry. He urgently enquires, "What's wrong what's happened?" The two young women couldn't speak with any sense that he could understand. A voice calls out aloud from the main house door, "William..."

"Ranald," exclaims William, "What's going on, what's wrong?" He urgently demands an answer as the two women cling to him as though they're in fear for their lives. He sees in their eyes a look of sheer terror; they appear dishevelled and totally distraught. "Come in, come, quickly," beckons Ranald, "There's been a terrible visitation been put upon our family." Ranald comes over at a pace towards William; Aunia throws herself at Ranald and clings on while Uliann refuses to let go William. With the two women holding on to William and Ranald for dear life, they quickly enter the main house and go through to the kitchens, there William sees True Tam talking quietly to himself and some of Ranald's attendants boiling water and soaking bloodied pieces of cloth to clean and re-use. "What's going on here, what's happened, where is everyone?" demands William as he tries to understand the scenes before him. "Will somebody tell me what the fuck is going on..." William rages in circles around the kitchens demanding answers. "Sit down boy and I will tell you," commands Ranald. "English soldiers came to Ach na Feàrna yesterday about noon and they took away all of the livestock, animals and horses. They said it was a lawful requisition for their garrisons in Glasgow and Ruther's glen. Then they told everyone to vacate the place or they would be imprisoned for sedition." Dumbstruck, William looks at everyone, they all have the same grey pallor etched in their faces, he sees True Tam usher Uliann and Aunia through to another room. William demands with a sense of urgency "Where's Margret, Malcolm óg, Andrew... wee Maw?"

Everyone looks at each other; Ranald puts his hand on William's shoulder, but William shrugs it away and shouts as he slams both fists onto the table "Is somebody going to fuckin' tell me what happened here, where is everybody?" Ranald says, "William, stay yer temper, your cousin Malcolm óg lies unconscious, he has been badly beaten and both his legs are broken. When the English took the livestock, Malcolm óg tried to stop them, but they beat him senseless with staves, he is in a very bad condition, but True Tam here has been tending with great care to his needs." William enquires, "What of wee Maw, Andrew and Margret?" Ranald replies, "Apparently they rushed to the gates to try and prevent the English leaving with everything, but the English simply ran them over them and trampled them down with their horses, then the soldiers beat them, but Margret..." William's head is in a spin, he can't grasp or understand the enormity of the situation. "What about Margret, what is it with Margret, is she still alive?" Ranald replies mournfully, "They violated her after she was injured, you know she was with child and… she lost the wee soul. William, I must tell you, they violated all the women here." William gasps "All of the women, you mean… naw… this cannae be true?" He looks at Ranald who shakes his head mournfully. "All of the women…" William exclaims desperately, "Even wee Maw…?" Ranald simply nods his head then he looks away. William sinks his head into his arms on the table; this is almost too much to take in. He mumbles, "Where is wee Maw?" Ranald replies, "Wee Maw is cribbed in the next room." Suddenly William feels a panic in his chest, "Is she…?" True Tam says, "Wee Maw will be fine if we gain time enough to let the potions take affect."

Ranald puts his hand out, "All still live William, but they are badly broken and hold loosely to life, they will be needing the greatest of care for a long time." William rises from his seat, "I want see them now?" Ranald gets up, "Come with me, but yie need to be as quiet as yie can be." They walk tentatively into a darkened room, where William is instantly hit by a heavy pungent smell that makes him want to retch. Ranald sees his reaction, "It's the herbs and potions True Tam and the good women who came to help are using to ease the pains of the wounds." Peering into the darkened room, William sees three rough looking makeshift cribs where Margret, Malcolm óg and wee Maw are being tended. He walks slowly and silently over towards his family. As he gains closer, suddenly he recoils in shock, Margret and Malcolm look like creatures from some hellish butchers bench, both their heads are swollen and bodies pulverised, making them almost unrecognizable, though thankfully they didn't appear to have consciousness to be aware of anything, particularly the pain. Terrible waves of convulsion course through William upon seeing their condition, the awful smell of blood, open wounds and the herbal elixirs being used repulses him. He approaches the crib of wee Maw where he sees deep cuts and bruising on her face and arms, but she does not appear as badly injured as the others. He whispers to Ranald, "What can I do, I mean who did this… why? Ranald, I don't understand what's happening in my head. Who would do this to us and for what reason?" Ranald shakes his head despondently, he has no answer to give. William simply stares at him in pained disbelief.

Kneeling silently between wee Maw and Margret, William reaches out and takes Margret gently by the hand, but there's no response. He reaches out with his other hand and lifts wee Maw's tiny hand, he sits awhile trying to gain some form of understanding, but there is none that would make sense of this, then he hears wee Maw moaning. He quickly turns to her and clasps her hand with both of his and whispers, "Its me granny, William." She speaks with a voice so quiet that he has to put his ear next her lips. She says, "Is that you Billy?" He feels the tears of unbridled emotion well up in his heart, he replies, "It's me Granny, it's William." Wee Maw sobs hearing the familiar voice, she cries, "Oh William I am so pained; will you go fetch Billy for me?" William glances at Ranald then he looks again at wee Maw, "I will, I'll see if he's here Granny." Still clasping wee Maws hand, she lets go and reaches out to gently stroke his long hair; she says with a very weak smile, "I know you will son."

He sits watching wee Maw till she falls back into a deep sleep, he waits awhile longer then he kisses her hand gently, stands up and pulls her mantle cover up to keep her warm. He looks at Margret and kisses her on the forehead too, then walks around Margret's crib and kneels beside his cousin Malcolm óg. He whispers, "I will wreak a terrible fuckin' vengeance upon whoever did this to us Malcolm, I swear to you by my life…"

Standing up William looks at Ranald then they both leave the room and make their way back to the kitchens. William notices Uliann and Aunia are busily boiling linen bandages beside True Tam, who is frantically creating his healing elixirs for the injured members of his family. Everyone has something to do to help the injured members of his family except him. True Tam looks up and acknowledges William, but he says nothing, though his presence here is a great relief. William feels that if his family has any hope of recovery, then it will come from the ancient skills and knowledge of True Tam, he doesn't know why, he just has a feeling. True Tam looks up again as though reading William's mind, "You are a true born blood from an Aicé Wallace, be sure that I will do all I can that is within my given powers to ease the pain for your family, for I owe your grandmother a great debt of life, and I will look to her and hers as my own, never fear." William feels a sense of understanding and calm when True Tam speaks, he's beginning to understand why wee Maw and the elders of the clan have such a love of True Tam as a friend, yet there is no rationale for this feeling he now has for this virtual stranger. William walks over to the door and looks out across the empty yards of Ach na Feàrna, his mind races as he searches for an answer to this nightmarish cruelty being dealt out to his loved ones, "Why Tam... Why do the English treat us so? We have done them no harm, why Tam, why do this to us?"

True Tam looks up at William with an expression in his face as though he already knows the answer. "Wallace, I have seen many things in my life, I've seen things that has made men want to kill me simply by my very being, not because I would offer them harm, but because they see me as different. This evil that descends upon this land has long gnawed at our shores and border marches. Now, in our time of greatest weakness, this malignancy and violence spreads throughout our realm like a plague. If we fail to resist this creeping pestilent evil born of earthly men, then all our people will suffer obscene cruelties of mind and soul for a thousand years and beyond." William feels calmness and peace descend upon his frantic mind as True Tam continues… "Scotland has long suffered terrible cruelty by its own hands, we are no different from any other kingdom that suffers the pains of birth, and yet as one, we've courageously resisted all invaders, but now, now our nobles are so easily deceived into yielding up our sovereignty like drunken parents who have no care for their children, our realm is delivered up to another without even a struggle nor a murmur of indignation upon this betrayal of our trust in them."

Shaking his head; almost demoralised, William says, "I cannot understand why our nobles are doing this to us Tam, or letting it happen, why do they betray the common man like this?" True Tam replies, "Ordinary people throughout the land are sharing this pain Wallace, most can scarce understand or believe it possible. Their precious freedoms so dearly bought is all but gone in moments of wanton brutality till our kingdom of Scotland is near no more. A proud realm worth less than the poorest shire of England, all because a few nobles lick coin from England's table."

"What then is to become of us the ordinary folk Tam? Are we to become hungry slaves in the fields of the rich or a source of battle fodder for these few noblemen of greed. But why this Tam, why all the barbarous cruelty that I've witnessed upon others that now visits my own family, I don't understand?" True Tam appears forlorn, "The famishing nobles of Norman blood accept this powerful English king at a price yet to be paid Wallace. They may be satisfied now in having retained their possessions, for they covet their wealth and little territories of land with what they believe to be privileged entitlement, simply to satisfy the avarice in their hearts. But for the mass of the common people of this land, we must now suffer an evil so deep, so malicious and so sullen, that our existence at the very hands of those we ever trusted to protect us would now ravage us unto a cruel and untimely death…" William enquires, "Who is there to protect us from this English king and his lackies?" True Tam replies "We are a people betrayed Wallace, but we are not a people conquered, take this hope with you into the dark days to come."

Their eyes meet for a moment in time. Really hearing and understanding the meaning of True Tam's words creates an electrifying moment of shared understanding with this mystical man. William has always felt something right about this unusual character ever since the first time he ever saw him, unnerving and uncanny at first, but he knows now that True Tam's very being has constantly nourished trust and faith from his family and anyone who has truly known this curious man for many years, now William is finding great solace in his words and life giving deeds.

Suddenly the door opens and one of Ranald's trusted guards rushes into the kitchens, the guard exclaims, "I just found these ringed messages on two birds in the doocots." He places two strips of velum based homing pigeon messages on the table. For a moment they all just stare at the tiny little messages, then Ranald picks them up and reads from them, "It's from auld Tam…" He reads the messages aloud, "English troops are billeted in Glen Afton." The other message says; "The English commanders are lord Cressingham and a Marmaduke de Percy." William exclaims, "De Percy, that's the name Affric…" He stammers "Mharaidh, Katriona, the wains…" A realisation of the potential danger everyone is in at Glen Afton strikes a fear in William he has never known before, he jumps up and cries out, "Malcolm, Sandy and Stephen are on their way there now, I must leave, if there are English soldiers there, the folk o' the Afton could be in bad trouble... and the name de Percy, that's the name responsible for the slaughters at Corserine, Dunveoch and Duibh hill... I have to go..." William races for the door. "Wait..." shouts Ranald. "You can't go there on your own, it's too dangerous, sit down and we'll work out a plan."

Impetuous in his haste, William will not wait a moment longer. "There's no time for a fuckin' plan," snarls William "So far, we've all been unprepared for this English takeover, what they intend for us all is clearly demonstrated by bathing their horses hooves in the blood of our kinfolk." Standing up beside William, True Tam says, "He must go Ranald, he has no choice. I'll stay here with the family for I have medicines here that must be administered to the injured, that is the only hope they have to recover. You fly young Wallace, but be sharp, be cautious and many more may live as you would wish it to be." Ranald speaks with a great sense of urgency, "Tam... Richard Wallace o' Craigie will be here soon, tell him to go bring his men and make speed for Glen Afton, I'll go to Crosshouse and fetch my men. Tell Richard to rendevous with us at Comunnach castle with great haste, from there we will lead our combined force into Glen Afton."

Pacing the floor and extremely anxious, William exclaims. "Fuck Ranald, hurry up, I need to get goin'..." True Tam says, "Wallace, take Fleetfoot, he's as your own horse Warrior, sired from Areion. Listen to me, take the main road over to the pass of Strathaven, that way you may avoid most of the English troops. Now you heed my next words Wallace and the spirits of the sídhe will aid you, trust me... you stay in plain sight, do not hide away. When the English see you they will not be aware of you, hide away your face and they will find you." Although William's mind is in complete turmoil, True Tams meaning is crystal clear and understood. Ranald and William know that any other deliberations would be futile, they quickly set to carrying out True Tam's advice. Ranald says, "William, tell lady Marjorie to make sure she arms all fighting Gallóbhet and Ceitherne in the glens about Comunnach. Now listen to me, I want you to scout Glen Afton first, if the English are gone from there and all is well, get auld Tam to send messages here and up to Crosshouse. If, God forbid, things are not as they should be, then we need you to keep watch and await our arrival, we should only be a few hours behind you." Looking at True Tam, Ranald says, "Take care of them Tam, and yourself." True Tam replies, "Don't be worrying about your kinfolks here, I will take good care of things and look after the family, it's just as important that you both take great care too, for your family and this realm do need you both."

As Ranald and William exit the main house and rush for their horses, Ranald says, "William, I know what True Tam said, but you watch out for those English patrols. Give them no reason to stop you nor any reason to delay or harass you, I'll soon follow on from Crosshouse without rest nor delay as soon as I have gathered my men, hopefully Richard and his men will be with us soon too."

William quickly gathers his longbow and four quivers full of goose-wing arrows with hunting barbs. He then fixes them to the tack on Fleetfoot, a brother stallion to Warrior, so obvious by his markings and bright outlook. William releases the reigns from a halter ring and is ready to mount and leave, when True Tam comes rushing out of the house with Billy's old brown leather battle jack, a thick triple-wolf-skin mantle and an old Claymore. "Take these too Wallace, some protection is better than no protection at all, these were your grandfathers. This was his guardians brand (Sword) he used at the battle o' Largs." William takes the rolled jack and mantle and quickly ties them to the back of his saddle, then he takes his grandfathers claymore and holds it high, he looks at it for a moment in awe, then he lowers the brand to rest on his shoulder.

"The perfect Guardians Claymore when it rests easy with its owner thus," says True Tam "When you return here Wallace, and you will, your people will be the better for my care, I promise you this. Now remember, you keep going, hide in plain sight and none shall see you, then Glen Afton will be yours by dusk." Placing his hand on True Tam's shoulder, William says, "I know you not stranger, yet you are like an elder brother from another time. I feel that whatever happens next, our future is entwined as kin." True Tam smiles, "Fly like the wild geese Wallace, the sídhe is with you." William mounts Fleetfoot, he thinks a moment then turns to face True Tam, "What about young Andrew, where is he?" True Tam looks at William then replies, "Andrew is away safe and unharmed to Crosshouse, but the girls…" William is puzzled, "What about the girls?" True Tam looks down at the ground then he says, "They will heal of body, but their minds…"

William is perplexed; then a cold realisation sweeps over his mind… "Naw Tam, naw, naw, naw… don't say it…" In a rage, William turns Fleetfoot who responds instantly as though they both have been soul friends from the womb. Fleetfoot nimbly turns again, his soft mouth responds instinctively to the lightest touch. William nods at True Tam who says, "You take care and mind you to be stayin' in plain sight…" William replies, "I will." He leans forward in the saddle and Fleetfoot immediately begins to canter towards the gates, then he breaks into a gallop on leaving the high wooden walls and palisades of Ach na Feàrna. Once clear of the fortalice, Fleetfoot strides easily at a pace gallop. William soon sees Glasgow in the distance.

The journey is fraught with danger as there are English soldiers and patrols everywhere, but he notices that none look at him nor give him a second glance. It appears to be as True Tam had said it would be. He rides on till it's not long before he is at the smithy Balloch of Gobhain on the banks of the river Clyde, there he turns east, past old Poloc church and through the villages of Pooktoun to Bogleshaugh then connects with the main droving road past Ruther's glen Castle, the most formidable Castle in the west of Scotland. As he rides on, William sees many English horse troops and patrols canter back and forth, hundreds of marching troops and streams of English supply trains moving through the land, yet none seem to have a care for his presence, if noticed at all. William rides unhindered through to the Strathaven drover's road, till finally, he arrives at the summit of the Ardochrigg pass. From there it's but a fast ride through the Lanarch woodlands to Comunnach castle and then on to his beloved Glen Afton, nestling on the edge of the Wolf and wildcat forest. William thinks of True Tam's words, to hide in plain sight, and it appears to be working, allowing him to hold to the most direct and quickest route towards Glen Afton.

In the distance, Loudoun Hill beckons. He clicks his tongue and Fleetfoot immediately kicks into a seemingly effortless pace gallop that most horsemen would be happy with as a top speed. His thoughts are a mixture of fear and desperation that he may be too late, he hopes and prays that perhaps not all the English are prepared to use the cruel devices that he has already witnessed, but unfortunately that has been his repeated experience on every encounter he ever had with English Peacekeepers. It also appears it is their pleasure to be so cruel, but for the exception of one Englishman… Fellows. William spurs Fleetfoot south into the lands of Lanarch county and Cumno. Having travelled almost thirty hard country miles at a fast pace, William notices Fleetfoot is beginning to falter, he listens to the rhythm of the gait then he sees Fleetfoot pinning his ears back and can feel the horses hip beginning to drop. William thinks it best to rest soon, for he has travelled relentlessly for such a long distance in roughly an hour and ran Fleetfoot so hard and fast… a slower pace will get them to their destination quicker. William sees a clearing in the woodland where there is a water flow to rest Fleetfoot. He takes his time to slow down till he eventually halts.

Dismounting, William takes a water bladder from the saddle and slakes his thirst. He waits impatiently till Fleetfoot has cooled and his breathing returns to normal, it's only then that he leads the horse to a stream to drink after such a hard pushed run. While Fleetfoot drinks, William examines the hooves for stones, checking he hasn't lost any shoes; then he leaves Fleetfoot awhile longer to drink and rest his heart. William sits impatiently on a large rock as dusk begins to approach. He looks around and notices the stoic landmark of Loudon Hill protruding over the tree top canopy, not so far in the distance. For a moment he feels a slight respite of relief, knowing he will be in Glen Afton very soon. Suddenly a forceful nudge at his back breaks his thoughts, quickly followed by another aggressive nudge, shoving him completely off the rock. He turns to see Fleetfoot looking at him as though he is questioning why he delays any longer. William reaches up, takes hold of the reigns then looks into the horse's black almond eyes… he says, "I know you will take me to Glen Afton Fleetfoot, even though you will let me burst your heart in the attempt... I know you would do this for me." Fleetfoot watches William as though they both understand something that rationale can never explain when men and horses bond. William mounts Fleetfoot, strokes his neck, then he leans forward slightly and the horse begins to walk-on.

Fleetfoot stops abruptly then pricks his ears forward, William feels Fleetfoot beginning to back up as though he's spooked. He squeezes the flanks of Fleetfoot and clicks his tongue, then he says, "Walk on..." but Fleetfoot is reluctant, hesitant, his ears are constantly flicking forward, then he begins to whinny and snort. Suddenly an English knight and seven mounted soldiers gallop round a sharp bend at speed hurtling straight towards them, it's too late to move aside, by the time William has his wits about him he's surrounded by aggressive looking Englishmen on horseback, with their weapons drawn in earnest. The knight in charge has no humour nor a kindness in his voice as he speaks, "How come you by such a fine beast Scotchman?" William doesn't reply, he sits sullenly and watches as the English circle him on their horses. If one momentary gap appears, he will kick-spur Fleetfoot and take his chances to break free. The knight barks an order, "You men, dismount and take the horse from this felon then hang him, he is clearly a horse thief."

Two soldiers dismount and walk towards William. The first soldier takes a hold of the reigns just below Fleetfoot's bit, while the other draws his sword and thrusts it up towards William who doesn't move a muscle in response. For a moment, no-one moves in the clearing, the air is still, no birds are singing... suddenly Fleetfoot bites into the neck of the front soldier, snapping the unfortunate soldiers collarbone; the soldier screams in pain as Fleetfoot rears into the air, still gripping the soldier by the neck and throwing him into a side ditch, bleeding profusely from a large gaping bite wound in his neck. Without hesitation William spurs Fleetfoot, the proud stallion immediately barges forward with such torque and power into the knight's horse he easily pushes it over on its flanks to roll over the top of the knight, crushing him underneath. Fleetfoot launches himself over both horse and knight who are frantically rolling about on the ground, while William hangs on for dear life. He regains control as they gallop away down the drove road and out of sight. "For fuck's sake Fleetfoot…" gasps William as they ride like the wind. "Do you and Warrior read minds too?" Gaining speed down the drove road, William glances behind to see in the distance that the English horsemen are pursuing him. He *clicks* his tongue and Fleetfoot accelerates to a gallop so fast, William has never ridden a horse at such speed before. He glances back again and sees that the English pursuers are falling back into the distance.

The incredible pace of Fleetfoot makes everything except that which is in front of William a blur. After what seems like mere moments, he rides out of the forest and finds himself at the northwest face of Loudon Hill. He pulls to a halt to let Fleetfoot gain breath. He doesn't want to stop, but he knows the quickest way he could get to Glen Afton is to break a few moments and let Fleetfoot cool down and breath easy. Dismounting, William looks away up the drove road but he sees nothing. No more pursuing English soldiers, thankfully. He assumes the English soldiers must have given up the chase. A few moments more and the sense of urgency presses hard on William's mind, he knows he must force a relentless pace upon Fleetfoot yet again and it's time to ride on. He thinks that only two more short stops and he will soon be at Comunnach Castle, where he can warn Marjory and get everyone to be on their guard to help if his kinfolks are in trouble. As he prepares to mount Fleetfoot, the horse appears agitated, then William hears another horse whinnying away to his left. Suddenly Fleetfoot bolts before William can catch the reigns, but the stallion only runs a short distance then stops. His ears prick to the side and he looks around for something, then he too begins whinnying. William hears the other horse whinny not far from where he is standing. Walking quietly up behind Fleetfoot, William grips the hanging reigns, then he notices standing on a small ridge at the base of Loudon Hill a horse he instantly recognises as Warrior. He thinks… Malcolm must be close by?

Walking towards Warrior, William sees an arrow sticking in the stallions bloodied neck; then he sees two more sticking in his rump. William whistles on Warrior, who instantly recognises him. The stallion bucks and kicks as he canters towards him, then he suddenly stops, turns away and canters back over to the ridge edge and begins whinnying once more. Another horse whinnies away to William's right-hand side; grabbing at his sword hilt he quickly spins around and sees a horse and rider standing a little distance away, William instantly recognises the outline, "Sandy…" he calls out, but Sandy doesn't stir. William looks at him curiously, he can't understand why Sandy sits so still on his horse with his head bowed and doesn't appear to hear his name being called out, "Naw…" mumbles William. He runs towards Sandy, but the closer he gets, the more certain he is that something is badly wrong. Sandy's horse looks up from feeding and sees William approaching. William halts abruptly to let Sandy's horse walk up to him…

"Awe naw, no' you Sandy, please no' wee Sandy…" His heart sinks and his stomach turns, for William can see that young Sandy is dead. The arrows in his thigh has pinned him to the saddle and he can see another is buried deep in the side of his chest; another is protruding straight through his throat. William walks-easy up to Sandy and grabs the reigns of his horse, he then walks back to tether the horse to a nearby tree that he may attend to Sandy. Slowly and carefully, he removes the two arrows from Sandy's thigh and gently pulls the body from the horse and lay's him down. He kneels beside his young friend, cradling him and stroking Sandy's hair away from his face; then he removes the other arrows from his body and throat. He hears Warrior whinnying again. Suddenly he thinks in a panic, Uncle Malcolm… Immediately he jumps up and sprints as fast as he can to where Warrior is running about in circles, stopping, rearing and bucking. As William approaches the restless Warrior, the horse runs down the embankment a few feet then he stops. Cautiously, William approaches Warrior and grips the reigns firmly, when a slight odour wafting in the air catches his attention, he scans the lower side of the Loudon Hill, then to his horror, he sees down in the pasture, a bloody dead body, naked and hanging upside down from the bough of a tree, like a butchered old hog. His mind begins racing, then his fears and realisation strikes like blacksmiths forge hammers…

"No, NO, NO, NO, NO… it can't be…" He runs and stumbles down the slope of Loudon Hill towards the oak tree near a small running burn. Upon reaching the hanging body, he instantly falls to his knees and buries his head between his knees, he looks up and cries… "No… no, this cannot be happening…" William slumps down and sits on his hunkers for what feels like an eternity below the body hanging from the oak tree, he wails through blinding tears, "Dear Malcolm, ma dearest Malcolm, what have they done to you… why… why… I don't understand… why did they do this to us, why?"

Raising himself from the ground in a daze, he walks over to Fleetfoot to collect his grandfather's mantle, then brings it back and lays it on the ground. He returns to Fleetfoot and walks him to where Malcolm is hanging. He mounts then stands on the saddle, reaches up and cuts the rope tied through Malcolm's heels then gently lowers his body to rest across the saddle. William dismounts and takes Malcolm's body to the ground and prepares to wrap him in his grandfather's mantle. It's then he sees in close detail the full extent of the heinous torture and cruelty inflicted upon his uncle, it causes him to weep uncontrollably. Malcolm's back, chest, legs and head has been flayed raw, his arms dislocated, his tongue has been cut from his head and his body is riddled with arrow holes. Tears flow down William's face as he looks into the dead eyes of his father figure, this man who loved him like a son. *'How is he going to tell the family and wee Maw? How could even begin to describe what he has found.'* William screams at the heavens, "Why… why would any man inflict such vile atrocities upon others? Where are you God… where the fuck are you…" William breaks down again as he slowly closes the last of his grandfather's mantle across Malcolm's face. William weeps, caused by the great sorrow unfolding before him.

Eventually, William has Malcolm and Sandy both wrapped and lain them across Warrior and Sandy's horse, he removes the two arrows from Warriors rump but he leaves the neck arrow embedded as it appears too deep to pull, he snaps the shaft next to where it had entered Warrior's neck. William knows he must get moving fast to reach Glen Afton, for no matter how he feels in grief, time no longer matters for Malcolm and Sandy, it's the living that need him. He ties the horses in train and walks them back up the slope towards the woodland drove rode leading to Comunnach Castle and Glen Afton. Once at the top of the rise, he spends a few moments securing the knots and ties on the horses when he hears the sound of horses galloping close by. He sees through the trees in the distance, three mounted English soldiers riding hard and fast. William calmly takes his longbow from his horse, strings the bow, hangs three arrows between the fingers of his pull hand, nocks a barbed hunting arrow then waits... It's not long before three English horse-soldiers thunder out of the woods to be met by William standing with an arrow ready to loose and three hanging from his draw hand. Surprised at the sight of this audacious youth standing so boldly before them, the English soldiers pull their sweating snorting horses to an immediate halt and look at William curiously. During this momentary standoff, William studies the faces of these Englishmen, he can see the first soldier is obviously a veteran, with a ruddy battle scarred complexion and wearing a saffron tabard with the three golden leopards of England's king on his chest. The other two are about the same age as himself, wearing bleached-white tabards with the red cross of saint Edward the confessor.

"What do you want of me?" demands William. The veteran soldier laughs out loud, "We don't want you Scotchman... what we really want are those fine bred horses you have there; then we'll hang you as a roadside brigand." For a moment there is no reply, then William says, "Leave now Englishmen, if you don't, your lives will end here by your own choice. Leave me in peace... and I will leave you in peace." The veteran English soldier shakes his head and laughs, "I am afraid I cant do that, my Lord wants your horses, and then we shall hang you. But I promise you Scotchman, it will be a swift and merciful end if you surrender to me... if not, we will have great pleasure watching you strangle awhile at the end of a rope." The veteran moves his horse forward slowly while pulling his sword lazily from its scabbard... William looks into the Englishman's eyes; he can see the confidence of this man and knows he is not going to be stopped. The Englishman looks around him then he says, "Now I do want you Scotchman, I want you to get on your knees, crawl over here and kiss the hooves of my horse; then I want you to kiss its arse, maybe then I may let you live, if you do not do as I ask, then we will kill you slowly and take great—" *Zzzup...* is the last sound the Englishman hears as William's arrow strikes him in the face and exits straight through the back of his head. Curiously, the veteran soldier remains seated upright in his saddle; then his body begins to shake and shudder as blood and brain tissue pumps out the tiny hole in his face and the back of his head. The other Englishmen appear frozen and petrified as they stare at their master still sitting upright, but dead in his saddle.

"FUCK OFF..." screams William with utter venom. The shout startles the horses, causing the dead Englishman to fall to the ground. One of the English soldiers nervously pulls his sword from its scabbard, but he drops it on the ground, William watches closely, voices scream in his head for the soldiers to leave so that he may continue on his desperate journey to Glen Afton, but the nervous soldier persists and pulls a mace from his saddle pack then spurs his horse and charges towards him, William looses an arrow that strikes the soldier in the chest then looses another that pierces the soldier's heart, causing the soldier to fall dying from his horse. William yells "Why?" The other young Englishman is sitting polarised while gazing at William, then he frantically pulls on his sword, but it is stuck in its scabbard. William looses an arrow that strikes the young English soldier just below the throat, then he looses second arrow that strikes him almost in the same place, then, like his master before him, the young soldier sits upright in his saddle simply staring at William in utter disbelief. Slowly he topples from his horse and falls to the ground, where he writhes about while gripping at the hunters arrows lodged in his throat. William walks over and looks at the young Englishman lying face up with blood trickling from his mouth. The dying young soldier stares up at William, gasping like a fish out of water.

With tears in his eyes, William looks at the young Englishman, but they are not tears of pity, they are tears vented by anger and frustration, tears of fear, hatred and rage. His emotions are causing his head to ache so much he can hardly focus or think. He kneels by the side of the dying Englishman, "Why do you do this to us Englishman, why are you even here…?" But there is no reply from the youngster as he desperately gasps for air. William looks into his eyes; then he mumbles, "This didn't need to be…" Just then, he hears more horses coming down the North road; they are close and gaining fast. He knows there is nowhere to run or hide, even if he cared, all he feels is anger and absolute cold determination. Wiping his eyes, he takes a quiver of arrows from the back of Fleetfoot then methodically sticks fifteen more arrows into the ground at his feet, he then lays his grandfathers sword behind him and nocks an arrow just as the knight he barged from the horse earlier comes galloping around the corner, with another three mounted soldiers following closely behind. Instantly, William looses a tracer arrow, striking the knight's horse deep between the eyes, causing it to jerk and buck, throwing its riders to the ground. The other soldiers try to avoid the falling horse and knight but they become entangled.

At lighting speed, William looses and strikes the lead soldier with an arrow into his head. He quickly looses a tracer arrow and strikes another soldier deep in his chest. The third soldier quickly jumps from his horse and runs at William, who calmly nocks another flight and looses a tracer arrow that rips clean through the running soldiers eye and exits the back of his head, causing him to run blindly past William as though he were in some manic fit, William spins around and looses another arrow that easily penetrates the soldiers skull from behind, curiously, the English soldiers body keeps on running until he falls dead somewhere deep in the dense woodland.

Bereft of any emotion, William pulls his dirk from his belt and walks over to where all the soldiers lay, they are all appear to be dead, all except the one he hit in the throat earlier, who groans and gasps out loud. William kneels beside him, puts a hand over the soldier's mouth then slowly he sinks his dirk deep into the soldier's chest, deep enough to pierce his heart. Instantly, the soldier arches his back and stares at William in terror, another few moments and the look of terror begins to fade. They both look at each other intensely as death creeps into the eyes of the young Englishman. William jerks the dirk out as the soldier's eyes turn misty blue, soon he will pass from this life. A noise behind William causes him to quickly spin around and sees the knight who had been stunned initially by the fall from the horse, staggering about in a daze. He turns and sees William staring at him. The English knight blurts out, "You... I shall have you imprisoned and hung for this grievous attack upon the King Edward's men." With no obvious response, William just stares at the knight, who shouts at him once again "Didn't you hear me Scotchman?" As if snapping out of some mesmerised state of mind, William exclaims, "Imprisoned... do yie mean imprisoned as they do in Ireland, or imprisoned in some other fashion?" The knight is confused by the question, "Are you insane Scotchman? I will have you flayed alive..."

Instantly, William reacts to this taunt and throws his dirk, striking the English knight under the chin. The powerful torque of the throw drives the needlepoint long blade deep into the knight's throat, easily penetrating through the back of his neck. The knight gasps and points at him. William walks over and stands in front of the knight who falls to his knees, sits upright and clasps desperately at his throat with both hands. The knight gargles and attempts to spit out blood. William sneers, "Flayed alive?" He reaches down and jerks his dirk out of the knight's throat and says to him with utter contempt. "Fuck you…" William spits on the ground then turns and walks away, wiping the dirk blade clean and shoves it back in its scabbard. Walking in a daze, William's mind is partially in a mist of desperate insanity, but the greater part is clearer and sharper than its ever been before, he knows the world has now changed beyond all recognition, the setting sun shines brightly, but everything is darker, harder, colder, more real, more savage, more brutal and more evil than he could ever have imagined it to be in his blackest of nightmares or most vengeful of thoughts.

Emotionless and bereft of feelings for the men he has dispatched, he goes back round all the English dead, swiftly cutting their throats open to be certain they are all dead and pulling his arrow shafts from their bodies, minus the barbed arrow heads still lodged inside the Englishmen's bodies. Finally, William goes back over to the horses where he ties his bow and quivers tight to Fleetfoots saddlebags, he slides the claymore inside the haulier rings in the flank leathers, mounts Fleetfoot then pulls Warrior and packhorse close in tow to train and resume his journey. Before today, William would have tried to talk his way out of the situation, but he knows now it is the same sentiment that may have been what had gotten Coinach, Bailey, Lihd and the Wildcats killed at Invergarvane, or what had nearly got him killed at Auchencruive when the English knight wanted to take his fish catch then cut his hands off. Never again will I kneel to the command of an Englishman… After a few miles of hard riding, William brings Fleetfoot to a walking pace as he clears the Lanarch woodlands. He sees he's within a few miles of Comunnach Castle, and beyond, the canopy of the Wolf and wildcat forest and the Black Craig gateway to Glen Afton. He slows his pace and begins to walk the horses slowly towards Comunnach castle… it won't be long now, he thought, even though his brain is still trying to make sense of everything, from the first outbreak of civil war in the south many years ago and the atrocities he had witnessed, to how much his life has been forced to change since the English had came into his country with wretched brutality, torture and cruel death following them.

William is beginning to understand how Coinach felt at the Corserine where his friend had lost his entire family. For a time, Coinach's mind was lost too, but William's sense of urgency to get to Glen Afton is tearing his mind apart with frustration, desperation, he prays he will reach his family and kinfolks in time to warn them to be on their guard. Fleetfoot stops in his tracks and pricks up his ears, as do the other horses. Sitting dead still for a moment, William knows that a horses ears are like a second pair of eyes, he's also acutely aware that such a simple sign from his sensory companion may save his life. Slowly he takes his bow in his hands, nocks another arrow and hangs three for the draw, he knows never to sense what is wrong with his horse, but to look out for what the horse senses is wrong.

Fleetfoot is focused straight ahead while William scrutinises the road and follows the direction to where the horses prick and move their ears, it's then William sees about twenty riders exit Comunnach Castle, led by a rider on a white mare. "Lady Marjorie…" He immediately spurs Fleetfoot towards the confluence bridge to Comunnach Castle. When Marjorie sees William, she orders her men to wait then turns her horse and canters over to meet him. As they close on each other, William becomes aware Marjorie's features and her body language look peculiar, somehow different. Perhaps she senses who is hanging over the back of his horses. They soon meet, both halt and dismount. "Oh William..." she cries. William can see in her face that she's in shock, her tear stained cheeks and blood red eyes are sending a message he doesn't want to hear, perhaps if he doesn't hear it, then it can't have happened. An ominous shock streaks through his mind as Marjorie falls to her knees at his feet weeping and wailing. She reaches out to hold his hand, "NO..." he yells at the top of his voice. He pulls his hand away and turns from her, but he sees in the distance the Loudon Hill. It's too much... he sinks to his knees, whatever way he looks, he is surrounded by death and he knows it. "I..." Whispers Marjorie in a croaky broken voice.

"NO, NO, NO..." shouts William "Don't say it..." He can't let himself think the impossible. He can't accept what may come from the mouth of Marjorie or his mind will disintegrate into total chaotic insanity if he allows her to speak. He can't break down if he doesn't know. Then he feels the gentle touch of Marjorie's hands upon his shoulders. Sobbing forces itself to swell in his breast no matter how hard his mind refuses to accept the inevitable truth. William slumps down the bridge wall, pulls his knees up and buries his head in his arms. Marjorie gets up and walks towards the bodies wrapped on the horses; she lifts the first sheet about the head, when she sees that it's young Sandy she shakes her head in sorrow. She then walks over to Warrior and tentatively lifts up the covers... immediately she recoils in disbelief, shock and horror. William looks at Marjorie as she collapses to a squat, weeping and crying with her arms outstretched towards him, but William defies her plea for comfort. Marjorie suddenly springs to her feet and runs at him wailing, she throws her arms around his shoulders, pulling him close, it's too much for William and they both break down weeping and sobbing uncontrollably.

After what seems like an eternity, Marjory eventually whispers, "I... I'm so sorry William..." he doesn't lift his head to respond, he can't, he simply enquires, "Alain, Mharaidh, Caoilfhinn..." he sobs, "Am, am... Am I too late?" Marjorie weeps profusely as she tries to give him an answer. She holds William to her bosom then stammers, "They are all gone..." He enquires in desperation "Graham, Tam, Jean... everyone?" Marjorie couldn't speak nor reply, her heart and mind is all but lost in grief, her sobbing becomes erratic as she forces her courage and sanity to acknowledge William's question. She stammers, "They have all flown with the wild geese..." Immediately the two become inconsolable as a spiritual mother and son embracing infernal suffering together in the dreadful wretchedness of loss. They both embrace in grieving till dusk falls to darkest night.

Eventually William and Marjorie compose themselves as much as is possible, then they try to stand up. Helping each other to their feet, William enquires, "Stephen of Ireland, is he..." Clasping his hands, Marjorie says, "He's alive, but his senses and wit have left him to be replaced with the spirit of a wild mountain wolf who has lost his mate. He's drawn his weapons and will let none go near the bodies of Katriona and his family, nor those of Alain, Mharaidh and little Caoilfhinn. He guards them all as that self same wolf that protects his litter from the hunters." William looks towards Glen Afton as Marjory continues, "When my men tried to recover the bodies, Stephen attacked them and he wounded many, the only thing we could do was leave him be and try to recover all other souls lost to us by the hands of evil-doers." Picking up the reigns of the horses, they walk slowly and in silence towards Comunnach castle, followed at a discreet distance by Marjorie's mounted bodyguards. William and Marjorie share sentinel comfort in a heartbreaking alliance, it's all they have left in this universe for a moment in time. The packhorse, Fleetfoot, Warrior and Marjorie's white mare walk behind them like a funeral cortege, carrying the bodies of Sandy the stable lad and his uncle, sir Malcolm Wallace, the proud knight of Ach na Feàrna. Upon entering Comunnach castle, Malcolm and Sandy are taken away and temporarily interred in the castle icehouse. Warrior is led to the farrier to tend to his wounds. William and Marjorie decide to make their way to the hellish scenes awaiting them in Glen Afton.

They ride tentatively along the drove road in the black of night, lit solely by an ominous illuminating glow emanating from the Glen Afton funeral pyres. William's senses are numb, they have to be, for the futility of all his fury and rage within and none yet known to exact a vengeance and retribution upon, would surely tear his heart and mind apart. He mutters under his breath, "The fires of darkfall…" Marjorie says. "William, my people are recovering all of the bodies that they can find, but…" she falters, then continues, "I must tell to you before we enter the glen proper, that all of the bodies without exception have been cruelly defiled or torn to pieces, many have been deliberately left asunder, intended I believe for the wild beast to feed upon. There's no other way that I know that I can make this less for you, or for any of us. I only prepare you for what you are about to see. We have gathered most that we could find for the fires, except the bodies of those that Stephen will not give up and those in the furthermost corners of the glen." William can find no words of reply for Marjorie as they pass by many destroyed outlying obhainn's and bothies, William can see her words are now becoming all to real. He steels his fortitude as they approach the corrals at the foot of Wallace Keep. He can now plainly see the funerary flames of darkfall are reaching high into the night sky, taking with them the mortal remains of his kith and kin to a better place. He looks around the glen, and from the glow from the many funerary fires, he can see everything in all its horrific gory detail as the men and women of Comunnach carry the remains of his friends and his clan towards the source of the flames.

Many of the bearers weep openly as they stoically adhere to their grizzly task. He sees others kneeling on the ground, overcome by the horrors they have witnessed that has been so cruelly inflicted upon the men, women and the children of his glen. Marjorie nervously points towards the doors of the Keep. "Stephen is up there…" Taking his eyes from the depraved scenes of hell, he looks up to the promontory and then the Wallace Keep. In the flickering red glow of the fires, he can see Stephen frantically pacing to and fro with an axe in each hand. But William has nothing left by way of any sympathy or emotion, for his eyes catches a glimpse of something that disturbs him even more than he could ever have imagined. He prays to any deity that will listen to his soul crying out, to take away the demons attacking his very being. He slowly dismounts and moves with grim intent through the cordon of Marjorie's men and begins walking up the bloody steps on his long tortuous journey towards the Keep doors. Stephen suddenly appears at the head of the steps like a monstrous satanic follower of hell. With the flames from the funeral pyres flickering on his dirty tear stained face, he stands defiantly blocking the route past him and confronts William. Stephen raises a cocked crossbow in one hand and a vicious broken shaft spartaxe in the other. "COME NEAR ME WALLACE, AND I WILL FUCKIN' KILL YA, I SWEAR TO THE GODS, I WILL FUCKIN' KILL YA…" Ignoring the madman's threats, William keeps on walking up the steps towards his morbid destination, never taking his eyes away from the doors of the Keep. Stephen screams and aims the crossbow and bolt directly at William's heart, "I MEAN IT WALLACE, I'LL FUCKIN KILL YA IF YA MAKE ONE MORE STEP…" But William walks on as though Stephen isn't there, Stephen shakes the volatile hair-trigger crossbow in William's face, but he simply pushes the crossbow aside and walks past Stephen and speaks in a calm deliberate voice, delivering a chilling message…

"Go on then h'Alpine, kill me…" William steps on to the promontory and continues walking across the flagstones, till he stops and stares, fixated by what he is seeing on the doors of Wallace Keep… Stephen collapses sobbing and weeping behind him. Running his dirty fingers through his matted tresses, he utters between sobs, "They fuckin' boiled them alive…" but William is undisturbed by anything else in this world, he continues to stare at the oak doors of Wallace Keep, Stephen cries out behind him, "The murderin' bastards, they've boiled me son, me wife and me unborn child alive…" Stephen weeps as he moves slowly up against the cold cauldron where the remains of Katriona and his family are contained, he gently runs his fingers around the rim of the cauldron then spreads his arms around it, begging and crying desperately for the love of his family to be his once more, so cruelly interred and torn from his loving touch for ever… he cries, "They boiled me family alive Wallace…"

Stephen curls up like a child, sobbing, cursing, raging… but William's focus remains upon three naked, boneless, eyeless human pelts nailed to the front doors of the Keep.

He knows it is Alain, Mharaidh and his half-sister eight year old Caoilfhinn before him… *'What pain they must have suffered…'* thinks William… *'But now they are free. He visualises what awful torment and heinous torture they had endured, but now they feel no pain, William has no more tears, he can't feel anything as he gazes at the sight before him, he has nothing left to give…'*

The thoughts going around in his head are cold, emotionless and bereft of any kind of pity, or love. What he sees now are simply the mortal remains of the people he still loves, once loved… will always love… It has to be this way he thought. For what he is looking at now has no feeling, no pain, nor any more suffering to bear. He cannot let himself accept any hint of emotion, to accept this awful reality other than as a witness… *'Then I must join them'*. He knows if emotion is to come to him now, he will draw his dirk and take his own life, but if he remains locked of heart, then vengeance most severe will be his. Behind him, he hears Stephen walking about clumsily; then he senses Stephen stopping by his side. Stephen stands sobbing beside William, he wipes his face with his sleeves, "What are we going to do Wallace, what are we going to fuckin do?" William's own disbelief that something like this could ever happen is beyond his comprehension.

An ice-cold sensation cruelly grips his heart, like powerful freezing fingers from an evil wraith of the apocalypse as he continues to stand staring, transfixed, trapped inside his own hellish emotionless world, where the walls of carnage and macabre scents of death relentlessly take on a cruel life of their own, from which there is no escape. His senses are spinning, he tries in vain to rationalize or understand, but there is nothingness in his heart where emotion used to dwell. William is disturbed when hearing a voice cry out nearby, pleading pitifully somewhere in the distance,

"Wallace… what are we going to do?" He hears the anguished cry repeat the same question over and over… Finally, William turns and looks coldly into the eyes of the wretched, tearful features of Stephen, a look that somehow brings Stephens senses to an equally cold and sinister place… William says simply, "Coinach was right…"

FIELDS OF SORROW

itting forlorn on the desolate promontory of the Glen Afton Keep, William stares inanely at what appears to be millions of tiny little snowflakes falling from a bleak pre-dawn sky. Fascinated by the phenomenon, he observes intently as the tiny gray flakes float gently past his face to land all around him to form a great thick snow-like blanket on the braes and glen floor. He slowly raises his head and looks to the heavens above, still captivated by the little dancing particles as they fall endlessly all around the Glen of Afton, transforming its normal lush green springtime appearance into what seems like a wondrous idyllic mid-winter scene from the fabled Tír na Findargat stories of the otherworld. The blizzard of little gray flakes and heavy scents of burning meat, contrasts eerily with the illumination caused by the hellish glow being cast out from the many funerary pyres spread throughout his homeland glen. Sitting back on his haunches, William holds out cupped hands to catch some of the little gray particles; then he rubs them together between his fingers, turning the little grey-scale flakes into a fine chalky powder. He wipes his palms on his bare forearms, creating the same chalky effect on his skin. Soon, the fine ash begins to burn his eyes... eyes that are already swollen and irritatingly hot with the pain of tears past. His throat and pallet begin to dry up, producing a gummy residue and a sickly alkaline taste in his mouth. He tries to swallow but his throat burns, his breathing shortens and becomes extremely painful. Even when he drinks copious amounts of water, there is no relief from the burning sensations in his throat, nor does it remove the bittersweet taste in his mouth.

Peering around the darkened glen, William feels a gut-churning malevolent connection with the surreal amphitheatre of nature. He senses his beautiful Glen of Afton may never wish to bask in glorious sunlight or witness joy, mirth or laughter ever again, such is the sorrow he's feeling in his nightmarish harmony with these ancient hills of his clan, these same hills that now surround him in a claustrophobic atmosphere, where everything he observes appears to share the same anguish and despair of the once-proud people who had celebrated their fruitful lives in his beautiful glen, a rich life gained from their diligent toils and labours while tilling the land and working in partnership with Magda mòr to provide a continuous source of sustenance for generations of his people. He raises his head once more upon hearing the baying of night wolves and feral dogs somewhere in the distance, they each howl their territorial harmonies to compete with a melancholy chorus of cackling carrion crows and ravens... all sensing a great feast awaits them as the scent of death hangs thick in the air... A brutal reminder that the relentless forces of the animal kingdom have neither a care nor a thought for his earthly emotions.

Soon, he notices a morning mist descending as a grey funerary shroud from the peaks of Craig Branneoch, S'taigh am Rígh and the Black Craig, slowly engulfing both the living and the dead scattered throughout the great glen pastures. Occasionally, through smoke and mist, he sees a crescent moon on the morning wain, appearing to be blissfully unaware of the awful tragedy hidden beneath the human fog that now cloaks and smothers his glen. Suddenly, a faint breeze caresses his cheeks and begins to cool his face. Finally… now the troubled spirits lingering in our glen may begin their journey to Tír na nÓg…

His thoughts of spiritual solace are interrupted when he hears a groaning sound nearby, he turns his head to see Stephen still hunched over the large cauldron, his head buried in his arms as though protecting the macabre contents from the outside world. Sensing William's gaze, Stephen raises his head and stares directly back at him with bloodshot emotionless eyes. The two friends share a cruel bond, though both have neither feelings nor any emotions that would be familiar or recognizable to most normal folk. The light breeze becomes noticeably stronger; it appears the wind spirits know the souls of the glen are refusing to leave their land and those they love behind. The breeze turns to forceful blustery gusts as William continues to observe what he believes to be a battle between the good Sídhe and the incensed souls of Glen Afton demanding retribution and justice for all the tortuous atrocities they have suffered. He senses their spiritual resistance against the powerful beating wings of the many unseen angels gathering overhead to carry away the defiant souls to a better place. He thinks it will be an almighty struggle that even the gods may lose, such is the power of the indignation caused by the atrocities enacted upon the innocents.

William knows he favours neither as a victor in this otherworld struggle; he will let his emotional outcome decide what action he will take next as the battle between nature and the lost souls is enacted all over the glen, with little gusts here and roof shaking moments of angry storm there. He pulls a brat over his shoulders and lays down on the ground with his head resting on clasped hands. For the remainder of the dawn break, he watches, he waits... and he thinks deeply. Time passes slowly by until the fabric of dawn breaks completely through the clouds to reveal the true extent of the barbarous carnage and destruction that has descended upon the homes and people of Glen Afton, his people. William observes the men and women from the nearby township of Cumno and surrounding glens stirring from where they had fallen asleep the night before, but they are still utterly exhausted from their previous funerary duties. He watches their slow painful movements as they force themselves once more to commit to the nightmarish task of collecting all that remains of his kinfolk, then laying all they can find to rest upon the great funeral pyres that are still smouldering after a day and a night.

The pyres, now being replenished with more macabre human fuel, emits monstrous tongues of flames high into the air, causing the fine grey ash to fall once again upon the distraught people, accentuating the tear stains of pain and sorrow on each individual face as they scour the glen while collecting remains. Curiously, William notices folk suddenly look towards the North road, he too looks up and sees Lady Marjorie Comyn returning from Comunnach castle, bringing with her, sustenance and provisions for all the weary clan folks who have dutifully travelled to assist with the funerary rights and sun-fire cleansing of Glen Afton. When Marjorie's cortege arrives at the corral situated below the promontory, William notices than none come to greet her, food is not what anyone could stomach as they meticulously go about their grim task of recovering each and every piece of flesh and bone they can find this morn. He continues watching everyone go about their tasks, with the exception of Stephen, for nothing will detract him from his vigil over the cauldron containing his beloved wife Katriona, his son Stephen and their unborn child, all entombed in a macabre mixture of solidified human remains and animal fats. Marjorie approaches William and Stephen with food and water; then she places it on the ground nearby, she glances at William, who simply nods but says nothing. She looks at Stephen, who glares back at her as though she is a stranger who has brought him poison.

Glancing back at William and seeing a similar expression, Marjorie knows to leave the young men to their thoughts. She smiles weakly and returns to help her people with their grim task. William stands up and drinks water from a flagon, picks up a bannock and takes a little bite... he recoils instantly and spits it out; no food can replenish the hunger he feels deep within his soul. He walks over to Stephen and offers him the flagon, but Stephen just glares back at him with empty manic eyes, his face coloured a ghoulish grey and severely etched with deep lines of pain and grief, accentuated by the funeral ash from the pyres, but William is unconcerned as he looks back across the glen. Eventually Stephen releases his grip on the rim of the cauldron and takes a long drink of water to quench his thirst, then the two friends look at each other... they know it's time to help with the gruesome task.

Slowly they make their way down from the promontory to the glen floor and contribute to the search for anything that should be put to the fire and cleansed. For the rest of the day, everyone continues to meticulously search back and forth, looking in every Bothy, Obhainn, sheilin and shelter, often repeated to ensure that no mortal piece of humanity remains hidden. Even the dead animals of the glen merit their own fire of purification. Wherever tools and utensils of the inhabitants are found, they are deliberately broken and placed upon the pyres to release the spirit energy within, that they too may also travel with their deceased owner to their new heavenly realm in a better place than this. Many hours pass by for William and Stephen, who have not spoken a word to anyone, nor to each other. Finally, fatigue and exhaustion becomes so overpowering, they climb back up the steps to the Keep, far enough away from everyone where they can rest awhile.

As they slump to the ground exhausted, William speaks, briefly telling Stephen that he had found the murdered bodies of Malcolm and Sandy. There is no obvious reaction from Stephen, other than sharing a deeper state of melancholy as they both fixate on the funerary pyres with blackened faces. Their hair and clothes are covered in the dirty gray ash, eyes blood red from weeping and morbid facial expressions displaying a sorrow that could never truly reveal the overwhelming devastation they feel, nor convey the void and sense of futile loss in the hearts and minds of the two young friends… "Why?" cries Stephen, "Why Wallace, why?"

William can't answer, he doesn't have an answer, he needs an answer himself. With his mind racing, he screams inside his own head looking for an answer to the most simple of questions, Why… Why did this have to happen, Why our people? His thoughts are almost out of control, no matter how many ways he tries to rationalise the irrational, the answer always returns to one little irritating word… Why? Nearby, Stephen growls, "We have to kill whoever did this Wallace, we have to kill every single bastard who had a part to play in this…" William mutters, "I know." Stephen continues in a low faltering voice, "They boiled them alive Wallace… they fuckin' boiled them alive…" he buries his head in his hands, sobbing. A moment passes then he raises his head, wipes his face with his léine sleeve, then looks at William in despair, "They flayed and skinned your father, Mharaidh and God please help me… they even flayed wee Caoilfhinn…"

William doesn't reply, he can't, he can't even reach out to console his friend as he squats on the ground while rocking back and forth, watching all the scenes below. Stephen goes silent once more and resumes his sentinel guard over the cauldron.

After a while, William stands up, turns... he stares at the naked boneless bodies and mortal remains of his Father Alain, step-mother Mharaidh and his half sister little Caoilfhinn. The hot dry air from the funerary pyres is beginning to sweat, cure and shrink their skins like a velum parchment, pulling at the crude thick horseshoe nails that pin their drying flesh to the doors of Wallace Keep. Their eye sockets are vacant and mouths hang open wide, as though gaping at him in tragic wonderment and also demanding an answer. Shaking his head mournfully, William utters "Its time..." Stephen looks up at him in subdued resignation, there is a feeling shared by both the young men that they are now beyond grief and in a dark hellish place, somehow both realise they've now stepped across a supernatural threshold into a forbidden realm of evil thoughts, where no birds sing, no children laugh, no flowers blossom and no sun will ever shine... not until the vengeance blood tax is collected one hundred-fold and in full measure from those that have not only perpetrated this barbaric evil, but also upon those who have sanctioned it. They begin to retrieve the remains of their families while wrestling with their sanity and the emotional enormity of such a grim duty to the dead.

Both of them are also aware that should their spirits break now, they may never recover their whole wit ever again, but they care little about losing their senses as they struggle with the heartbreaking task of recovering then placing their families remains on the cold slab flagstones in front of the Wallace Keep in preparation for the cleansing fire.

All throughout the glen, the last mortal remains of the auld folk are being put to cremation, followed by the bodies of the children of the glen. The labour of duty to the dead has been near the breaking point of everyone's sanity; only the duty of cleansing the victims keeps any minuscule notion of reality alive in the thoughts of the living.

Suddenly screaming is heard. William and Stephen immediately turn to see the Cumno folk point towards the north entrance of the glen... William looks to see about a hundred horsemen in shining armour, bright colored tabards and chain mail riding towards them at speed. The thundering rhythmic sound of the approaching cavalry can be heard and felt underfoot like an ominous earth drum. People carrying their macabre cargo place it gently to the ground then run at speed to the steps and up to into the sanctuary and protection of Wallace Keep, there they urgently search for stones, rocks, sticks... anything they may use as a weapon, for they will not give up their lives cheaply. Their fear is palpable, as is their defiance and will to live. The two young friends grab their longbows and swords as they run forward to the edge of the promontory, notching an arrow then hanging three arrows in their draw hands, preparing to fast loose and flight. Lady Marjorie runs up the stairs from the corral and stands between William and Stephen. They watch the riders gain ever closer, Marjorie calls out, "It's sir Ranald and sir Richard... I see by their pennants..." William and Stephen lower their bows and sit back down, everyone from Cumno sits behind them or lays down somewhere safe to give their exhausted and very weary bodies a moment's respite.

As the riders enter the corral, Marjorie goes down to greet them. William sees his uncles Ranald and Richard look up at him, but he's too fatigued and bereft of any emotion to acknowledge them. As his uncles dismount, Marjorie hastily relays everything she knows, weeping when telling them that sir Malcolm and Sandy's bodies are interred in the icehouse of Comunnach Castle. Although Ranald and Richard are men of great experience and are certainly no strangers to the brutality of man, but this utter destruction and desecration is their own blood, butchered and murdered. The impact of unbridled grief is etched deep in their faces.

As the rest of Ranald and Richard's troop arrive and dismount, they desperately try to understand what or who has caused this scene from hell that they have just ridden into. All around them, they see little piles of flesh and bone where they were placed only moments before... Some gaze at the large funerary pyres in disbelief, while others throw up where they stand. Marjory composes herself when Richard enquires, "How are William and Stephen taking this?" They all look up at the promontory to see the young men stare back at them, like two mawkish birds of prey. Marjory stutters, "I don't know, I... I... I just don't know" But there is no way of knowing what the young men are thinking, their ghoulish appearance masks any sign of emotion, their blood-red eyes simply stare back with a pinpoint accuracy that begins to unnerve Marjorie.

Ranald calls out to them "Come down boys..." but there is no response, they don't flinch, they just stare... Ranald calls out to them again, "Come down and we may talk of this..." but it's apparent they are ignoring him or oblivious to his appeal. Ranald looks around the glen of devastation and fields of sorrow. The stench of death is everywhere, mixing with the putrefying scent of human gut and turning remains that hangs heavy in the air, adhering to cloth, skin and hair. Ranald soon feels the sticky taste of death in the back of his throat, he swallows hard and spits out a grey bitter phlegm, then he looks back up at William and Stephen, calling out to them once more, "William... Stephen, come down..." but the two friends continue with their manic glare as though Ranald and Richard are their mortal enemies. Eventually William calls out... "What's the fuckin' point...?" Ranald shakes his head and glances at Richard and Marjorie, but he sees they're both in deep shock. He says, "Marjorie... Will you take us for Malcolm and Sandy, we'll bring them back here and lay our kith and kin's souls together upon the sun-fire, William and Stephen will likely come down and talk with us in their own good time." Ranald gives his men orders to stay behind and help the Comunnach people gather up any remaining body parts they may find, everything from little clumps of hair, bloodied clothing, bone or broken skulls and torn flesh from the Kailyard's and hog pens... all must go to the sun fire, ensuring the spirits of the dead will rise to the heavens complete and purified, to be carried on the divine winds blowing westward towards Tír na nÓg, island of the Cruathnie spirits.

While mounting his horse, Ranald glances up at William; in that spontaneous moment, both understand something unspoken between them. William stands up and calls out to Stephen, "Get a horse Stephen, hurry, we're going to fetch Malcolm and Sandy." They prepare to rush down from the promontory when Stephen stops and looks back at their families remains, lying still on the cold stone flagstones in front of the Keep. Stephen says, "It's a fine and proper duty to be keeping all the families together Wallace." William replies, "Aye, It is..." They hastily cover the remains with shawls, mantles, brats and plaid, then they leave the promontory and run down the winding steps to the corral. William catches the reigns of Fleetfoot and walks him out of the corral. He stops in front of Marjorie and enquires, "Will you shroud our people for us?" She puts her hand to William's cheek,

"Go you with Ranald and fetch back to us dear Malcolm and young Sandy, we'll lay the greatest care of the Aicé upon your people William, and with your permission too Stephen…" With his dark mousy tangled hair hanging over his blackened eyes, Stephen nods his head in approval. He wipes the long greased locks from his face and looks at Marjorie proudly, "Aye Marjorie, Katriona would wish it to be so." Reaching out with both hands, Marjorie briefly holds the hands of William and Stephen. As they part, she makes her way up the steps to organise the last of the shrouding on William and Stephen's families, preparing them for the sun cleansing fire where their spirits will be raised to the sky on their final journey to the other world… and a better place.

Pulling gently on the reigns of Fleetfoot as he mounts, William says, "Jump up behind me Stephen, I'll come back on Warrior, you ride back on Fleetfoot." Both young men clasp wrists and grip each other firmly. William pulls hard as Stephen jumps on the back of the horse to sit behind him. William presses Fleetfoot to walk-on. Ranald, who is still looking over his shoulder, meekly smiles as William and Stephen catch up with them on their journey to the icehouse of Comunnach Castle, to collect their much loved family member sir Malcolm and his brother in death, young Sandy, the stable lad of Ach na Feàrna. Marjorie watches them leave, a single tear rolls down her cheek… How could any God set such cruelty and evil upon these wonderful people… She thinks of Mharaidh, Caoilfhinn, Alain, Tam, wee Graham, Jean, Katriona and everyone else of Glen Afton, more tears begin to flow as she remembers how much joy and happiness she has shared with them for most of her life, but now they are gone. How must William and Stephen be feeling? How is it possible that anyone may keep any wits about them after such inhumanity? Marjorie knows she can never truly comprehend their particular reality. Turning away, she sobs quietly to herself while she walks toward the flagstones in front of Wallace Keep, where she gathers all her kinfolk and prepares them to commit to their last funerary task of the fire cleansing. Marjorie's lady of Comunnach castle, Mary Burris and two of the older goodwives, begin to bathe the remains of Alain, Mharaidh and little Caoilfhinn, others cleanse the bones of Katriona, young Stephen and their unborn child. The gentle maternal and caring hands of the good women set to the task of preparing the remains of Auld Tam, wee Graham, Jean and little Jamie for the final funeral pyre of the cleansing sun.

As night falls, the Cúr na re' cleansing of the bodies is all but complete. Marjorie wraps the last remains in muslin hemp shrouds and binds them tight. Such is the few remains of Katriona, young Stephen and her unborn child, that Marjorie has only one course but to wrap their mortal remains in one little bundle and place it alongside Katriona's mother auld Jean, her father wee Graham and their lifelong companion Auld Tam. All the women weep silently as they tend to their friends remains. As one of the younger goodwives washes little Caoilfhinn's face, a piece of Caoilfhinn's blond hair tugs away from her scalp, tangled in the fingers of the young Goodwife. She screams in horror and staggers back, tripping over her long skirts, her spirit broken, she kicks and wails like a woman demented. Marjorie, Mary and the other goodwives calm her, then they tearfully resume their spiritual tasks till all the Wallace and Graham families of Glen Afton are honoured in shroud.

The Comunnach cortege soon arrives back at the corral, along with Sean Ceàrr, keeper of the Kings hunting dog's of Glen Afton, driving a hay cart that carries the bodies of sir Malcolm and young Sandy. Everyone dismounts and takes the bodies from the back of the cart. Ranald and Richard lift Malcolm's body and follow William and Stephen who are carrying young Sandy up to the promontory; there they lay the bodies beside their kinfolk where Marjorie and Mary Burris begin to cleanse the bodies of Sir Malcolm and young Sandy, making them ready for the sun fire. William and Stephen watch intensely as the ancient funerary rights are being applied to their loved ones. Richard and Ranald go back down to the fields of sorrows to speak to the men and women of Cumno, Ayr and Riccarton. Sean sets the horses to feed then returns to sits beside William and Stephen. He says "I'm so sorry fella's... if only I hadn't been away in Ayr town... maybe I could have done something..." They both look at Sean and see that he too is in shock at the barbarity of his witness. William puts his hand on Sean's shoulder, "There's nothing anyone could have done Sean..." Stephen says, "We're just grateful your family were no' here when the English came a callin." But Sean feels deep guilt, shame and rage... then he breaks down and sobs. William and Stephen cannot see to anything other than consoling their friend.

The funeral pyres in the glen begin to dwindle as a dark night cloaks Glen Afton. The Riccartoun, Crosshouse, Cumno and Comunnach men and women collect faggots of wood for the final funeral pyre when a watchman calls out, "Riders on the southern pass..." Everyone reaches for their weapons as the riders gain close. William drops his guard when he sees it's his uncle Bryan from Galloway leading a large troop of Gallóbhet. He also sees Crauford banners held by Ranald's sons, Ranald óg and Billy... then he notices the pennant of the Red Comyn and two of his retainers. The oncoming horsemen ride fast and recklessly until they arrive at the corral in a flurry. William, Stephen and Sean go down to greet them, when William notices Lady Marjorie and the red Comyn walk away from the gathering. William watches as Comyn speaks quietly to Marjorie; then he puts his arms around her as she collapses weeping. Comyn looks around and catches a glance with William; it's obvious that whatever he said to Marjorie has finally broken her heart.

By the time William joins everyone at the Corral, he hears more terrible news. Ranald says, "William, this is sir Tam Halliday the husband of your aunt Dorinn." Halliday's face appears strained and fatigued. He says, "Our families have suffered the same fate as has happened here... we've also sent my beloved Dorinn our children and our kinfolks to Tír na nÓg." Halliday falters, then he continues, "When we got back to our homes from the Norham conference, we found that English soldiers had paid a murderous visitation upon our people at Ceann Corriechd estates..." Halliday stammers, "They... they murdered everyone... We were too late... We found everyone had been butchered and then hung high in the barns, the old men, our womenfolk, even all our wains... none were spared."

No one would speak, the grief and rage felt by everyone is becoming numbingly impossible to comprehend. William sees that his uncle Bryan looks similarly bedraggled in appearance. "Our families too..." says Bryan, "The English swept up behind us from the long shores in the Rhinns and Machars. They didn't attack at first, nobody was of a mind or even thinking they would... fuck, they rode into our Balloch's and shielin's with warrants, held mock trials then hung or beheaded all the chiefs and their son's... but many of the Gallóbhet chiefs and their families still managed to escape though. We were settin' out all o' our sun pyres when news came to us o' what had happened here in Glen Afton... Seoras stayed behind to martial the remainder of our Gallóbhet families; he's leading them deep into the southwestern end of the Wolf and wildcat forest to the old fortalice of Glen Lochar. All the other Gallóglaigh are making their way to safe hides near Taliesin, the hills o' Barr, Glen Trool, Torr Point, Kirkennan and the Munchie clearin's. We rode up here as fast as we could to see if we could be of assistance when we met Halliday at the Silver Flowe, that's where he told us what happened to Dorinn and everyone at Ceann Corriechd." Ranald enquires, "Was there no negotiating with the English at all?" Bryan sneers, "Fuck Ranald… there are few enough in Galloway who speak the English tongue, far less any who understands the Norman French that many o' the English soldiers used. Most in Galloway are Dálriatan Ghaeltacht and had no way of knowing what was being said, it was on that pretext of guilty by silence that they were brutally tortured then executed."

William rages "Are the fuckin' English trying to kill all the Wallace?" Red Comyn, standing nearby comforting lady Marjorie, steps forward and speaks in anger, "It's not just the Wallace who are being murdered… as far as we know its also the Comyns, Graemes Douglas', Marshalls, MacDowells and all of the Galloway Gallóbhet Clans, even Dougal MacDougall of Gairachloyne and his younger brother Fergus… their families and kinfolks have all been slaughtered. The MacDougall brothers signed the fuckin' Ragemanus too, just like your own father Wallace. The English seem to be intent on killing all the families of the native Scots who held any position of rank in Alexander's army, in particular officers of our late Kings personal household and the Garda bahn Rígh. Many of my own kinfolk have been murdered under the pretext of breaking this English martial fuckin' law." Richard shouts out, "This is war, we must take up arms…" Uproar ensues amongst the men and women gathered below the promontory. Amidst the chaotic scenes of over a hundred warrior

Gallóbhet furiously clamouring for revenge, William calls out for calm, but no-one takes any notice, he quickly runs up the promontory overhang and shouts above them all at the top oh his voice "HOW CAN THIS BE FUCKING WAR…?"

Suddenly everyone falls silent as they look up to see a giant muscular frame looming over them, like some mystical leader of the ancient Tuatha de Cruinnè cè. William continues… "We have no king… we have no army… who is to protect us from this evil?" Stephen walks up and joins William on the overhang, then he speaks, "You Scots must surely bring everyone together as one, for I have seen all this happen before in my Ireland… there the English carried with them death lists of all those who served or supported Irish Kings, Clan chiefs and all others deemed to cause the English a sleepless night. They impose the laws of England on subdued territories, for they see the Scots and Irish as bleedin' slaves to do with as they will… Know this me friends or yee will all surely die, the laws of England applies wherever their army lights a fire, and any poor soul, even though they be ignorant of these English laws, will be executed for sedition or treason without a trial. Those lucky enough to escape are branded as outlaws." Bryan shouts out, "Who will stop them?" The desperation in his voice is painfully clear. He continues, "We have no army, our nobles have sold us out, who will seek justice for us that we may not be deemed outlaws or hunted like rats to the slaughter in our own land? Who will to stop the English when they come to our homes to murder us? Who will protect us?"

Everyone looks at each other, but none has an answer, not Even Ranald or the Red Comyn. Stephen spits on the ground, "The bleedin' English army and damn few of your cosseted fuckin' nobles… this is your protection now…" Everyone clamours for justice, revenge and retribution is on everyone's lips. Lady Marjorie walks up to the promontory and stands between William and Stephen. She stands proud, "My friends…" Her calm voice seems to have been heard by everyone vying to have their own voice heard above all others. Everyone falls silent to listen to her words, "My dearest friends… I have no words that can comfort you for what has happened here and elsewhere by evil men… but I know that while our tempers are hot, the laying to the sun and wind of your dearest beloved family kith and kin is now upon us." There's a murmur of embarrassed approval when hearing Marjorie's thoughtful words, all reconcile themselves to the duties of the last funeral pyres to be lit on the promontory of the Black Craig.

The gathering disperses, then silently they walk up the stairs to the flagstones where they courteously make even space on the little plateau, till all are gathered solemnly around the bodies of William and Stephen's families. William gazes at the shrouded bodies waiting to be placed on the funeral pyre, an uncontrollable wave of terrifying emotion sweeps through his mind, but then he sees Stephen walk over and kneel beside the shrouds of Katriona and his children, the scene tempers William's emotions. He looks on as Stephen dutifully places broken food and rests a hand gently at the head of the small shroud, sobbing quietly as he mutters a last solemn prayer to his loved ones. William wants to wake from this hellish nightmare, but instead, he feels himself walking towards the shroud wrapped bodies of Alan, Mharaidh and Caoilfhinn, as though he is in some dark evil dream. He stops briefly beside a food platter and picks up some food then kneels beside Stephen and places the broken food on the shrouds of his father, Mharaidh and Caoilfhinn. He puts his hand gently upon their heads while raising his other hand to cover his eyes. Composing himself,

William gathers into his arms the shrouded body of little Caoilfhinn. Stephen holds the remains of Katriona, Young Stephen and the little one. Richard walks over and gathers the remains of Alain. Ranald carries Mharaidh. Red Comyn carries Wee Graham. Sean Ceàrr carries auld Jean. Ranald óg carries auld Tam, followed by his brother Billy carrying young Sandy. Bryan gathers little Jamie; then collectively, they walk forward and place their charges side by side on the large unlit pyre platform. Ranald and Richard return to carry the remains of Malcolm then place him on the left of Mharaidh to rest her between the two Wallace brothers.

Everyone lowers their heads, each saying a private prayer to their deity; then everyone from Cumno, Ayr and surrounding villages gathers food, vittals or drink to place carefully around the shrouds. Soldiers of Richard and Marjorie's bodyguard with Ranald's Ayr town guard bring lit torches forward and hand them to the family bearers. Marjorie's chailleach (Wise woman) Mary Burris, begins to sing a Ceantrachd (Kowntra) accompanied in delay by other female voices, creating a beautiful soulful harmony of unusual rhythms as the men of the Wallace light the funeral pyre. Red Comyn's men, with two drone and pennant bagpipes, begin playing a solemn funerary air and lament of souls from the ancient score-scripts of Iona.

While the pyres flames quickly take hold and ascend toward the heavens; a flock of wild geese rise from the marsh grounds and fly towards them in a great majestic spiral. The flock of geese circle awhile then they fly westward, a sign to all who believe, that the birds have risen to carry the souls and spirits of the departed away from Glen Afton to take them on their long journey to the otherworld island of beautiful souls and eternal peace. Watching the flames, William and Stephen sense a moment's peace momentarily replacing their hunger for an answer. The ancient sun fire, usually reserved for Artur's Aicés and Chiefs, has cleansed everything for the auld faith kinship of Glen Afton. Eventually the time comes to pass when everyone begins to wander away from the pyre after honourably paying their respect and tributes, till William and Stephen stand alone on the steps of Wallace Keep watching the sun-flames lick skyward.

The pyre ceremony has brought a minimal form of closure to the great loss they must now endure. With their families safe from further harm, William and Stephen sit down to rest as Marjorie approaches them, "William, Stephen… we're all going down to Comunnach Castle to continue with the wake, will you join us?" William looks at Marjorie's pained features… "Marjorie, I surely do thank you and yours for all you are doing for us, but I think that I'll be staying in Glen Afton this night." Stephen agrees, "Aye Marjorie, I'll be staying here too, but I will surely be thanking yie for the humours yie have shown to us." Marjorie pulls William and Stephen close in a loving embrace. She says, "I understand… I'll return by first light in the morn."

As everyone departs for Comunnach castle, Comyn approaches William and Stephen, "Boys… do yiez mind me staying here with yiez awhile? For I am not of a mind for being inside this night." William looks at red Comyn, "I'll no' be much company this night Comyn, though your presence in the glen is most welcome. You'd better ask Stephen here his thoughts, for I don't know what I'll be doing, sleep, walk, run, fuckin scream, kill…" William pauses then speaks softly, "I'm sorry that you too have lost kinfolks Comyn." Stephen says, "You're welcome by me'self Comyn fella, though me wits are in no better mettle than those of the Wallace." Comyn puts out his hand in friendship, "I'm pleased to meet you Stephen of Ireland, Wallace has told me much about you.

I just wish..." Comyn falters, Stephen quickly takes Comyn's offer of friendship and shakes his hand, he says, "Aye Comyn, and I you... I wish it had been under a better circumstance." Stephen turns and walks over to the doors of Wallace Keep and sits down on the steps. William follows and sits beside him, both watching the pyre. William says, "Sit with us Comyn and share a dram, but I'm warning both o' you fella's, if I get up and walk away into the darkness, don't follow, for I'll want none around me." Stephen picks up the whisky canter, drinks from it then hands it to Comyn, then he says, "I think that we are all o' the same mind Wallace." Comyn drinks from the flagon then passes the whisky to William.

Many hours pass and nothing is said, not till William looks at the Comyn curiously, he sees that Comyn has the same lines etched in his face as all those who have suffered the tragedy of Glen Afton. William enquires, "I saw you speak to lady Marjorie earlier and I saw her reaction to your words..." Comyn stares at the pyre, then he answers, "I was travelling down to our clanlands to visit my kinfolk... I arrived at one of our Clachans not long after English soldiers had been there under the direct command of Robert de Brix and an English knight called Graystoke. Almost everyone in the Clachan had been tortured and executed for treason or sedition, even the children, many were close relations and friends with Marjorie..." William exclaims, "What the fuck is happening?" Comyn shakes his head, "I don't know Wallace, I cannot fathom out why there is so much killing of the native Scots and why your family, the Galloway Clans and Gallóbhet have suffered too; unless its true that all of the families who served Alexander loyally are now being put to the sword." William enquires, "This surely cannot be the orders of the English King... can it?" Comyn sighs, "No-one knows, our nobles are powerless, the fools have given up our castles and strongholds over to English governorship and support the imposition of martial law." William says, "Maybe then the wee folk like us should rise up and rebel against the English and our own fuckin nobles… We need to do something about what's happened here Comyn, I'll try to do it by the law, but if not…" Comyn interrupts, "What are you going to do Wallace? We're fuckin' helpless… I'll tell you this fact though, if our Comyn clan rise as one, both North and south, there will be hell to pay in this country." Stephen comments defiantly, "I'm wit ya Comyn, for I won't stay here when there is a blood tax to be collecting." William listens as he looks intensely at the pyre that is now burning down to a bright glowing mound of embers. He sees that the bodies of his kin have been completely consumed by the fire. He looks at the red Comyn "I am with yie too Comyn…"

The three friends grip each other's left hand in a timeless bond of camaraderie between soldiers of faith. As they sit by the last pyre, they fall to silence once more, each of them dwelling upon how they may find justice, then they hear voices nearby. They peer into the darkness, and see Bryan Wallace, followed by the two Crauford brothers. Bryan enquires, "How are you fella's doin?" William replies, "Ach, it is what it is. What are you fella's doin comin' away up here?" The kinfolk sit on the steps, then Bryan replies, "We couldn't stay inside Marjorie's castle, it's a fine enough place she has there, but it's too comfortable for us, we need to be outside where we belong." William smiles, "Ah know what yiez mean." Billy Crauford enquires, "What are we going to do about this Wallace?" William shakes his head, "Ah don't fuckin' know…" Billy gazes at the glowing pyre awhile, then he says, "The English rode through our country just west o' here, they were savage, ah'v never seen the likes afore. They held mock trials then hung or beheaded most folks they came across, then they stole all our livestock and horses." Bryan says, "Aye, It was the same down about the Rhinns and Machars…" he pauses then shakes his head as he recalls, "They herded all the families together then they took all the young men they could find and hung them from trees or from the back of carts, all for not obeying English orders, but most o' the folk couldn't understand what the English were fuckin' sayin'. And do yie know what else fucked me up? It was our own religious clerics who were in attendance, sittin' there to confirm that the English actions were lawful and just. If I ever see a priest again I swear I'll gut the fucker. We barely made our escape into the forest's, for there we knew the English wouldn't follow us, if they had, we would have easily taken the bastards out one by one."

William and Stephen look at each other curiously; then Stephen enquires, "What about the Gallóbhet, I mean, where were all the fighting folk?" Bryan shakes his head, "Orders had came from the nobles for us all to stand down as the English were only here to keep the peace, but the English had many of de Brix and Graystoke's knights and soldiers with them. They began singling out the Gallóglaigh chiefs and their sons… they never stood a fuckin' chance, no-one expected or even thought that the English would turn on them. Many of the chiefs welcomed them in with food and good cheer, as is our custom. The English ate and drank plenty, then held their trials and murdered the defenceless hosts." William exclaims, "Fuck… What are we going to do?" Bryan replies, "Well, we're going back down to meet with Seoras and see how many of the Gallóbhet escaped into the forests. I reckon the Gallóbhet will come out fighting though, that's an absolute fuckin' certainty, for this is now a fuckin' blood feud, especially after de Brix carrying out what they call legal reprisals and retribution for the civil war… and it was him that fuckin' started it." Ranald óg agrees, "Aye, for sure about that, we'll never be caught cold by the English ever again. The bastards will soon rue the day the put their feet down in Galloway, for it'll be a slow and joyous toes up on those fucks… they think they can massacre and murder here and not expect us to react? Ah don't give a fuck who-ever is arse-lickin' the English king… we're on our own now, and we'll sure make all o' those duplicitous the bastards pay dearly for all o' this." William smirks to himself hearing that expression, "Toes up," it reminds him of when Bailey used the same term to describe his vengeance and retribution down in Wales, but that seems like a lifetime ago. For a moment he sees the smiling faces of Bailey and Lihd…

Suddenly his thoughts are interrupted when he hears a harsh and raised voice beside him, Comyn rages, "I feel the same way as you fella's do, I'm going to find and kill that fuck Robert de Brix and his fuckin' son Brus of Carrick for what they've done." Bryan says, "De Brix is using legal writs to murder as many of our folk as he can, all under the pretext of peace-making through their martial law, and he's using English knights and soldiers to back him up to do his bidding and carry out all o' his dirty work. If de Brix attempts to become our King, then I tell yie this. This country will be torn apart in total war." Ranald óg glances at William, "What are you going to do?" William replies, "I don't know." Stephen exclaims, "Well oi know what I am going to fuckin' do Wallace…" he turns and looks intently at Bryan and the Crauford brothers, "If you fella's will have me, I'm goin' down to Galloway wit' ya, and oi'm goin' to be joining your Gallóglaigh as is me blood right through me kinfolks. And when my wits are fit and level, I'll hunt down the bastards who did this to me family. By the life o' me, I'll dedicate my whole lifetime to slowly killing the bastards… are you wit' me

Wallace? And what about you Crauford's?" Ranald óg and Billy look at each other, "Aye we're with yie." Stephen turns to William, "Is it Galloway we're to be going Wallace?" William thinks for a moment, then he replies, "I can't Stephen, I've got to look to the safety of wee Maw and the family up in Ach na Feàrna first. After that, I'll see if Ranald can find out who is responsible, for he's a Sherriff and he'll soon find out who committed these murders, then I'll let yie know then what I'll decide to do."

Stephen is dismayed to hear this from William, but he nods in understanding. He says, "If I find out anything on me hunt Wallace, I'll let yee know." He turns to Comyn, "What about you?" Comyn shakes his head, "I have got to get back up North and report all I have seen to my father." Turning to Bryan, Stephen enquires, "When is it you'll be leavin' then?" Bryan replies, "First light o' the morn we're heading back down to the Rhinns." Stephen nods, "Then oi'm comin wit ya." Bryan says, "Glad to be havin yie Stephen, this is a blood tax now and only death will stop me, mine or theirs." William says, "I heard almost all of those same words used by Coinach when his family was massacred at the Corserine, I thought I could empathise and understand what Coinach was going through at the time, but I never truly knew the gravity of what it could be like to be finding myself now in the same situation, now I do, and it hurts bad, so fuckin bad…" William takes a sharp intake of breath, "Ah don't think that nobody and nuthin' could ever prepare you for this… fuck…"

The young men all nod together in forlorn agreement, then they talk through the night till dawn breaks over Glen Afton. As the first light appears, they gather more wood and place it upon the pyres, ensuring that nothing but ash remains on any of the funeral pyres in the Glen when they finally burn down.

The last of the faggots have been thrown on the pyres when Lady Marjorie, Ranald, Richard and Halliday arrive with their troops from Comunnach. Ranald dismounts and walks up to them. "William… we must leave for Ach na Feàrna now. We need to make sure everyone up there is safe from any further malice." William stares at the pyre and sees that there are no longer any remains of his kinfolks existence left on this earth, only their love and memory remains.

William enquires, "Will you go up without me uncle?" Ranald looks at William curiously as he continues, "When the fires are scattered I'm going to torch what's left of the Balloch's and the Keep o' the glen, for who could live here now with the ghosts and spirits of the past here to haunt them?" Ranald understands what William means by burning the place to the ground. William continues, "True Tam is with the family up in Ach na Feàrna… ah don't know Ranald, but there's something about that fella's demeanor that makes me feel we have nuthin' to be worrying about the family not being safe up there." Ranald looks around the empty Glen, it makes his heart heavy; in his mind he hears the laughter and music of his kinfolks echo mutely in the surrounding hills of Glen Afton. It seems just for a moment, everyone is in spiritual unison, seeing the same happy faces, sharing the same fond memories of good times past, happy memories that will remain in their hearts forever.

The dwindling rancid smoke from the pyres reminds them that those halcyon days have now brutally and ominously ended. Eventually the time comes for William to be saying farewell to his kith and kinfolks from Crosshouse and Craigie. He watches as Ranald, Richard and the Red Comyn leave with their troops to go north, while everyone left behind goes about burning down the last of the pyres to a fine ash. William instructs everyone to clear all the remaining bothies;

obhainn's and shielin's then torching them too. Anything else that's found that may be of use to Outsiders, is to be burnt on the last of the pyres, ensuring no human remains or artefacts escape the cleansing.

It's late in the afternoon before the last fire is but a glowing heap of pure ash to be extinguished and scattered. Everyone congregates to say farewell to both the spirits, and to each other. A little while later, when all had departed, William looks up to the west road on the side of the sentinel hill of Black Craig, there he notices the fading silhouettes of Stephen, Bryan, Halliday and his Crauford kinfolks as they make their way over the high ridge to forge deep into the safety of the Wolf and wildcat forest on their long journey into southwest Galloway. He sits down exhausted on the charred steps of Wallace Keep and scans across the glen, when a single tear rolls down his cheek. His emotions are becoming overwhelming with no-one nearby to witness, he attempts to remain stoic, when suddenly, the tears of unrestricted sorrow and the hurt of a great loss breaks free. He lies down on the edge of the promontory and curls up like an abandoned child, soon he feels a chill breeze freezing his skin with the heat of the cleansing fires no longer in existence…

'Like my family' he thinks, but natures cold wind pales to the chill of the iron constitution now locking his emotions away deep inside his heart. He pulls his brat over his head and lays awhile, then he hears the baying and howling of the night wolves and wild dogs in the distance, but they no longer sound like base scavengers hunting for a feast, they cry as his brothers and sisters who now sing their own song of mourning in respect of their collective glen families demise. He realises that in nature you cannot hide the truth, but it all becomes too much for William, the chains of the iron guard around his heart breaks, causing involuntary sobbing and tears to flow, till a long deep sleep finally comes to him, bringing peace.

"Wallace..." A voice in the distance calls out to him, "William..." He feels his heavy brat being pulled back, but he has no care be it friend or foe. He opens his eyes and flinches, to his surprise he sees Marion, he tries to jump up but his body is aching and racked with pain. Marion cries out, "Oh my love..." she cradles him in her arms. "Marion..." He looks into her eyes and he sees that they too are swollen from weeping and grief, he can also see she has been severely traumatized by the evil visitation. He says, "Come here my love..." He puts his arms around her waist and pulls her close, clinging to her like a son who needs a mothers nurture, but he has no more tears left for grieving. He slowly sits up and drapes his brat around her shoulders and pulls her close as darkness envelops them.

A few hours pass by while they sit silence, then William looks into her eyes... "My love... we must seek shelter soon, for it looks like storm clouds are closing in and we cannae be staying out here..." Marion raises her head and kisses him on the cheek, then she speaks to him with a care, "William, Marjorie told me to bring you back to Comunnach castle when you're ready, she say's she will provide all the shelter and warmth we need, and we can stay with her as long as we would wish." He looks at his bonnie Marion, her beauty and gentle demeanor fills his heart with love, but he feels fear too, fear at the thought that anything could happen to her. A realisation strikes him, "Marion... how did you get here? I mean, what are you doing up here on your own?" She cradles her head into his chest then says, "We were all in Lanark at the Bruin hoose when we heard rumours about what had happened here, so Brannah, Brian and I travelled across country as fast as we could to be with you."

William enquires, "Marion, you've risked everything to be here…" Marion replies, "Without you Wallace, I have nothing." William pulls Marion close and they embrace for a long, long time. William looks at Marion and sweeps a strand of her long jet hair away from her face, "I love you so much Marion, I don't know what I…" Marion sits up, "I love you so much too William, nothing is going to happen to us, remember, we have a wee one on the way." William shakes his head … "I don't know what I would do…"

The young lovers embrace one more time, then William says, "Come darlin' we'd better get yie back to Comunnach as quickly as possible." He helps Marion to her feet; then he enquires, "Where's Brian and Brannah?" Marion replies "Brian is in your Obhainn I think, he said he would light a fire there to keep it warm and wait for us there… he watches over us William. Brannah, she's up in Comunnach castle waiting with Lady Marjorie, she also sent her personal guard here with us." William smiles and clasps Marion by the hand. "Let's go Marion, for it's no' safe to be out here on our own. We'll collect anything the English have no' taken from my Obhainn, for it's the last to be put to the fire, then we can go to Comunnach."

As they walk towards his obhainn, he enquires with concern in his voice, "How are you anyway?" she replies with a little smile, "We're fine." William throws his arms around her, "Marion, I don't know what I would do if…" She puts her fingers to his lips, "We should go now my love." William leads her carefully from the Keep and down the steps to the glen floor where Brian and the guard greet them warmly; then they share a moment of sorrow and grief together. Brian says, "I've taken as much from your Obhainn as I could find and loaded everything on the cart." William thanks Brian as he looks at the little pile of clothing and chattels he'd accumulated since his arrival in Glen Afton. "Wait here a moment…" says William. He goes into his Obhainn to see that it's been thoroughly ransacked. He goes to the far corner and throws back brats and hides to reveal a flagstone, he pulls it back then digs his fingers into the earth to reveal another flagstone, He pulls the heavy flagstone up to uncover a cyst, much to his relief, he sees his grandfathers 'Royal' dirk, wrapped in saffron linen on top of his father's bull-leather battle-jack. His sword and Anam-Crios are laid out meticulously beside his grandfather's dragon helm and haubergeon. As he thoughtfully lifts out his hereditary possessions, he runs his fingertips over the spread-wing Dragon on the chest of the old battle-jack, then carefully lifts the royal dirk and unwraps it, revealing the exquisite detail of workmanship etched in the polar-white ivory-handled blade, with the inscription in Latin and Ogham, I tell you this truth, the best of all things is freedom, never my son, live under the bonds of slavery… He pauses for a moment, thinking upon the words of his Uncle and Grandfather. He quickly wraps everything up and hurries back to Marion then he and Brian put his obhainn to the flame.

It takes a few hours of slow walking of the horses and rickety cart before they eventually reach the lower drawbridge of Comunnach castle, the tall curtain walled fortification appears imperially foreboding below a star bejewelled night sky, intimidating and hunched like a giant primeval forest ghoul, guarding the confluence of the Rivers Nith and Afton. Marjorie's guard and Brian walk the old cart over the drawbridge and in through the castle portcullis gates while William and Marion take a moment to rest awhile, sitting on the drawbridge wall. He glances towards Glen Afton and sees there is no longer an evil ochre glow emanating from the funerary fires above the glen, in its stead, hovers a black fearful-looking night sky, brooding over a place now bereft of any humanity, haunted by young wraiths of death as its new tenants. William shudders at the thought. Marion looks meaningfully into William's eyes and whispers, "I love you Wallace…" He sobs quietly as her words touch him deeply. After everything he has experienced these last few day's, those three simple little words I love you, mean more to him now than he could ever have imagined… he pulls her close and holds her dearly… "I love you so much Marion, I really do… but, I must leave you now for I can't stay here." Marion exclaims, "What, you can't leave me here William, not now…?" William says, "I don't want to leave you Marion, but I must. I want you, naw, I need you all to stay here, and don't even be thinking of leavin' till I get back, unless you're under a well-armed escort from Marjorie, you'll be safe here with her. Marion my love, I have no choice, I must get back to wee Maw and the family."

Marion looks curiously at William, she places his hand on her stomach then says, "Please think about us before you decide what you are going to do… Oh William, I couldn't live without you… please don't go." Holding Marion in a protective and loving embrace, William sees in the distance behind her, the vague silhouette of Loudoun hill, peaking through the forest canopy, the place where English soldiers had murdered Malcolm and Sandy only a few days ago. "I have to go my love, there's something I must do…" Marion draws back from their embrace, she takes hold of both his hands and places them on her stomach. "We need you too William Wallace…" He embraces her once more, for he wants nothing else but to take her somewhere safe and be away from this tortuous madness that's engulfing his life, even though he has a burning fever in his mind to seek revenge for his families murder and the massacre of Glen Afton…

but foremost to that, is his concerns for the safety of wee Maw and the surviving members of his family up in Ach na Feàrna.

"Please don't do anything rash William," says Marion, "I beg of you." he replies, "I…" Suddenly Brannah comes running out the castle gates towards them, "Marion, Wallace…" He looks at Marion and a feeling of overwhelming love comes to him. He whispers, "I promise you Marion, I'll do everything within the law to bring the perpetrators to justice. I will no' be the cause of hurt to you or the little one." Marion holds William close in a vice-like grip and sobs gently, "Oh my love, I… I… don't want you to leave us, but I know you must." Brannah approaches and throws her arms around both of them, "Wallace, I am so sorry for what has happened. I, I…" Lost for words, Brannah weeps profusely. William pulls her close too, "I thank you for your care and thoughts Brannah, I really do…" Brannah and Marion clasp him by the arm then they slowly walk through the gates into the courtyard, there they meet with Mary Burris waiting to greet them, she says, "Wallace… Lady Marjorie has retired to her chambers and there's only the night guards awake, I'll tell them to have your horses stabled, fed and groomed, if you would like to follow me…"

Looking at Marion, William goes down on one knee and holds her gently by the hands, "Marion, please understand… but I cannot be staying here this night, I must to get back to Ach na Feàrna to make sure wee Maw and the family are safe. I cannot have peace till I know they are all protected from this evil. By travelling at night, I may avoid any English patrols…" Marion gazes into the eyes of her handsome lover and sees how deep the pain of grief is etched into his face. Tears begin to roll down her cheeks as she pulls him close to where he feels the warmth of her stomach in nature's cradle of their unborn child. "Oh William I don't want you to ever leave me, but I know you must… please… just don't get into trouble. When you're back through the gates of Ach na Feàrna, send me a message to me to let me know you're all safe from harm."

Marion looks down upon his head cradled against her stomach; she gently runs her fingers through his long hair. The loving caress and warmth, the safety of a mothers touch, William fights off the nurture he so desperately needs, it is almost breaking his heart. He forces himself to get back on his feet, "I must go now Marion, for if I stay here and something happens…" Marion says, "I understand my love." William turns and calls out, "Brian… Bring me Warrior and Fleetfoot, I'm leaving for ach na Feàrna right away." Brannah runs back over to them, still weeping, "Wallace please, stay with us, we need you here." Hearing Brannah's plea, William feels enormous sorrow, his mind is racing as to what he should really be doing next, but whatever he does, it must be on his own, he knows Marion and Brannah will be safe here staying with lady Marjorie in Comunnach castle, rather than leaving with him. His gut instinct is telling him he will never have peace until he is certain that wee Maw, Margret and the family are also safe and well. He puts his arm affectionately round Brannah, "I'll return to you all soon, I promise… when I know everyone up at Ach na Feàrna is safe and free from any further harm or any danger, I will meet with you all soon after, ah promise yie this."

Brian soon arrives with the horses. William says, "Look after your sisters Brian, don't leave for Lamington unless you're with lady Marjorie or Blackbeard's retinue. I'll find you all as soon as everything is secure up at Ach ma Feàrna." He turns to Marion and puts his arms lovingly around her. She looks up and their eyes meet, they kiss passionately.

The feeling of her soft warm lips and her sweet scents sends waves of loving emotion through his body. He pulls back and looks at the beauty of his love, "By my oath Marion, I vow and promise to you my bonnie darlin' that I'll come back to you in peace, I swear to you… I'll keep away from anybody and anything that may cause me to break my vow. I'll seek justice for what has happened in Glen Afton and Loudon Hill, not revenge." With tears running down her cheeks, Marion says, "I love you so much William… my Wallace." He smiles and wipes the tears gently from her face, "I love you too my bonnie Aicé, to the stars and back…" Saying these words and holding his love so close, brings a smile to William's heart, the first real smile he has known for a long time… and it feels good. They kiss passionately once more; then they pause for a moment, both knowing that he must leave now or he won't leave at all. He breaks the magical spell of their lovers embrace and mounts Fleetfoot. He pulls gently on the soft-mouth stallion, "Mary Burris, please be thanking lady Marjorie for all she has done… tell her I'll be returning here as soon as I can, and you Brian… I need you to protect them all." Gentle Brian smiles at his given responsibility. William looks down at Marion and sees tears in her eyes. Mary and Brannah put a brat around her shoulders as William pulls gently on the reigns of Fleetfoot, he trails the wounded Warrior and walks-on towards the gates of Comunnach castle. Marion waves frantically, but he doesn't look back… he can't look back…

Coming Soon

The fifth thrilling instalment in
Wallace: Legend of Braveheart

CPSIA information can be obtained
at www.ICGtesting.com
Printed in the USA
BVHW040234130223
658272BV00036B/179